Novel Possibilities:
Fiction and the Formation of Early
Victorian Culture

University of Pennsylvania Press
N E W C U L T U R A L S T U D I E S
Joan DeJean, Carroll Smith-Rosenberg,
and Peter Stallybrass, Editors

A complete listing of the books
in the series appears at the
back of this volume

Novel Possibilities

Fiction and the Formation of Early Victorian Culture

Joseph W. Childers

University of Pennsylvania Press

Philadelphia

Library of Congress Cataloging-in-Publication Data

Childers, Joseph W.
  Novel possibilities : fiction and the formation of early Victorian culture / Joseph W.
Childers.
    p.   cm. — (New cultural studies)
  Includes bibliographical references (p.   ) and index.
  ISBN 0-8122-3324-7 (alk. paper)
  1 English fiction—19th century—History and criticism.
2. Culture in literature.   3. Literature and anthropology —Great Britain—History—19th
century.   4. Politics and literature—Great Britain—History—19th century.   5. Religion and
literature—Great Britain—History—19th century.   6. Literature and society—Great Britain—History—19th century.   7. Great Britain—History—Victoria, 1837-1901—Historiog-
raphy.   8. Social change in literature.   I. Title.   II. Series.
Pr878.C84C45   1995
823'.809358—dc20   95-24893
                                                                                          CIP

In Memory of Q. N. Childers

1964–1984

Contents

Acknowledgments

Although we often hear that writing is a lonely occupation, in trying to thank everyone who helped bring this book to fruition, I realize that I, at least, almost never wrote alone. I have benefitted immeasurably from mentors and colleagues who have generously offered their time and advice. This project began as a dissertation at Columbia University, where I was fortunate to have the support and direction of Steven Marcus, who encouraged my desire to become familiar with the "extra-literary" aspects of the Victorian period. I am indebted to Edward Said, Jonathan Arac, John Rosenberg, Howard Horwitz, Andreas Huyssen, Charlotte Bonica, and the late Alice Fredman for at one time or another agreeing to read—or more selflessly, listen to—early versions of parts of this book. I owe much to the *Critical Texts* collective for providing a stimulating intellectual community at Columbia and to Charles Biggs, Jon Anderson, and Richard Moye for their willingness to read and comment on my work at any time.

I am extremely grateful to the University of California Dickens Project for allowing me to present portions of this book at two of the Project's annual conferences. I have profited enormously from my conversations with Catherine Gallagher, Hilary Schor, Regenia Gagnier, Martha Vicinus, Fred Kaplan, Murray Baumgarten, John Jordan, Robert Newsom, Peter Logan, Gerhard Joseph, and Robert Polhemus. Of my colleagues at UC, Riverside, Peter Mileur, John Ganim, Ralph Hanna, Carole-Anne Tyler, Traise Yamamoto, Carlton Smith, George Haggerty, Katherine Kinney, Ruth ApRoberts, Edwin Eigner, and Parama Roy have all read large sections of different drafts of *Novel Possibilities*, and their criticism has been most constructive. I especially want to thank Deirdre David, whose reading of an early version of this book helped me to rethink its presentation and its scope, and Helena Michie, who offered me encouragement and insightful suggestions while I was in the midst of that rethinking. I am also grateful to Robert Patten and James Buzard, whose thoughtful commentaries on the entire manuscript contributed to making this a better book now than it was when it first landed on their desks.

The University of California at Riverside Committee on Research has underwritten this project with several generous grants. Kate Watt and Josh Stein provided invaluable assistance in preparing the manuscript for publication.

My parents Neal and Bonnie Childers have never faltered in their support. My "other" parents, my in-laws, Joshua and Elaine Shapiro, and my wife's aunt, Millicent Groman Benwitt, have provided both encouragement and material assistance that have allowed me to complete this project. My son Rhys, who was born at the very beginning of this project, has helped me to remember what it was like to discover my love of stories, and my daughter Olivia, whose birth is imminent as I write these acknowledgments, bodily punctuates my sense of closure. Finally to my friend and wife, Estelle, I owe an intellectual and emotional debt that I can never hope to repay in full. Without her, this book would never have been completed.

A version of Chapter 1 appeared as "Politics as Interpretation: 'Progress,' Language, and Party in Early Victorian England," *CLIO* 17.1 (1987). Parts of Chapters 4 and 5 appeared as "Observation and Representation: Mr. Chadwick Writes the Poor," *Victorian Studies* 37.3 (1994). Those portions are reprinted by permission of the Trustees of Indiana University. A version of Chapter 6 appeared as "Feminine Hygiene: Women in Edwin Chadwick's Sanitation Report," *Prose Studies* 17.2 (1994).

Introduction:
The Possibility of the Novel

Making Claims

This book is about change: the way understandings of the world change; how new understandings affect material change, and vice versa; the effects such change has on subjectivity as a cultural function; and changes in the ways we might view early Victorian culture and the role of the novel in its formation. At the heart of this consideration of change is a theoretical position lying between a conception of language as completely constitutive on the one hand and on the other as corresponding directly with "reality." In many ways this position supports arguments contending that the implementation of any way of seeing the world, what one might call a paradigm for making the world knowable, is less concerned with describing or interpreting the object at hand than it is with rediscovering the possibilities of its own content. Certainly it accommodates the premises that a cognitive activity must be self-conscious, always calling itself and its presuppositions to account, and that any interpretive act alters the configuration of language within which the novelist, politician, writer, or critic is working. Not assumed or supported in these pages, however, is a fundamental implication of this sort of argument: that because we work from within the confines of an interpretive model (or "interpretive communities") the possibility of any articulation already exists and nothing new can ever come to be, that there is no other way of seeing. Nor do the arguments and readings in this book rely upon suggestions that only descriptions that in some, albeit "hidden," way already exist within our cognitive conventions are available to interpretation, or that interpretive paradigm can only change by expressing itself in a way that seems different but is really just a permutation of what already exists.

Instead, in *Novel Possibilities* I want to insist that all interpretations engage the world and that through this engagement ways of understanding change. New descriptions come about when lacunae in the paradigm are exposed and filled. When an interpretive enterprise does call itself to account and find itself lacking, the discursive forces shaping both interpretation and the interpretive moment converge to produce a description to meet that need, not out of some "already-present-but-unsaid" mist, but through the discovery of something that could not have been perceived without a specific implementation of the paradigm. The act of interpreting, therefore, contributes to change in its engagement with something that is outside the interpretive paradigm, something that is *perceived* as other, even though it is the paradigm itself that constitutes it as such and thus controls that perception.[1]

When attempting to theorize change, we often find ourselves bound to a causal model and thus confronting the paradoxes that so commonly accompany accounts of agency. Is it the interpelletive function of interpretation and representation that instigates change, or is it those subjects whose activities are circumscribed by discursive boundaries who are "responsible" for material and epistemic shifts? Rather than seeking to resolve this paradox and thus indenturing my argument to causality, I prefer to use it as a starting point for making clear my own position regarding interpretations and interpellations of the world. I do not want to be understood as arguing for a return to some sort of reductive empiricism in which texts exist outside an interpretive paradigm. By the same token, I wish to avoid a naive idealism that depends on language as *the* constitutive element for all objects of interpretation. As Fredric Jameson says of Althusserian history, simply because history is a text does not mean that the referent does not exist (*Political Unconscious* 35). Material changes do take place in the world of people, institutions, practices, and things. But those changes are not available to us except through our interpretations of them. Nor do our descriptions of those changes ever adequately reproduce them in all their multiple causes and ramifications. Rather, descriptions are limited by the language available to us and by the forms descriptive language takes, forms that seek resolution and closure, and that, because they do seek resolution and closure, must constantly be revised.

Here it is important to emphasize the distinction between ideology and discourse throughout this book. Lawrence Rothfield writes in *Vital Signs*: "One broad difference between ideology and discourse is that while ideological presuppositions form a part of a widely shared everyday knowledge, discursive assumptions are esoteric. . . . Discourse tends to nest within an institutional framework that at once delimits and supports it. A discursive practice will be organized not only textually or lexically (dictionaries, manuals, handbooks, and encyclopedias) but also technologically and politically" (45). Ideology, then, is articulated through discursive practices, but is not necessarily identical to discourse, per se. It is important to remember that the institutionalization of practices is a defining characteristic of discourse, making it possible to examine the tectonics of discursive activities. Class difference, for example, may in fact be an ideology that exists as a "consensus of unconscious valuations" (Eagleton, *Literary Theory* 15), but it is also a discourse implemented through a number of institutional measures such as literary productions, parliamentary and radical politics, the sciences (e.g., sociology, statistics), religion, and so forth. The assumptions governing these specific discursive practices are unique to them, formulated according to institutional demands.

The constant formulation and reformulation of these assumptions constitute cultural change, for they make possible new ways of seeing, understanding, and thus participating in the world. Often in the instances I discuss, a discourse will discover its own shortcomings and begin to look to other public discourses as means of shoring up its enterprise. At other times, it will focus upon the failings of a competing discourse and offer interpretations that "better" explain the issues at hand. In all cases, these interpretive projects operate with a certain degree of autonomy. That is not to say they are self-contained systems. Rather, like language in general, they may appear systematic but are often arbitrary in their signifying practices. Further, their autonomy is always relative, finally, to their existence within the larger network of practices and discourses we call culture. Each of the interpretive enterprises I discuss is generated and granted whatever authority it may hold by a convergence of competing interpretive models.

Among these discourses I would place the novel. By the mid-1840s, the literary production of fiction had become highly institutionalized. Also, the ideological impulses operating within novel writing and publishing had established a palpable, if tacit, set of presuppositions about what could and could not be said within the pages of a novel intended for the general reading public. Such institutionalization can also be considered in light of the notion of interpretive communities, which exist both to reinforce and to re-examine the principles of noticeability and relevance by which they make sense of the world. The texts produced as novels in the period I consider in this study, and especially those novels I examine in the following pages, all participate in this community. They respect the limits of paradigmatic utterances, as long as those utterances serve the functions the interpretive community perceives as its own.

Based upon these theoretical suppositions, I am making a substantially different claim about the function of novels, in this case "social-problem" novels, in the early years of the Victorian period, than do most of my precursors. While I accept Raymond Williams's assertion that these works were a way to make sense of the world, and Catherine Gallagher's that a number of contradictory exigencies such as freedom and determinism, public and private, are played out in these texts, I am suggesting that these works are not merely epiphenomenal. In beginning with the conception of novels as discursive, I want explicitly to grant them constitutive status. Not only did the novel undergo "basic changes whenever it became a part of the discourse over industrialism',' as Gallagher has said (*Industrial Reformation* xi), but the discourses revolving around the issues of industrialism were themselves shaped and informed by their intersection with novelistic discourse. Thus, novels not only attempted to describe the "reality" of the early Victorian world, they also participated in the formation of that world.

Such a claim obviously begs a certain number of questions about the status of realism and representation, both as we now discuss the issues and for the Victorians themselves. As George Levine has pointed out, the Victorians were well aware of the epistemological problems and moral imperatives involved in "truth telling." "Realists take upon themselves a special role as mediator and assume self-consciously a moral burden that takes a special form: their responsibility is to a reality that increasingly seems 'unnameable' . . . ; but it is also to an audience that requires to be weaned or freed from the misnaming literatures past and current" (12). Thus while there is always an essentialist undercurrent in realist depictions, an attempt to know the "thing in itself," in the fiction as well as in the narratives of someone like Edwin Chadwick or James Kay-Shuttleworth, there is also a self-consciousness of the failures of language to engage the actual, the "real," completely. The texts discussed in this book share these attributes, attempting to produce new ways of knowing even while they fall into the inevitable trap of realism—self-referentiality and the subjectifying of their audiences in terms that ultimately reaffirm their epistemological and moral goals.

In dealing with these issues, *Novel Possibilities* dovetails with but does not duplicate the work of Nancy Armstrong. Like Armstrong I often rely heavily on the insights of Michel Foucault for theoretical guidance. Yet I stop somewhat short of the "crisis of representation" that Armstrong identifies in her important and influential *Desire and Domestic Fiction*. Armstrong adopts a theoretical position that has become commonplace in contemporary criticism. For her, representation is more important in its constitutive than in its referential function. Indeed, the referential possibilities of language are called into question. Novels, therefore, are not so much ways of referring to the world as they are ways of knowing, and ultimately of creating, the world. As Armstrong states, she is specifically concerned "to show how the discourse of sexuality is implicated in shaping the novel, and to show how domestic fiction helped to produce a subject who understood herself in the psychological terms that had shaped fiction." She goes on to write that fiction "both as the document and as the agency of cultural history. . . helped to formulate the ordered space we now call the household, made the space totally functional, and used it as the context for representing normal behavior" (23–24).

In a number of ways I agree with Armstrong's assertion that fiction is both "document" and "agency" of cultural history—at least in the nineteenth century in Great Britain—and that it does indeed create its own context and thus relegate "vast areas of culture to the status of aberrance and noise" (24). For me, however, an important historical question remains: where is it that new or different ways of seeing come from? Armstrong, of course, also asks this question, but for her the answer always works back to a discursive "first moment," for the links in her argument, women-desire-sexuality-domesticity, privilege the discursive over the material conditions of those categories. And it is in this aspect of her work that she distances herself from critics like Gallagher, and even more so from Mary Poovey, who depend heavily on the recognition of certain material conditions that compel specific middle-class, masculinist, discursive positions.[2]

Like Gallagher and Poovey, I too part company with Armstrong on that point. For while I often argue for the constitutive effects of discourse, and not only "fictional" discourse, I have tried always to keep in mind that fiction and other public utterances of the nineteenth century were inextricably bound up in making sense of those material conditions of existence out of which they sprang. We only have access to the "real" through language, and thus through flawed representation, but there is a constant attempt on the part of language and its users to access that which is *not* discursive. The junctures I attempt to map in this book are as much informed by various interpretive enterprises' attempts to describe "reality" as they are by the points of competition and contact I identify among two or more of those descriptions.

Concerning Choices

In many ways, the largest text considered by this study is a particular historical moment in England, that period of intense political, industrial, religious, and literary activity between the 1829 Catholic Relief Act and the 1851 Crystal Palace Exhibition. In those years Britain underwent a series of unprecedented changes as diverse, yet connected, as the creation of a Metropolitan Police Force, the extension of the franchise, the institution of the railroad as an accepted and even preferred mode of travel between distant points, and the reformation along Benthamite lines of the laws dealing with the poor. As much as this was a period of great political, economic, and social change, it was also notable for its production of great literature, especially great novels. During these few years the novel established itself as the dominant popular literary medium. Dickens was flourishing, inaugurating his fame with *Pickwick Papers* and following with novels such as *Oliver Twist*, *Dombey and Son*, and *David Copperfield*. Thackeray and the Brontës were establishing themselves on the literary landscape, producing works like *Vanity Fair*, *Wuthering Heights*, and *Jane Eyre*. In these years a distinctive and compelling subgenre of the novel began to appear, variously labeled "social-problem novels," "industrial novels," and "Condition of England novels."

Three social-problem novels, Benjamin Disraeli's *Coningsby*, Elizabeth Gaskell's *Mary Barton*, and Charles Kingsley's *Alton Locke*, provide the framework for a discussion of the "possibilities" of this book's title. Except for a brief analysis of *Pickwick Papers*, this study avoids the literary promontories of early Victorian fiction in order to focus more intently on texts that, despite recent efforts to the contrary, have been relegated to the less well traveled glens and dells of Victorian novel criticism.[3] The relatively marginal position of these works combined with their cultural significance may be reason enough to choose them as a way to begin my analysis of early Victorian culture. But my decision has less to do with issues of canon formation than with the effects of their intersections with other kinds of public writing of the period. These three novels are at the center of a torrent of discursive activity in the second quarter of the nineteenth century, activity that partly informs the conditions of possibility they can articulate but that is also shaped by the social-problem novel itself. Certainly the genre was popular, as well as provocative, and these three particular novels were fairly well received. *Mary Barton* "made" Gaskell's career as a novelist. *Coningsby* went through five editions in five years, and *Alton Locke* went through four editions between 1850 and 1856. Indeed, the very reception these novels enjoyed hints at the kind of discursive reciprocity and textual power at work across public writing in the early years of Victoria's reign.

In selecting these three texts as literary focal points for the argument of *Novel Possibilities*, I hope to foreground them both as problematic cultural artifacts that offer us a specific vision of Victorian life and as participants in a competition among a number of interpretive discourses. In this contest for interpretive primacy it is possible to begin to imagine a counter-memory of the Victorian period, one that depends on interaction among specific discourses, one that considers the literary in terms of social and political as well as aesthetic effects. Perhaps, too, it is possible to begin to move away from a preoccupation with the "reflective" function of literary texts and consider their constitutive roles more carefully—in terms not only of the interpellation of individual subjectivities but of larger social formations as well.

Because I want to emphasize the constitutive possibilities of the novel, I have also written about a number of texts that were in direct interpretive and interpelletive competition with the novel, especially the social-problem novel. And just as *Coningsby*, *Mary Barton*, and *Alton Locke* are signal examples of that subgenre, the work that is central to the argument put forth in the following pages is also a "classic" of its kind and time: Edwin Chadwick's 1842 *Report on the Sanitary Condition of the Labouring Population of Great Britain*. Other non-literary texts examined in the present study are Robert Peel's "Tamworth Manifesto," a number of political and historical essays and parliamentary speeches by T. B. Macaulay, the letters and memoirs of Disraeli, Kingsley, and Gaskell, and reports, articles, and summaries from special interest publications and the popular press. The decision to interrogate such texts speaks to my wish to challenge some received ideas and orthodox habits of mind about what literary criticism can and should do. Until quite recently, literary critics have often been guilty of assuming that the significance of certain texts is indisputable, that tradition and conventions of taste have authorized the scrutiny of those texts and have isolated them from other kinds of writing and other means of knowing. Designating a text as "literary" often leads to closing it off from the forces that converged to create it. In choosing the primary works for this study, I have tried to avoid such suppositions and their resultant effects by deliberately fixing upon documents that in various ways accentuate their intersection with discourses that compete with and in some cases borrow from literature as explanations of the world. This competition, this impinging of interpretative paradigms and agendas upon one another, is a primary focus of this work.

In this aspect of my undertaking I have found myself traversing "traditional" disciplinary boundaries, and I have found that this disciplinary tourism, the effects of which Dominick LaCapra and others have called "cross-cultural montage," allows me to articulate another aim of this project. Much as the texts addressed exist at the crossroads of a number of interpretive discourses of the nineteenth century, this study similarly resides at an intersection of cognitive disciplines that provides more than just a vantage point from which to read particular documents; the work produced at such a juncture suggests ways of reading culture that might otherwise be closed to us, ways of reading which—in fact—offer alternative histories and understandings of how culture functions and produces itself as well as how it works to constitute the subjectivities, and thus the very existences, of those who participate in it.

Because this essay does concern itself with reading and interpreting selected features of early and mid-nineteenth-century culture, and because it links itself to recent work in anthropology and ethnography, to considerations of Marxist and neo-Marxist explanatory paradigms, to sociological inquiries, and of course to historical studies—specifically, studies of Chartism and of religion in nineteenth-century England—certain issues arise that pertain to the writing of a critical literary history such as this one. It has recently become fashionable to "return" to a historical approach to literary studies, yet for most critics of Victorian literature the question of whether to historicize has never really been much of a question. At least since Louis Cazamian, if not the majority then a significant number of critics of nineteenth-century literature have been concerned to examine the literature *and* the society of Victorian England. Yet the question of *how* to historicize has proven problematic. In response to that question, scholars such as Mary Poovey, Catherine Gallagher, D. A. Miller, Rosemarie Bodenheimer, Nancy Armstrong, and Daniel Cottom, to mention only a few, have offered models of how a "new" historical criticism can work.[4] And while not all these critics would label themselves new historicists, their projects attempt in diverse ways to re-examine representations of middle-class or patriarchal Victorian society, to challenge descriptions of the period as one of consensus, and to reconsider accounts of Victorian literature as the product of a shared pool of ideas and goals for society. Like those students of the English Renaissance who have been actively re-evaluating what had been handed down to them as "Elizabethan World

View," scholars in nineteenth-century studies now refute the assumptions underlying the notion of a "Victorian Frame of Mind." They argue that positing any singular description of Victorian society is totalizing and teleological and either marginalizes or denies the existence of a number of ways of thinking, speaking, and writing that may not fit precisely within a definition of any general "frame of mind," yet were vital, productive, and integral to how people lived their relations to their world.[5]

One of the primary theoretical objectives of this study is to keep this issue of totality in the critical foreground. In examining the discursive cultural artifacts I have chosen, I assiduously try to avoid a concept of totality as inert and non-dynamic, its parts occupying some fixed position in an unchanging whole.[6] On the other hand, however, I also posit and make considerable use of what Fredric Jameson has called "dynamic total-izations," heuristic fictions that are only apparently unified cultural texts (56–57). These sorts of generalities, it should be remembered, are always suspect, always changing and disintegrating, even as they provide ways of discussing representations of progress and change.

In this study "dynamic totalities" exist most importantly in my con-ception of interpretive enterprises and their statements, and depend upon accepting that they sometimes function in unified ways, that whatever dif-ferences exist within them are temporarily overcome by needs, desires, or compulsions to concentrate on similarities and to make the world under-standable to as large a number of people as possible. Thus I often discuss parliamentary politics, religion, class, morality, and the novel as though these concepts are homogeneous, codified wholes. Such, of course, is never the case. No public discourse, no matter how apparently unified, is with-out internal differences. In spite of their internal conflicts, however, such discourses do frequently *present* themselves as unified, so that when one discusses them and their functions, questions of "difference" are less impor-tant than a discourse's overall effects upon individuals and society. There-fore, while I understand the need for recognizing the heterogeneity of the several interpretive enterprises I identify and analyze, I also suggest that concentrating *solely* on difference in any analysis is more an ideal than a possibility and can sometimes hinder important discussions of a necessarily broader nature.[7]

As I stated in the beginning of this chapter, the primary broader issue for this book is change: how it can be described and theorized. And it is this project's occupation with the topic of change that distances it from most new historicist work. Any historicism should at least implicitly provide some theory of change, not necessarily in a linear, teleological way, but certainly in a manner that does not merely identify the anomalies within a given way of ordering the world. Explaining how attitudes, descriptions, and understandings of the world can change is difficult, however, for literary studies such as D. A. Miller's *The Novel and the Police* or Catherine Gallagher's *The Industrial Reformation of English Fiction*, which emphasize the containment of oppositional activities and statements by some dominant interpretive paradigm. This is precisely the obstacle facing (and foiling) many new historicist accounts of culture, for at work in these studies is a perception of the "power" of any "system" of order or of any means of describing the world as monolithic and all-pervasive. No matter how unconventional or oppositional a statement may seem to be, it is always reabsorbed into some dominant discourse. Yet a strategy of this kind of discursive "recuperation" assumes conditions that do not necessarily obtain. It assumes that the text is participating in and indeed is already constituted by a monolithic perception of the world in ways that always *reaffirm* that perception. While ostensibly relying on Foucauldian discourse theory, such an assumption misuses Foucault's genealogical conception of discourse by failing to attend to the specificities of a number of competing ways of seeing the world. Thus Foucault's injunction that power needs "to be considered as a productive network which runs through the whole social body, much more than as a negative instance whose function is repression" (*Power/Knowledge* 119) goes nearly unheeded in favor of a conception of power "as repression, ... a law which says no,. . . taken above all as carrying the force of prohibition," what Foucault calls a "wholly negative, narrow, skeletal conception of power, one which has been curiously widespread" (*Power/Knowledge* 119). Every statement within a culture is unique, contributing to the protean shape of the culture itself. Furthermore, the material conditions within which each statement is made are never the same and must be considered accordingly, for it is through these statements' engagements with ever-mutable material conditions and the ways such conditions can be known that new statements, including the texts we study, take shape.

On Presentation

Because I am interested in a discursive charting of the intersections between competing interpretive enterprises, this book often follows digressive, disruptive lines of argument. Rather than state a simple thesis in these opening pages and then demonstrate it, deductively, over the course of several chapters, concluding with its restatement and impact, I have chosen to offer a more metonymic text, one whose arguments are reflexive and overlapping, and often as shaped by contiguity as by transition and syllogistic justifications. The result I have striven for is a book that can be read both as a genealogy, where connections are multiple and complex, and in the more usual linear fashion, in which argumentative threads can be traced throughout the entire text, only occasionally, I hope, leading to cul-de-sacs. In keeping with its metonymic aspirations, the text is divided into five distinct portions: three large segments or "parts" bookended by this introduction and an epilogue. And in the spirit of symmetry each of the segments is divided into three chapters, each examining a different aspect of the interpretive enterprises that are the subject of the segment.

I begin specific discussions of how different public interpretations of the world work upon one another in Part I, "Trading Places: Novelistic Politics and a Political Novel." Chapter 1 in that segment is concerned to demonstrate that parliamentary political language is both interpretive and self-conscious. My readings of Peel's 1834 "Tamworth Manifesto" and several of Macaulay's speeches and essays from the 1830s and '40s show how legitimated political language is responsible for interpreting immediate social needs, looks forward to future needs, and, in order to align itself with the tradition out of which it has come, also examines its past. Because of this tripartite activity, political discourse finds itself forever searching for new normative boundaries and continually re-examining significations that at one time may have seemed unalterable to its participants. Peel, for example, casts his Tory arguments in rhetoric that is increasingly moderate yet nonetheless attempts to preserve its conservative tradition. Ultimately, the term "Conservative" replaces "Tory" as the label of his and his followers' political beliefs. Macaulay's political utterances, while more suited than the Conservatives' to the ideology of progress that becomes the standard against which all political idioms must measure themselves, are finely interpretive and often attempt to discover the direction of "noiseless" revolutionary currents that Macaulay sees at work in the seemingly inconsequential and mundane activities of day-to-day life.

Of course, political discourse, which includes Macaulay's and Peel's utterances, is not only interpretive, but representational. Whichever idiom —Conservative or Whig—one may prefer, each purports to offer an account of the way things *really* are. Chapter 2, "Fiction into Fiction," considers yet another perspective on how the reality of society and parliamentary politics may be understood. This portion of the book examines *Coningsby, or the New Generation*. This 1844 work is important for a number of reasons. Besides being arguably the first English political novel,[8] *Coningsby* combines and examines two major interpretive systems of nineteenth-century Britain: the novel and parliamentary politics. In doing so, it maintains not only that political representations of the world may be "factitious" but that the truth claims of fiction often may carry more weight than their political counterparts. This is particularly momentous for the status of the novel in Victorian England. For, in spite of Disraeli's often paradoxical explications of social and political change, *Coningsby*'s assertion that novels can offer workable (and sometimes preferable) explanations of the rapidly changing world helps establish the genre as an instrument of social criticism and an interpretive discourse that actively informs Victorian culture.

Chapter 3, entitled "The New Generation, the Political Subject, and the Culture of Change," investigates the ways in which the political subjectivity of *Coningsby*'s main character is directly linked to how he and the novel theorize political change according to a conservative agenda. Such theorizing provides a political subject position for the character, but his political *agency* remains in abeyance, existing beyond the limits of the text. This problem of conceiving of oneself politically yet not being able to *act* politically is the paradox that drives this text, but it also has other important ramifications for the constitutive work of novels and politics as interpretive discourses. Perhaps most importantly it points up the necessity for establishing characters' political subjectivities within novels—a contention that directly opposes Nancy Armstrong's assertion that the subject in the novel is figured either as politically subjugated or as apolitical. Further, *Coningsby* demonstrates that the intersection of the novel and party politics is a space that accommodates resistance and agency.

The argument that the novel was instrumental in the formation of Victorian culture has for the most part been taken for granted by literary critics. They assume the importance of the novel in Victorian society, and, consequently, their analyses tend to concentrate on how works of fiction represent that society. Books such as Patrick Brantlinger's *The Spirit of Reform*, Sheila Smith's *The Other Nation*, and Ivanka Kovacevic's *Fact into Fiction*, for example—while important studies of political and industrial fiction—subordinate the novel to the social discourses surrounding industrialization, religion, or reform. These studies stress the ways novels use bluebooks or party politics as sources for making their representations of the world more socially, politically, and economically effective. Useful as such studies are, they assume that the novel's relation to other interpretive enterprises is unilateral, and they tend to forget that the novel in its own right provided interpretive possibilities for political, religious, and reformist discourses.

In Part II, "Observation, Representation, and the *Report on the Sanitary Condition of the Labouring Population of Great Britain*," I avoid that tendency by reading Edwin Chadwick's *Sanitary Condition Report* with an eye to how the novel as a discursive model might have contributed to certain strategies of representation used by the report. Chapter 4, "The Novel and the Utilitarian," establishes the connection between novelistic discourse and reform writing. As I have already noted, the 1842 *Sanitary Condition Report* is one of the classic social documents of the Victorian period. In addition to its unprecedented distribution (perhaps as many as 100,000 copies were sold or given away), it was comprehensive in its collection of data. As secretary to the Poor Law Commission, Chadwick used the bureaucracy that he helped to put in place to gather information from all parts of Britain: Scotland, Wales, and England, village, town, and city. The amount of material for collation was astronomical, and he needed some method for ordering and presenting it persuasively.

Statistical analysis served part of that need. As with most bluebooks there is all manner of tables and charts in the *Sanitary Condition Report*. But there are also hundreds of pages of direct testimony from the poor themselves and from Chadwick's informants (usually Poor Law Union administrators and medical officers), which invariably takes the form of narrative. Even when the testimony is presented as interrogation and answer, a narrative is quickly discernible. The laboring population—or those who found and observed them—are telling their stories, and Chadwick assumes the responsibility of presenting those accounts as some sort of unified text that tells a tale of its own—the story of the "demoralisation" of the British "labouring" poor, the causes for that condition, and the need for the middle classes to recognize and help to rectify the situation both for the sake of those less fortunate than themselves and to protect their own interests.

The tales Chadwick and his informants tell are presented to the *Report*'s readers as "real." That is, despite being mediated through hundreds of middle-class interlocutors, the workers' stories and the conditions that produced them have concrete referents that can be known—if sometimes only third-hand—by readers of the *Report*. The techniques of textually reproducing this real world, which had been "hidden" from many of the upper and middle classes, already existed in fiction. In works like *Pickwick Papers*, *Oliver Twist*, and *Sketches by Boz*, for instance, Dickens had effectively used metonymy to establish the connections of people to their surroundings. This type of representation, in which people become "of a piece" with their surroundings, is particularly suited to the *Sanitary Condition Report*, for it allows Chadwick's text to accomplish a number of ideological objectives, which are examined in the following chapter, "Mr. Chadwick Writes the Poor."

Because the *Report* directly links one's intellectual and moral existence to one's physical surroundings, Chadwick can blame what he and his informants perceive to be the lax morals and inferior work habits of the laboring classes on their deplorable working and living conditions. Using the same logic of representation, he is able to suggest remedies: clean up the environment in which the poor must live and work, and a corresponding rise in the "respectability" of the working classes must follow. In offering his findings and solutions, it is important that metonymy gives way to metaphor as a strategy of representing the working poor, for such a shift highlights the dangers that Chadwick found festering throughout Britain. When a member of the lower classes becomes one with her surroundings, it may seem that she is only outwardly affected: she fails to wash regularly and is negligent in her personal appearance. But her essence is also altered. The representation of this, or any worker, then changes from metonymy to metaphor. The poor come to be described as wild beasts, feral dogs, "swine," "worse than savages," and as such they pose a grave threat to England's civil order.

Chadwick's use of metonymic representation also allows him to raze material and discursive barriers that kept the conditions of the poor out of sight (and out of the minds) of many in early Victorian England. By emphasizing the contiguous construction of British society, Chadwick pushes the poor out from the shadows of their existence and into the light of English social consciousness. It would be foolish to assert that the middle and upper classes did not see the poor every day.[9] But seeing and recognizing are significantly different activities. With Chadwick's *Report*, the poor become the focus of the public gaze rather than a social Medusa from which the nation must avert its eyes at all costs. The effect of such discursive cover snatching is not just a hegemonic restuffing of the poor into new categories; it also suggests possibilities of resistance and agency for the poor, possibilities that Chadwick often overlooks, but that nevertheless expose his own presuppositions and give us a glimpse of the residual culture of the poor that his report attempts to repudiate and replace with concepts of middle-class respectability and, above all, cleanliness.

Chapter 6, "Feminine Hygiene: Women in the *Sanitary Condition Report*," takes direct issue with Mary Poovey's argument about the effects of the *Report* on gender construction, class, and middle-class hegemony. Rather than adopt Poovey's contention that Chadwick's promulgation of domestic ideology is primarily a controlling mechanism that insists upon the consensual participation of working-class women (and men), I maintain that the conception of domesticity functioning in Poovey's account fails to consider the differences between working-class and middle-class domestic ideologies. I further argue that it is in these differences, as well as in Chadwick's promulgation of a middle-class conception of domesticity, that working-class women are often empowered and assume an agency they might otherwise be denied. Rather than eliding class distinction and reifying gender inequities, the effects of Chadwick's work underscore both gender and class difference and indeed raise the possibility of resistance even in trying to coopt it.

In "Washed in the Blood of the Lamb: Religion, Radical Politics, and the Industrial Novel," the third and final part of this study, I return my scrutiny to two literary texts, *Alton Locke* (1850) and *Mary Barton* (1848), and their interaction with two of the principal public languages of the period, religion and radical politics. It is only fitting that a discussion of these works follow the chapter on Chadwick's *Report*. First, *Mary Barton* and *Alton Locke* were published some years after the *Report*. Further, like the *Report on the Sanitary Condition*, these two novels "discover" the urban working classes and their conditions of existence. After they are discovered, however, it remains to be seen what can be done for them. In the brief introductory chapter, "Religion, the Novel, and Speaking for/of the Other," I suggest some ways in which religion functions as a means of social control of the working classes and as a medium for speaking about and for the poor. In its connections with the discourses of radical politics and religion, the novel provides a discursive arena for constructing the poor, to be sure, but also for analyzing that construction. And while the problem of the working-class subject beleaguers both these works, and each in its own way "raises" its title character to a recognizably middle-class ethos, these two novels also attempt to make working-class life knowable in its own terms to their primarily middle-class audiences.

As I point out in *"Alton Locke* and the Religion of Chartism," Charles Kingsley's novel works toward bridging the gap between classes through its insistence on making the working classes "worthy" of being electors by raising them above the economic or political circumstances that disenfranchise them. In *Alton Locke*, radical politics and religion coalesce into a new discourse of understanding that authorizes a "Chartism of the Future" in which laborers are no longer slaves to their stomachs and their purses but are devoted to the progress of humankind toward a society where morality and righteousness take precedence over the "merely political."

Kingsley can make this sort of argument because, after all, the novel was written *after* the 1848 London Chartist rally that really did strike fear in the hearts of some London residents. Comic and overreactive as the response to the Chartist gathering now seems, it was not for nothing that the aged Duke of Wellington was called upon to lead the regulars and militia should the rally turn to riot. *Alton Locke*'s perspective on Chartism and the mélange of public languages through which it is articulated point up this work's importance. Fixing retrospectively on a social and political failure, *Alton Locke* nonetheless attempts to accommodate Chartism, as cacophonous a group of discourses as it is, by reworking it in light of other interpretive enterprises of the period, especially religion. Kingsley's "Chartism of the Future" is a religion of humanity for which the charter is unnecessary. True understanding goes beyond the outward signs of a world of things to communion with the world of ideas, of immutable universals. Once the working classes come to this point of understanding, revolutions can be averted, and positive social, political, and spiritual change can do its work.

Elizabeth Gaskell's *Mary Barton* is the obvious companion piece for *Alton Locke*. Like Kingsley's novel, *Mary Barton* is about the conditions of the working poor; one of its main characters is an intelligent and somewhat alienated laborer who becomes a Chartist activist. Also like *Alton Locke*, Gaskell's novel is explicitly concerned with religion as a discourse instrumental in the formation of English society. Each of these novels examines religion from the perspective of the working classes and Chartism. And in each, religion, or idioms of it, are found to be insufficient to meet the spiritual *and* material needs of the poor. *Alton Locke*'s solution for improving the conditions of the working classes is to fill their spiritual pantries and moral coal bins. Once a person's spirit is provided for, material requirements will take care of themselves. As I point out in *"Mary Barton* and the Community of Suffering," Gaskell's novel addresses this problem quite differently. For

Gaskell material wants lead to unrest when it is unclear to those who are deprived *why* it is that they are cold and hungry. While she has no program for redistributing wealth, Gaskell does propose a new community based on communication. In such a community, compassion and understanding can help to mitigate the conditions in which so many of the poor spend their entire lives. Further, such a community offers a model of Christianity that employs respect and human sympathy as much as the promise of heavenly rewards as its basis of comfort and relief to all members of society. In contradistinction to *Alton Locke*, *Mary Barton* sees England's problem of the "two nations" as one that must be addressed communally rather than by individuals. True, in *Mary Barton* individuals have their place and can contribute to the overall direction a community takes in seeking to solve the problems dividing the classes. Finally, however, Gaskell's novel stresses the reformation of British society from an aggregation of individual and separate interests into a whole in which isolated concerns give way to the more important social needs shared by all.

In each section of this book, the emphasis, whether implicit or explicit, is on how particular discourses do their cultural work. Underlying the entire study is the assumption that literary criticism also does cultural work by offering us ways of reading texts and events that give us some insight into how other societies presented and understood themselves. Such an assumption may appear to privilege literary criticism, but that is not my intent. Rather, I wish to demonstrate the cognitive function of my discipline among other interpretive enterprises in the academic world and in society at large. I wish to show how our interpretive communities, in attempting to understand change, also contribute to change. This is the final but by no means least important objective of this study. We may work in ivory towers, but we do not live in them. Our work has some cultural effect. Our interpretive enterprises and communities should not be characterized as self-interested, self-perpetuating epiphenomena that stand somehow outside the vicissitudes of everyday life. Within the conception of literary criticism functioning in this study, not only is the interpretive community a force for provoking cultural and epistemic change, but the *social* is reinstated in an account of those transformations.

PART I
Trading Places:
Novelistic Politics and
a Political Novel

I
Politics and Interpretive Discourse

While Thomas Carlyle was in London in the autumn of 1831 searching for a publisher for *Sartor Resartus*, he wrote an article reviewing Thomas Hope's *Essay on the Origin and Prospects of Man* (1831) and Friedrich von Schlegel's *Philosophische Vorlesungen, insbesondere über Philosophie der Sprache und des Wortes* (1830), which in December of that year he published in the *Edinburgh Review*. In this review, "Characteristics," Carlyle is less concerned with discussing the relative merits of these books than he is with surveying the dominant features of the current intellectual landscape, which he finds gloomy and foreboding, dependent on political panaceas and physical and social "mechanisms," and in the grip of unhealthy passions for analysis, organization, and utility. Highly critical of many popularly held social and political notions, this scathing article so outraged and offended the *Review*'s influential Whig contributors that it effectively ended Carlyle's association with the journal.

Despite the content and tenor of the largest portion of the essay, however, "Characteristics"—especially toward the end of the piece—focuses on one particular over-arching issue that concerned Tory and Whig, Popular, and Philosophic Radical alike—change. "Change," writes Carlyle, "is universal and inevitable." "In Change . . . there is nothing terrible, nothing supernatural: on the contrary, it lies in the very essence of our lot and life in this world" (223). And while neither essential truth nor essential goodness ever dies or "can die; but is all still here, and recognised or not, lives and works, through endless changes," the primary impetus to social and political change is material: "The new omnipotence of the Steam-engine is hewing asunder quite other mountains than the physical" (224). Second, and directly linked to the changes in the material world, though perhaps with greater possible ramifications, change is caused by the inability of established institutions to cope effectively with society's increased potential: "What is it, for example, that in our own day bursts asunder the bonds of ancient Political Systems, and perplexes all Europe with the fear of Change, but even this: the increase of social resources, which the old social methods will no longer sufficiently administer?" (224). Nor should one consider change valueless; even change for the worse will eventually become change for the better; that is, all change is progressive, for "Out of all Evil comes Good; and no Good that is possible but shall one day be real" (222).

Thus even Carlyle, who perceives himself standing "yet in the bodeful Night," firmly believes that "Morning also will not fail." Certainly for many, the passage of the Reform Bill in December 1832 signaled the coming of rosy-fingered Dawn, and the large Whig majority ushered in by the election of 1833 prepared itself for an exceptionally sunny administration. The possibility of serious opposition seemed—at least to some—to have been completely devastated by the strong Whig victory. Observers like Charles Greville felt justified in arguing that "there exists no *party* but of the Government." To his eye there was no opposition of any account and thus no impediment to Whig policies:

> The Irish act in a body under O'Connell to the number of about forty; the Radicals are scattered up and down without a leader, numerous, restless, turbulent, and bold . . . the Tories without a head, frightened, angry, and sulky; Peel without a Party, prudent, cautious, and dexterous, playing a deep waiting game of scrutiny and observation. (2:361)

To those in power the future both politically and socially seemed particularly bright, and the political latitudinarianism already effectively begun by the repeal of the Test and Corporations Acts and by the granting of political freedom to Catholics, and extended even further by the passing of the Reform Bill, seemed to foreshadow a steady continuance of Whig-instituted reform.

It was not long, however, before the political skies began to threaten. The reformed Parliament was dissolved by William IV in November of 1834, and a new government was formed under the conservative Robert Peel, who had been Wellington's right-hand man during the high Tory '20s. The Whigs managed to retain control of the House in the ensuing election, and ultimately to force the dissolution of Peel's ministry in April 1835, but William IV's actions, together with an increasing divisiveness within the party itself, had made it clear that regardless of a reformed Parliament, the Whig stewardship was neither unified nor, at least for a time, "the Government." The enfranchisement of the urban ten pound freeholders had opened the floodgates of reform; and the Whigs, though somewhat more prepared than their Tory counterparts, were equally drenched in the subsequent deluge. The extension of the franchise, so long a theoretical possibility, had become a practical reality, and the implications of both the spirit and the letter of the Reform Act required politicians to take careful stock of their own—and their parties'—positions. Suddenly, or so it seemed, the rapid, powerful, and inevitable change that had appeared to be so well in hand became potentially uncontrollable. And while the actuality of material and social change redefined the conditions of persons' existence, the rhetoric and the language that informed the ways positive or ameliorative change could be thought of and discussed came to express as "progress" the way persons lived their relations to their new conditions of existence.

This perception of forward-moving change was lived at "such a depth" and so saturated society that it attained hegemonic status, constituting "the substance and limit of common sense for most people under its sway" (Williams, *Problems* 36). The post-structuralist (and especially post-Marxist) commonplace of assuming that the relations of a subject to his world are mediated and overdetermined seems especially well borne out by even a cursory overview of the function of "progress" during the Victorian era. At the risk of summoning forth more than two decades of debates over the "nature" of ideology, I would have to side, for the most part, with Louis Althusser's identification of those lived relations as ideological, expressing a will rather than describing reality (*For Marx* 233–34). Yet imaginary as we may assume the Victorians' lived relations to their world to be, the expression of those relations as progress corresponded to the *reality* of their social experience. By attaching positive value to the change that was affecting the lives of almost all its members, the majority of British society was able to encourage economic and material growth, while simultaneously taking steps to rectify the inequities that the institutions springing up in conjunction with this type of growth were perpetuating and often widening. Progress, then, whether characterized as ideology or as hegemony, expresses its will, but not as a univocal totality without contradictions. The institutions that were born of material change could not be easily reconciled to mitigating the opprobrium they produced. A few exceptions, such as Robert Owen's New Lanark Mills, prove the rule and bring up another important point in considering the contradictory elements of the nineteenth century's "practice" of progress.

New Lanark demonstrated, at least on a restricted scale, that a carefully controlled social and economic structure could provide both material growth and relatively good conditions for its workers. But Owen's paternalistic and highly regimented community, based on the principles that social forces shape the individual character and that the "working classes 'sustain the whole superstructure of society' without fully sharing its benefits" (Briggs, *Improvement* 288), changes little in the relations of laborer to manufacturer. The working classes partake of the benefits in Owen's scheme, but only insofar as the industrialist deems something to be beneficial. Progress in this case then, for the manufacturer means increased revenue and production *and* increased control over the lives of his workers, a situation he considers to be to their benefit, while the workers' social and political freedoms decrease.

The example of Owen also illustrates the recognition by early Victorians of the paradox inherent to a doctrine of material progress and of the need to institute corresponding social and political change to ameliorate certain conditions of life which had come to obtain in British society, especially among the working classes. It certainly was not the consensus, however, that increasing the political rights of the middle classes, let alone the working classes or "populace" was necessarily the proper course for instigating such change. Even the Whigs, who were more responsive to calls for political reform, agreed with the Tories "during the crucial debates of 1830–32 that democracy was an unpalatable and dangerous form of government" and that "the 'wild'—as distinct from the 'rational' part of the public should not be left undisturbed to exercise pressure on governmental policy" (Briggs, *Improvement* 239).

The real threat, for Whig and Tory alike, was from the lower orders, who were not considered ready to assume the responsibility of suffrage. T. B. Macaulay, one of many Whig champions of reform, emphasizes this point when during the height of the Reform Bill debates he argues for the importance of limiting the extension of the franchise. In an uncanny prefiguring of Arnold's "might 'til right is ready" argument of thirty-five years later and another Reform Bill, Macaulay avows that there may in fact be "societies in which every man may safely be admitted to vote." But England is not that society: "If the labourers of England were in that state in which I, from my soul, wish to see them, if employment were always plentiful, wages always high, food always cheap, if a large family were considered not an encumbrance but a blessing, the principal objections to suffrage would I think be removed" (House of Commons, March 2, 1831, in *Speeches* 2). For Macaulay and other liberal Whig supporters of the Reform Bill, nothing could be more dangerous to the health of the state than enfranchising the discontented: those who had inherited the undesirable portion of progress's legacy.

On the other side of the political coin, it would have been difficult for the staunchest of the Ultra Tories of the early 1830s to argue with Edmund Burke's 1790 admonition that "a state without the means of some change is without the means of its conservation. Without such means it might even risk the loss of that part of the constitution which it wished the most religiously to preserve" (106).[1] Yet few members of either of the two major political parties—not to mention the smaller though extremely influential factions such as the Irish Radicals or even the Utilitarians—would have been able to agree upon what exactly the responsibilities of properly maintaining the "entailed inheritance" of the liberties of the constitution implied, what those liberties were, or to whom they extended.

These issues, questioning the extent to which change must be effected, constituted an integral portion of the debates surrounding the political and social reform of the late 1820s and '30s and became the foundation for ways of thinking and talking about progress that informed the political and social practices of constitutionally empowered institutions, such as Parliament, the cabinet, the crown, and the church as well as the activities of more marginal, yet increasingly powerful, institutions such as the untaxed press, the Chartists, and the trade unions. This discourse of change, in helping to shape political and social action, continued to affect significantly the ways people talked and wrote about political and social issues. The obvious objection to this statement is that it seems to put the cart before the horse, that political and social reforms would not have been possible if the ability to think and speak them had not already existed. To an extent, this objection is valid; but it assumes a simple, unmediated linearity to social and political change that does not exist in real terms.

J. G. A. Pocock offers a way of confronting this difficulty with his conception of a history of discourse, that is, of a history that examines both the events constituting the text of what we traditionally call "history" and the way those events are represented contemporaneously as well as subsequently. Language, at least in its everyday use, is referential, and, as Pocock writes, "it alludes to those elements of experience out of which it has come and with which it offers to deal, and a language current in the public speech of an institutional and political society may be expected to allude to those institutions, authorities, value symbols, and recollected events that it presents as part of that society's politics and from which it derives much of its own character" (12). The language of any public speech act, no matter how oppositional, partakes of the historical, political, or social context within which it is situated. Language in this special, "Pocockian" sense is a set of rules prescribing both the way something may be written or said and the subject matter of the utterance. There is no separating language from those institutions it affirms or opposes, for even though language "to some degree selects and prescribes the context within which it is to be recognized" (12), social and political practices are always reshaping the contextual possibilities within which they and the language accompanying them exist. To this end, progress—inherent to the historical, social, and political contexts[2] of the institutions of the period surrounding the first Reform Bill—is not only an important informing *ideological* concept of the political language of the period, designating the way utterances may be made, it is also an important topic, a "prescribed subject matter," of that political language.

Since the complex and interdependent relation of political language to social and political action is always redefining the possibilities of political utterance, we find that political speech is always functioning in at least two ways. It is "of course practical and informed by present necessities, but it is none the less constantly engaged in a struggle to discover what the present necessities of practice are, and the most powerful minds using it are exploring the tension between established linguistic usages and the need to use words in a new way" (13). Change in usage, the emergence of new meanings, therefore depends on an antagonism between established, institutional, legitimated linguistic usages and social and political pressures that make new meanings possible, even necessary.[3]

Pocock's self-conscious use of the term "language" seems to sever the linguistic activities of politics from its "necessities of practice," but in fact what he is doing is identifying the operations of what another sort of critic might label political discourse. Language of course is discursive, but a number of signifying practices that cannot be reduced to what we usually call "language" can also be so designated. Votes on a bill, maneuvers to form coalitions, consolidations of power within parties, legislatures, or cabinets, even failure to act—not voting or refusing to align—all these and innumerable other practices both partake of and define political discourse. Politics especially is difficult to separate into the distinct spheres of speaking and doing, for in effect, speaking politics *is* doing politics, and often the equation works in reverse as well. Furthermore, politics is always self-referential. To participate in political discourse is always to comment on the discourse itself.

According to Pocock, then, political language (and I would argue all political discourse) is historical in its allusions to the institutions that shape its context, immediate in its active engagement with the necessities and limitations of its context, and forward-looking in its attempts to articulate the trajectory of the changes taking place within its context. These characteristics, however, do not imply that politics is always able to describe accurately its relation to its context. Consider the interpreter (historian, literary or social critic, or novelist) of political utterances. He or she knows the norms usually implied by the discourse informing the speech act, but because of his or her place in time relative to the utterance, may also possess "independent knowledge that these norms and the society they presupposed were changing" in ways and for reasons that the discourse could not yet recognize (13). From this example, we see that while human political existence is linguistically constituted, situations exist in which politics as an interpretive and constitutive enterprise in its own right is "catching up" with its new normative boundaries and the social intercourse prescribed by them.

Two important discursive enterprises find themselves in exactly such a situation by the middle 1830s. On the one hand we find that the novel, which at just this time is taking its place as the primary literary mode, occupies itself with many of the same issues and themes as politics. And while the novel's boundaries are often difficult to define, accommodating themselves to its borrowings from other discourses, especially the ecclesiastical and the political, it is at the same time establishing its own rules, and consequently its own way of constituting the world. This increasingly important discourse is the form, that "perhaps between 1730 and 1750 was temporarily dominant, but . . . from the 1830s . . . is regularly the form in which most major writers work" (Williams, *Writing in Society* 72–73). In the chapters that immediately follow, I will be investigating one particular novel, Benjamin Disraeli's *Coningsby*, as instrumental in establishing the novel as both participating in politics and constituting the way politics represents itself to itself.

Before taking up the intricacies of the multilateral discursive negotiation that goes on between *Coningsby* and parliamentary politics, however, it is useful to consider the self-reflexive and interpretive function of certain political utterances of the late 1820s and the 1830s, when politics finds itself in the Pocockian position of "catching up to itself." Engaged and informed as it is by a representation of society as progressive, parliamentary politics finds itself constantly reassessing the possibilities prescribed by a doctrine of progress to which all political utterances must reconcile themselves. Always at the root of any political discussion in this period are the questions: "How much change? How fast?" "Change to what end?" And "change based upon what model?" The political discourse of the "Age of Reform" can in part be characterized as the struggle of the language of progress to discover the necessities of practice, which themselves are difficult to establish because of the rapidity of material change during this period, and as a calling of itself to account, to explain and address real circumstances that on the one hand it has wrought and on the other is not yet able to articulate fully.

It is at this juncture, the point at which the politics of the late pre-Victorian and the early Victorian period begins to turn an increasingly critical attention upon itself, that we are able to see different possibilities of change assert themselves within the larger discourse of progress. As different political interest groups focused on progress as the prescribed topic of their utterances and attempted to answer the questions of control and extent that confronted any discussion of change in the nineteenth century, they established the rules of their own ways of speaking of progress. These rules governed the "party lines" of the Tories, Whigs, and other political groups, establishing models for speech and action which, while based on traditional interpretations of the party's interests, were continually being revised to meet the immediate needs of their contexts.

A significant example of this type of revision is Sir Robert Peel's famous "Tamworth Manifesto" of 1834, in which he realigns Tory rhetoric, accommodating it to the necessities of the time, especially the conservatives' need to respond more positively to the clamor for reform. Even before his return from a tour of Italy to form the 1834 government, he had been advised as to the wants of the country and the needs of the party. In a December 8, 1834 letter to Peel, Henry Goulburn had written, "all I see around me and learn from other quarters confirms me in the opinion that the property of the country desires a Conservative not an *Ultra*-Tory Government—meaning by that a Government deaf to all improvement that comprises change" (quoted in Kitson Clark, *Peel and the Conservative Party* 209).

The "property" of the country, of course, now also meant those who, under the Reform Act, met the property requirements of the franchise;

and because of the reapportioning of representation, especially the greater representation of manufacturing areas, it was politically prudent to hearken to the interests of the new electorate. On the other hand, the king had exercised his royal prerogative, dismissing the popular ministry and calling upon the opposition to form a new one. Peel was forced into a position of mediator between the "new" constitution and the traditional powers of the king. His address to his constituency of Tamworth is his interpretation of that role and an announcement of the measures that must be taken to accommodate reasonable change and traditional institutions.

After stating his intentions of offering a "frank exposition of general principles and views which appears to be anxiously expected and which it ought not to be the inclination, and cannot be the interest, of a Minister of this country to withhold," Peel describes the action of the king in dismissing the Melbourne ministry as one taken "in a crisis of great difficulty," which required his services (Peel 59). The middle course that Peel outlines in the rest of his address is foreshadowed in this early portion of the speech. While Peel implicitly justifies the king's actions, he makes it clear that as a minister he is also responsible to his constituency, that they have a right to question his policies. Also it is important that he first refers to himself as a "Minister of the country," not as a minister of the crown. By force of the Reform Act, the metonymic implication of this statement has become ambiguous. No longer are king and country necessarily synonymous. The extension of the franchise, based on property qualifications, has turned the country over to the people; they empower the ministers. Thus, Peel's description of himself in his introductory remarks as a minister of the country, though partaking of traditional rhetoric, assumes a new meaning by foregrounding a ministry's accountability to the people while still intimating its duty to the king.

Later in the address, when Peel does refer to the "King's ministers" and the "King's government," it is always with the implication of the government's answerability to the people. In closing, he accepts the office of prime minister in "the firm belief that the people of this country will so far maintain the prerogative of the King, as to give the Ministers of his choice, not an implicit confidence, but a fair trial" (67), thus emphasizing not only the constitutional power that lies with the people to affirm or oppose the actions of their king but also the power of maintaining those ancient institutions, such as the prerogative of the crown to dissolve the government, which for the conservatives are the portions of the constitution they "most religiously wish to preserve."

Whether Peel "held a new language" in this address—a charge by his opponents that he denied (see Peel 67–72)—is less important than the fact that this address was perceived as an utterance shaped by rules which up to that time had not governed conservative politics in England. The conservative organ *The Quarterly Review* supported Peel's address and noted the timeliness of it:

> In former times such a proceeding would have been thought derogatory and impugned as unconstitutional, and would have been both; but the new circumstances in which the Reform Bill has placed the Crown, by making its choice of Ministers immediately and absolutely dependent on the choice of the several constituencies . . . have rendered such a course not merely expedient but necessary. (53 [April 1835]: 266)

The moderate path of this "new conservatism" did not interpret the "spirit of the Reform Bill" as suggesting that "we are to live in a perpetual vortex of agitation; that public men can only support themselves in public estimation by adopting every popular impression of the day,—by promising the instant redress of anything which anybody may call an abuse; by abandoning altogether that great aid of government—. . . the respect for ancient rights, and the deference to prescriptive authority." Rather, according to Peel the act encouraged "a careful review of institutions, civil and ecclesiastical, undertaken in a friendly temper, combining with the firm maintenance of established rights, the correction of proved abuses and the redress of real grievances" (Peel 62). It reconciled the conservative interest to the unyielding doctrine of progress that had helped bring about the Reform Act without causing conservatives to give up completely their old rhetoric of protection of ancient rights. Peel's address attempts to coopt the notion of reform for the conservatives by calling for reasonable, cautious change. The party, with Peel as its spokesman, expediently and necessarily reinterprets the relation of its interests to the demands of its social and political context, accommodating itself to those demands.

In contrast, but not too much contrast, to Peel's reinterpretation of the conservative mission are T. B. Macaulay's expressions of the liberal Whig agenda, which like conservatism attempts to reshape itself to the ideological (that is, progressive) demands of the period. Seemingly in near agreement with the Peelite Tories on many issues, Macaulay is at great pains, from very early in his political career, to delineate the difference between Tory and Whig policies in an age of reform. The problem with the

Tory approach to reform, according to Macaulay, is that it is too slow to make necessary changes, and thus perpetuates social and political unrest. For Macaulay, the radicals (both the Popular Radicals and the Utilitarians) and the Tories belong together at the extremes of civil prudence. The conservative engenders the radical, and both are enemies of the orderly progress of society.

Nor does the emergence of a moderate conservative leader like Peel necessarily mitigate the effects of long standing Tory policy. For while he may be "free from the fanaticism which is found in so large a measure among his followers," the party itself "has become fiercer and more intolerant even than in days gone by" (*Hansard* 54:1355–56, June 19, 1840). In Macaulay's eyes, the Tories were at fault for not perceiving the present necessities of political practice, for not participating in "true statesmanship," and for being willing, as he argued, to sacrifice practical considerations for "general doctrines."[4] The ultimate result of placing conservative doctrine before practical necessity is the empowering of dangerous radical leaders. For "when men are refused what is reasonable they . . . demand what is unreasonable. . . .They lend a too favourable ear to worthless agitators." Thus it is that the true power of demagogues "is the obstinacy of rulers" and that "a liberal Government makes a conservative people" (*Speeches* July 5, 1831, 28–29).

The focus of Macaulay's attack on the Tories is on its recalcitrance in shaping its policies to what William Hazlitt and later John Stuart Mill labeled "The Spirit of the Age." True, Macaulay argues on the floor of the Commons in 1844, the Tories had made some concessions to change— most notably Catholic Emancipation. Yet even that important reform was not prudently passed in 1813, 1821, or "even in 1825," when such a change might have removed grievances and avoided indignation. Rather the act was passed four years later, for all the wrong reasons, at a time when it was absolutely demanded, with violence—possibly even civil war—the alternative to reform. And then, states Macaulay, the reform was "made reluctantly, and with obvious dislike" (*Hansard* 72:1176, Feb. 19, 1844).[5]

The paradox of the policies of Tory conservatism for Macaulay is that, in refusing to come to amicable terms with a changing society and effect moderate, controlled change, the Tory party is always too dilatory and too parsimonious in its attempts at concession. Thus inadvertently, though surely, it endangers both church and state by alienating even the moderate middle class and making radicalism a desirable alternative to political and social stasis. In conflict in Tory policies were the basic presuppositions that had informed party action from the time of Wellington's first ministry throughout the 1830s. On the one hand was the overarching discourse of progress that called for change and ameliorative measures and that, as Peel's Tamworth address indicates, must be heeded; on the other hand and in direct opposition to a general faith in progress was a nostalgia for times past, a nostalgia Macaulay viciously attacks in his famous review of Robert Southey's *Colloquies on Society*:

> Here is wisdom. Here are the principles on which nations are to be governed. Rose bushes and poor-rates, rather than steam engines and independence. Mortality and cottages with weather-stains, rather than health and long life with edifices that time cannot mellow. . . . Does Mr. Southey think that the body of the English peasantry live, or ever lived, in substantial or ornamented cottages, with box-hedges, flower gardens, bee-hives, and orchards? (342)

The incompatibility of Peel's and Southey's positions underscores what Macaulay sees as the primary struggle within the Tory party, which allows necessary changes to be made only in extreme conditions, that is, when the "very foundations of society" are threatened. A government attempting to reconcile these two polar positions, coupled with the Tory tendency to exert social control through suppressive legislation, in Macaulay's view, exacerbates and engenders rather than removes grievances (cf. Hamburger 40).

Macaulay's remedy to the extremes of radical and conservative politics was a flexible center that based its policies on symptomatic interpretations of present needs as they have been produced by society's "noiseless revolutions." These revolutions are those unguided changes that take place within a society but whose

> progress is rarely indicated by what historians are pleased to call important events. They are not achieved by armies or enacted by senates. They are sanctioned by no treaties, and recorded in no archives. They are carried on in every school, in every church, behind ten thousand counters, at ten thousand firesides. The upper current of society presents no certain criterion by which we can judge of the direction in which the undercurrent flows. ("History" 156)

Changes in morals, manners, and taste, economic and demographic shifts, changes in fashion, in religious beliefs, technological advances, changes in methods of philosophical and scientific inquiry are all examples of what Macaulay identified as "noiseless revolutions." And it is these, as much as military and diplomatic exertions, that bring about political change, establishing new institutions that reform the old order, but that in time will themselves need to be reformed.

Macaulay's interpretation of the nineteenth century was crucially shaped by the analogies he found between his own time and the seventeenth century. The history of that period and the mistakes of Charles I, "who would govern the men of the seventeenth century as if they had been men of the sixteenth century," had important implications for him. They "are written," Macaulay said, "for our instruction": "Another great intellectual revolution has taken place; our lot has been cast on a time analogous, in many respects, to the time which immediately preceded the meeting of the Long Parliament. There is a change in society. There must be a corresponding change in the government" (*Speeches* 79–80).

As is obvious from the earlier passage from "History," Macaulay saw these changes as moving forward, progressing. Political change, however, rarely occurs in the same ways as social change, and it is up to those in a position to initiate political change to do so through the careful, empirical observation of the "undercurrent of society" over a long period. Only through an empirical approach may one inductively formulate the criteria necessary to recognize correctly (and promptly) the direction of the undercurrent and coordinate the flow of the upper current with it, thus averting maelstrom and crisis.

From this brief examination of Peel's and Macaulay's utterances, which —despite their opposition—occupy the political middle, several conclusions can be drawn. First, and above all, we see that politics in attempting to determine the present necessities of practice is engaged in interpretive activity. Further, we see that the text with which parliamentary political discourse is concerned is not only the context of its present situation but also the intertext of its heritage. Thus the interpretative activity of an utterance from within this discourse is multiply bound. It must interpret and represent the conditions of society it intends to address, but it must also interpret its own legacy and tradition and attempt to formulate its perceived necessary course of action, its program, in accordance with the rules of action dictated by its past. To the extent that those acknowledging a specific political affiliation accommodate their utterances to the past, that is, talk in Tory or Whig (or radical, monarchist, or even anarchist) ways, they define their own positions within a group, Parliament, which in its own right subscribes to certain rules that regulate interpretation. Very schematically then, the participants in parliamentary politics of the late 1820s through the 1830s and '40s were members of an "interpretive community" that was divided into two main camps: those who interpreted the needs of society in terms that demanded dramatic redefinitions of existing institutions—yet who always worked to reform from within those institutions, even when calling for their ultimate demise—; and those who favored a less drastic change—a change that addressed the demands of the present, but not at so great a cost to the past.[6] And despite its internal variances and oppositions, the institution of Parliament remained, in practice, a unified community, defining a space for political utterances that, when taken together, were recognized as "legitimate" politics in Britain in the second quarter of the nineteenth century.[7]

Of course not all legitimate political statements are uttered within the walls of the legislature. Politics and its statements are public inasmuch as they address public issues and concerns, are available for public commentary, and are carried on by those who are not actually members of the cabinet or Parliament. Nevertheless, even in the public domain, the rules of political discourse are defined by its dominant institution, in this case Parliament, and consequently the discourse functions within the limits prescribed by those rules. These rules are informed by the shared presuppositions of those acting within the discourse and are "prerequisite to perception itself" (cf. Kuhn 113). The object of interpretation is already—in some ways—predetermined by the discourse available for interpreting it and can only be seen within the limits of that discourse.[8] For mid-nineteenth-century British politics this meant that the extent to which it was possible to address social problems was directly related to politics' ability to perceive and articulate those problems within the limits of interpretation available to it.

As I mentioned earlier, one of the discourses that competed with politics in perceiving and articulating those problems was the novel. The extent of the novel's reach in the early Victorian years should not be underestimated. Between 1800 and 1850 the population of England and Wales grew from 8.9 to 17.9 million; and the population of Scotland, an important market for English books and periodicals, grew from 2.09 to 4.5 million between 1821 and 1901 (Porter, *Progress of the Nation* [1912] 3–4; quoted in Altick 81). Raymond Williams has estimated that nearly 12 million of mainland Britain's 20 million inhabitants in 1840 were literate. As might be expected, the remarkable increase in the number of readers led to a substantial increase in the number of books published during this period. Between 1802 and 1827 the average annual number of published titles (new books and reissues) was 580; by 1850 that number had grown to more than 2600, many of which were novels (*Writing in Society* 69–70). Nor were the writings of extremely popular novelists, such as Dickens, limited to the literate: "Mrs. Hogarth's charwoman, who lodged at a snuff-shop, attended a monthly tea at which the landlord read the new number of *Dombey* to the assembled lodgers" (Tillotson 21).

It is entirely a propos that the charwoman should go to hear *Dombey and Son* read, for it is in this novel that "Dickens undertakes a comprehensive, unified presentation of social life by depicting how an abstract principle conditions all experience. That principle is change" (Marcus, *Pickwick to Dombey* 298). Indeed, the supposition underlying nearly all novelistic discourse during the 1830s and '40s is change, which "altered not only outward forms—institutions and landscapes—but also inward feelings, experiences, self-definitions. These facts of change can be seen lying deep in almost every imagination" (Williams, *English Novel* 12). Change became both the object and the informing ideological presupposition of the nineteenth-century novel, just as it had of politics. Yet because these two important discursive systems of early Victorian England are similarly informed ideologically, it does not necessarily follow that they are identical or that their perceptions of society are the same. Rather, politics and the novel are two major systems of interpretation and signification at work in this period, two systems that often overlap, each sharing certain aspects of its language and interpretations with the other, at times blatantly borrowing from the other in order to reinforce its own arguments. At the same time, each exists as unique and in many ways independent of the other; each exerts its power sometimes in unison with, sometimes against the other.

Most critics of the early Victorian novel, especially what has come to be called the "industrial" or "social" novel, have argued for the preeminence of political over aesthetic discourse, coopting the novel's own discursive space for the "political" utterances and practices surrounding the industrialization of England in the early and mid nineteenth century. Beginning with Louis Cazamian's assertion that "[the social novel] maintained a close relationship with political agitation, and its development mirrored the phases, and to some extent took on the pattern, of the Victorian era" (4), considerations of the constitutive force of the novel have taken a subordinate place to discussions of those discourses that inform the novel. Even Catherine Gallagher's original and important work, *The Industrial Reformation of English Fiction*, which focuses on problems of representation and the negotiations between the novel and other discourses, retains in its title the residuum of Victorianists' tendency to privilege the novel as "made" instead of "making."

Granted, novels are important historical social documents and are significantly shaped by the world that they try to represent and, as I argue, interpret. And the exercise of "reading history" through an investigation of the conditions that helped to shape this genre of document is useful for understanding the period. Certainly, that technique will be valuable in this study. However, studies that base themselves on the subordination of the novel to other discourses fail in one important respect; they fail to examine the discursive power of the novel itself in its relation to other discourses in a reciprocal rather than a unilateral way. If, as Clifford Geertz has argued, culture is a semiotic concept (5), then it seems unproductive to elevate one portion of the signifier to a privileged, a priori status, thus reducing other aspects of culture to derivations. Of course, the problems entailed in "thick description" prohibit considering all aspects of any cultural phenomenon, but the caveat against the temptation of considering relations between and among discourses within a culture as linear and (even implicitly) causal should be heeded. In the case of the relationship between the novel and parliamentary politics in the early Victorian period, a fruitful examination will be one that focuses on how each of these powerful interpretive enterprises works to inform, subvert, or reinforce the other and on how those working within these two signifying systems accommodate themselves to the rules that govern the articulation of statements, how these rules of articulation change, and how the lived experiences of those who are affected by both the novel and politics correlate with changes in these discourses. The best place to begin such a study is with an example of one who successfully accommodated his own utterances to the various demands of the rules of both the political and the novelistic, yet who at the same time is able to stretch the limits of those rules and infuse each discourse with new ways of speaking and interpreting.

2

Fiction into Fiction

After four unsuccessful attempts in five years, Benjamin Disraeli finally won a seat in Parliament in 1837 and almost immediately gave his maiden speech. The results were nearly disastrous. One observer recalls Disraeli beginning with "florid assurance," but "speedily degenerating into ludicrous absurdity" and "being at last put down with inextinguishable shouts of laughter" (Greville 3:404). Rising directly after Daniel O'Connell had been a mistake. The Irish leader and his followers created such an uproar that they succeeded in hooting down the freshman MP. In a manner that would become his political trademark, however, Disraeli was able to turn this initial embarrassment to his advantage. He writes to his sister Sarah of how R. L. O'Shiel, an Irish MP of longstanding and with little love of O'Connell or his tactics, overheard "a knot of low Rads" disparaging Disraeli at the Athenaeum:

> Suddenly Shiel threw down the paper and said in his shrill voice, "Now gentlemen, I have heard all you have to say, and, what is more, I heard this same speech of Mr. Disraeli, and I tell you this: if ever the spirit of oratory was in a man, it is in that man. Nothing can prevent him from being one of the first speakers in the House of Commons. . . . If there had not been this interruption, Mr. Disraeli might have made a failure; I don't call this a failure, it is a crush. . . . The House will not allow a man to be a wit and an orator, unless they have the credit of finding it out." (Quoted in Monypenny and Buckle 2:13)

Later that same evening Disraeli chanced to meet O'Shiel, who stood by his analysis of Disraeli's situation, advising him to "get rid of your genius for a session. Speak often for you must not show yourself cowed, but speak shortly. Be very quiet, try to be dull. . . . Quote figures, dates, calculations. And in a short time the house will sigh for the wit and elegance which they all know are in you" (Monypenny and Buckle 14).

Disraeli's dubious start is directly connected to issues of discursive competence. As O'Shiel intimated to the young MP, he overstepped the bounds of parliamentary political discourse, pushing against the usual confines of the public political speech act so strenuously that his performance was completely subsumed by its opposite—inarticulate, though signifying, shouts of laughter and derision. In taking the floor as speaker, Disraeli placed himself squarely within the matrix of relations and regulations that are both informed by and sustain parliamentary political discourse. Consequently, his subjectivity within that discourse immediately took shape, and he was summarily hailed into place as an audacious and somewhat dandyish new member of the House of Commons. Not only his speech and its performance but the topic upon which he spoke, his choice of time to rise, his response to the "low rads and repealers," and even his later meeting with O'Shiel demonstrate that however full he may have been of the "spirit of oratory" and however well informed he may have been about parliamentary politics as an object of study, as an agent within its discursive operations Disraeli was in unfamiliar terrain.

With the 1844 publication of *Coningsby, or The New Generation*, Disraeli made it obvious he had found his discursive footing and was sure enough of it to demolish the already dilapidated bridge spanning the broad political and personal chasm between himself and the Tory leader, Peel.[1] This novel, the first he had written since entering the House, attempts to expose the wrong-headed course of politics, especially Tory politics, since the advent of reform. It traces the beginnings of the party's troubles back to Liverpool's "arch-mediocrity" and Wellington's mismanagement, then fixes on what Disraeli considers the flaws of Sir Robert's administration, ferociously criticizing the prime minister for failing to establish sound principles of conservatism and for deserting the Tory standard in favor of Whiggish policies.

The novel's plot is thin and partly derived from some of Disraeli's earlier, pre-MP works, most notably *Vivian Grey* and *Contarini Fleming*. Following its eponymous hero's development from naive Eton school boy to newly elected, idealistic MP, the story itself is remarkable primarily for its typicality: Harry Coningsby, an orphan, is the ward and favorite of his powerful and rich grandfather, the Marquess of Monmouth. He falls in love with the daughter of his grandfather's oldest and bitterest enemy, parts ways with his grandfather, proves himself to his sweetheart's father by living in penury while studying for the bar, effects an uneasy reconciliation with his grandfather, marries his sweetheart (and her fortune), and is returned for Darlford in the election of 1841. At the end of the novel, Harry and the other young men of his generation stand on the threshold of public life, prepared to "denounce to a perplexed and disheartened world the frigid theories of a generalising age that have destroyed the individuality of man" and to "restore the happiness of their country by believing in their own energies and daring to be great" (503).

In the discussion that follows I will be putting aside certain vexed questions of genre such as whether *Coningsby* was the first "political novel"; whether it should be read as a "manifesto" of the Young England movement or, as Robert O'Kell has argued, as a psychological romance; and even what exactly we mean when we call a work a "political novel." Instead I will be focus more on what *Coningsby* does than on how we can label it. As unsurprising as its plot may be, in another register this work differs significantly from other novels of the period, for along with the tale of Harry's education and success, it tells the story of politics in England from Liverpool to Peel. And in this novel the discursive boundaries of parliamentary politics—its utterances and activities—are called into question and reassessed. It is this that makes *Coningsby* singular.

Peel and Macaulay, as I showed in the preceding chapter, were endeavoring to retrace the political genealogies of their respective parties and to extend the limits of what might be thought, said, and done in (and as) politics. But their attempts emanated from within the very discourse that had legitimized their ability to make those statements:they spoke (or wrote) from within parliamentary politics. Their interpretations, transformative as they were, also depended upon maintaining politics as a discursive system. Even as they called their affiliations, their parties, and their very political existences to account along the Pocockian lines that emphasize a connection between a statement and the material needs it seeks to address, their own statements were necessarily circumscribed by the limits of thought and action that define early Victorian Parliamentary politics, thus highlighting the paradoxes of their political subjectivities. Macaulay, the advocate of franchise extension, cannot conceive of universal suffrage in Britain as either a necessary or a desirable goal. Nor, for that matter, can Peel imagine his trimming stand between the crown and the electors of Tamworth as constituted by any "new" language; and his address ultimately affirms the power of the prime minister.

In contrast, *Coningsby* calls Parliamentary politics to account in terms of a competing interpretive enterprise, the novel. The discursive practices of the novel necessarily govern the articulation of its interpretation of political discourse; consequently, the political utterances that exist within the world of *Coningsby* will also subscribe to those practices and in that sense become "novelized" in the process. One result of the confrontation and combination of these two important early Victorian discourses is a synthesis of interpretive enterprises in which statements may still be recognized as "political," but are no longer necessarily constrained by the limits of "conventional" parliamentary political discourse. *Coningsby* becomes a space in which politics may dwell. But because it is a novel functioning according to the presuppositions of noticeability and relevance that define it as fiction, it can comment upon, interpret, *think* politics in ways politics cannot think or know itself. To this end, *Coningsby* opens up political discourse to new possibilities of transformation, and many of the statements within it have a dual affiliation. The result is a reshaping of the epistemological, and thus ontological, boundaries of both the novel and Parliamentary politics as each remarks and impinges upon the other.

In the pages that follow, I will examine the outlines of those boundaries and identify the ways in which discursive systems reinforce and diverge from each other in their competing interpretations of the world. I am not interested in demonstrating the "expressive causality" of either *Coningsby* or the novel as genre. Rather, I want to support my assertions from Chapter I by establishing the novel in a genealogy of discourses whose conditions of possibility define what we perceive as the culture of the early Victorians, and thus to place the novel on the same discursive and constitutive footing as other important interpretive enterprises of the era. As for *Coningsby* specifically, this novel connects itself to the social, the political, what one might call the actual, in a way that can hardly be said to have been done so effectively before. This novel forces its way in among the many competing utterances of Parliamentary party politics by dint of its very *fictiveness* and what that fiction, that narrative, has to say about a discourse—politics—that it presents as increasingly vacillatory and incompetent.

From its first scene, *Coningsby* criticizes the efficacy of current party politics, as well as its utterances. But in these early pages, its assault on Tory inadequacies is not frontal, that is, it is not operating within the discourse of Parliamentary politics but is cast in novelistic terms. No page one tirades on the state of government for *Coningsby*. Instead, the novel opens rather conventionally, describing a "youth of still tender age" being ushered into the waiting-room "of a house in the vicinity of St. James' Square" (31). The youth is Harry Coningsby and the house is the Tory Carlton Club, recently established by the Duke of Wellington. The description of the club as a house of "no very ambitious character" metonymically comments on the state of the party itself, a comment that becomes more explicit in later chapters of the novel and that will sound as a refrain throughout the work. According to *Coningsby*, not only is the conservative party unsure of what it means to conserve, but the pronouncement of stasis as the party philosophy in a time of unprecedented change further subverts any claims to ambition the party may have.

As if to underscore the pervasively stultifying effects of the Tories, Disraeli describes a young Coningsby, who, had opportunity offered, would "have found amusement and even instruction." In the house "surrounded by dead walls," however, Harry is reduced to pacing about the room and writing his name over several "sheets of foolscap paper," where he "drew various landscapes and faces of his friends; and then, splitting up a pen or two, delivered himself of a yawn which seemed the climax of his weariness" (31). Within the party and within the Carlton Club, both essentially "built" by Wellington, a youth of ability, enterprise, and promise seems able to find nothing to do except indulge his vanities. Yet Harry manages to find one useful task to set for himself. Just before Rigby, his escort and his grandfather's henchman, comes to take him to the marquess, Harry notices that a portrait of Wellington is askew, climbs on a chair, and adjusts it, signalling that while the party may be stifling to the promise of one of such remarkable character as Coningsby, certain tasks depend on Harry and his kind for their completion; once within its structure, Harry and those like him will realign a party that has gone awry.

Tory policy and practice are very much an object of presentation in this first chapter. Young Harry's "setting right" Wellington, the "surprise" announcement of the dissolution of Parliament, and Rigby's portrayal as a perpetual political spear carrier who believes himself to be on the inside but is always just out of the loop, all denote the topical primacy of Parliamentary politics. But *Coningsby* is not a party pamphlet or the text of a speech on the floor of the House of Commons. It is a novel. And Harry's housekeeping, Rigby's sanctimonious self-justifications, and the news of Lyndhurst's meeting with the king introduce the characters and the setting of the novel just as surely as they represent the condition of the party. If *Coningsby* is to function as novel—even in modifying the genre—it must create and populate a fictive world that has significance for its characters and its readers. Only when a world that shares common referents with the reader's world has been established can the work put actual political language in the characters' mouths, for only then can politics become a more central topic for the work.

The first several chapters of *Coningsby* describe only enough of the state of party politics in 1832 to establish the context of Harry's life. Characterization and plot occupy center stage. And although the characters who march across the pages of those early chapters are obviously, inextricably entwined in the web of party politics, the reader is never quite sure precisely what those entanglements are. As novelistic discourse subtly subsumes overt political discourse, party politics remains a hazy, somewhat removed narrative backdrop. Politics seems less important as romantic affiliations between characters begin to develop, though even the marriage plot is always subordinate to the *bildungsroman* aspect of the work. *Coningsby* thus begins to fulfill its reader's expectations of what a Victorian novel does: establishing relationships between characters, following the development of a protagonist, offering the possibility of plot lines to be explored, and either pursued or abandoned—in short creating an imaginary world, but not so imaginary that the reader cannot identify in some way with its workings.

This insistence on the novelistic abruptly changes in chapter 7, the first of many that are almost entirely devoted to an extended description, and therefore interpretation, of the novel's political context. The shift is so sudden that the chapter seems generically misplaced, an ultra-Tory diatribe in the midst of a novel. Beginning with a restrained attack on Wellington's actions just prior to the passage of the 1832 Reform Bill, it goes on to heavily opinionated exposition of the events surrounding the ratification of the extension of the vote. In the face of this short history lesson, the novel's main characters drop entirely out of the text and only reappear in the chapter's last three paragraphs.[2] And when they do come back into view, as suddenly as they disappeared, their connections to the political events just described remain as distant and indistinct as ever. Politics once again seems no more than novelistic dressing, a familiar setting in which the characters may develop:

> During this eventful week of May 1832, when an important revolution was effected in the most considerable of modern kingdoms, in a manner so tranquil, that the victims themselves were scarcely conscious at the time of the catastrophe, Coningsby passed his hours in unaccustomed pleasures, and in novel excitement. Although he heard daily from the lips of Mr. Rigby and his friends that England was for ever lost, the assembled guests still contrived to do justice to his grandfather's excellent dinners. (66)

Despite this scene's function as transition back into the fictional world of the novel, it seems particularly out of place. It comes at the end of an overtly "political" chapter in which the importance of current politics is urgently stressed. If politics was to become the dominant discursive mode in this chapter, that possibility seems subverted. Not only does the placement of the scene pull the figurative rug out from under political discourse, but the activities within the scene also contribute to the domination of the novelistic over the political. Whatever importance politics may have assumed in the foregoing pages of the chapter is undercut by the narrative's poking fun at Rigby's overemphasis of political events and by hinting at the true repercussions of the impending Reform Act on aristocratic mores and privileges. Further, the descriptions of Harry speak directly to the conventions of the silver-fork novel, the fictional subgenre upon which Disraeli cut his literary teeth. The text even plays with the word "novel," suggesting that both new and literary amusements occupied the protagonist's time and energies. In light of this sort of self-referentiality, the portrayal of Rigby as an overwrought and comic reactionary, and of Harry and the others stuffing themselves at the marquess's table, it is difficult to imagine how any legitimized political event might upset the order of things.

At another level, however, politics, while presenting no immediately dire consequences to any of the characters save perhaps Rigby, lurks in the background, managing such a "tranquil" revolution that "its victims" are scarcely sensible of it. At least a good portion of the ironic thrust of this scene is that Rigby is right, though he little suspects how right he is. Remember, the novel's contemporary readers have already lived through the effects of the first Reform Bill. Rigby's warning, however ridiculous it may seem to the other characters in the novel, and however overstated it may seem to pro-reform readers of the work, no doubt had some ring of truth to it for all who had experienced the political uncertainty of those days in May 1832. Rigby's fears have no material referent for the other characters in the novel. But they do reach beyond the confines of the novelistic world, and for contemporary readers his pronouncement exists simultaneously within novelistic and political discourse. The irony that encases Rigby's statement, an irony based upon what the characters cannot know and the reader cannot help but know, both undercuts *and* underscores the political content of the chapter.

The irony of this paragraph also performs the important function of allowing the novelistic discourse to regain control of the narrative. In this chapter *Coningsby* begins to tell the story of contemporary English politics in earnest, a telling made possible by conventions of fiction, but a telling nonetheless reliant on political, especially Tory, utterances. This becomes problematic, for the political language of the Tory party has as its referents "real" situations, events, objects. The referential world of this novel, how-ever, is fictive, imaginary despite its *roman à clef* characteristics. As author, Disraeli must negotiate between these discourses and their requirements. One way he does this is by giving political utterances a quasi-fictional refer-entiality. That is to say, in loosening the relations of the referents of political language in *Coningsby* from questions of veracity or truth testing, he creates a place for it in the novel. For the characters seated at the marquess's dinner table, the political events of 1832, at least at that moment, do not appear to have any real significance. Rigby's ranting about the loss of England only contributes to their interpretations of the events. Coming from the inept old pol who is invariably wrong and always overly reactionary, Rigby's pronouncements affirm the aristocrats' belief that little will change. At this point in the novel, the discourse of Parliamentary politics is self-contained. Its battles are fought with considerable vehemence, but it ultimately con-stitutes nothing beyond itself. It does not affect those dining in Coningsby Castle, nor is it expected to affect those supping elsewhere in the kingdom. The discourse of politics is presented as a sort of fiction in itself: its utter-ances are always esoteric, its representations always of itself and to itself, its factions and divisions paradoxically necessary for the overall coherence of its discourse but without correspondence to the world beyond it.

One way *Coningsby* supports this representation of politics is by ex-amining party affiliations and the statements reinforcing them. These are givens for the novel's characters, not to be questioned without upsetting the entire discourse of parliamentary party politics and forcing it under a scrutiny that, the novel argues, it can little bear. Up to the point when Harry becomes friends with the younger Millbank and begins to hear opin-ions that are new to him, he never questions the validity of the political legacy he has inherited. He considers himself a high Tory,

> which he was according to the revelation of the Rigbys, he was also sufficiently familiar with the hereditary tenets of his Whig friend, Lord Vere. Politics had as yet appeared to him a struggle whether the country was to be governed by Whig nobles or Tory nobles; and he thought it very unfortunate that he should probably have to enter life with his friends out of power and his family boroughs destroyed. (131)

Harry's political subjectivity is passively constituted, a formation of the "revelations of the Rigbys" and "hereditary tenets." He is bound by these utterances, unable to think of himself as anything but Tory. And since such discursive acts function both to fix the political subject and to reinforce the dynamics of the discourse of party politics, it is a matter of no concern if "conservative" has any referent as long as Toryism is accepted as a political philosophy. While in the course of the novel Harry and his circle do come to question the assumptions of the political allegiances they are expected to hold, they are clearly the exceptions. For most, politics is carried on as usual: Rigby at the end of the novel is still trying to be returned as a high Tory candidate, and the marquess, a few chapters earlier, exhibits his unwillingness to question the viability of party line language as a function of political discourse. "But what is the use of lamenting the past?" he concedes to Harry. "Peel is the only man; suited to the times and all that; at least we must *say* so, and try to *believe* so; we can't go back. And it is our own fault that we have let the chief power out of the hands of our own order. It was never thought of in the time of your great-grandfather, sir" (427; emphasis added).

Although clearly a pragmatist for whom the end of "all parties and politics" is to gain one's object, and who is aware of the inconsistencies and irrelevancies in current conservative practices and language, Monmouth will allow neither himself nor his grandson to act upon those conclusions. Quite to the contrary, Monmouth wants to follow Pascal's advice. But even when on his knees and moving his lips he cannot believe. Tory politics has proven utterly unreliable to him and his order. Recognizing the limits of one's politics, however, does not mean easily discarding them. Both he and Rigby are experienced in the intricacies of the old Tory party line, and both understand the difficulty of assuming a new political rhetoric. Likewise, they both fail to see how a different way of interpreting the political world would be any more effective. They have become symbolic relics of the old order, doomed, respectively, either to death or to defeat. As Sidonia tells Harry at their first meeting, "The Age of Ruins is past" (141).

By declaring the death of the old order and by enthusiastically affirming the irresistible progress it finds almost everywhere,[3] *Coningsby* achieves two very important effects, in part by exploiting a certain slippage between conceptions of the novel and "fiction." First, it establishes the quasi-fictional referentiality of high Tory politics, showing that the actions and principles of those who still proclaim themselves Tories have little relation to real world situations or needs. In this instance, fictionality functions pejoratively, insinuating falseness and deception. Second, the referential world of the novel, linked as it is to a society obsessed with moving forward, becomes increasingly immediate and "real." The "fictional" status of the novel, however, does not receive the same evaluation that political fictions do, precisely because it asserts itself as a more accurate version of lived experience. Thus, the "truth values" attached to the respective referents of the novel and politics essentially exchange affiliations: within the novel, the referents of political statements appear based in fiction and the referents of the novel come to seem factual.

To the extent that Disraeli is working within two distinct interpretive systems, he is also attempting to affect the way each orders the world it interprets. Using the interpretive conventions of the novel, *Coningsby* remodels fiction's connection to politics, making the discourse of parliamentary party politics more overtly the object of interpretation than any earlier novel ever had. If the importance of this link was not clear in the 1844 edition, Disraeli certainly left no room for doubt when the work was reissued in 1849: "It was not originally the intention of the writer to adopt the form of fiction as the instrument to scatter his suggestions, but, after reflection, he resolved to avail himself of a method which, in the temper of the times, offered the best chance of influencing opinion" ("Preface," fifth edition of *Coningsby*). The novel, particularly this novel, becomes a political tool and every message it conveys must be read within a political context, a context of interpreting and acting on present needs. At the same time, many of the presuppositions of that political context are questioned, especially those associated with the contemporary Tory party. According to *Coningsby*, the conservative party has severely declined since the "Archmediocrity" of the Liverpool ministry, and in an effort to save itself has forsaken its principles. The programmatic statements of *Coningsby* therefore present themselves as having a greater basis in the real than the utterances of those who call themselves conservatives. Claiming that the principles of the party never change and that those who claim Tory affiliations are not "true Tories," but in fact are "pseudo-Tories" (95), *Coningsby* asserts the gap that has opened between public needs and Tory policy. Even the nominal savior of the Tories, Sir Robert Peel, "who had escaped from Lord Liverpool, escaped from Mr. Canning, escaped even from the Duke of Wellington in 1832, was at length caught in 1834; the victim of ceaseless intriguers, who neither comprehended his position, nor that of their country" (108). According to *Coningsby*, Peel turns his back on the Tories when he issues the "Tamworth Manifesto." For Disraeli, as the narrator of *Coningsby*, this amounts to an articulation of a conservatism that "discards Prescription, shrinks from Principle, disavows Progress; having rejected all respect for Antiquity, it offers no redress for the Present, and makes no preparation for the Future . . . and the Conservative Constitution will be discovered to be a Caput Mortuum" (126).

The force of Disraeli's attack on Peel is in his insistence that the Manifesto's representation of the current political situation bears no resemblance to the immediate and ongoing needs of England; nor for that matter does it jibe with what, in Disraeli's mind, conservatism should stand for. Both referents—the needs of society and the tradition of conservatism—are replaced in the new conservative interpretations of the things most necessary for party solidarity and efficacy. For *Coningsby* these new referents are chimerical, without basis in the real, and consequently their function as the ground for Toryism increasingly weakens that political philosophy's connection to real world needs. In Baudrillardian terms Peel's Toryism is a simulacrum of conservatism, not the thing itself. As a simulacrum it may function within its discursive realm and may even have effects in that realm. But it is without access to the world that *Coningsby* claims to be better able to represent and understand. In this novel, the Manifesto becomes a fiction within a fiction, and its tenuous links to the material base of politics are highlighted. Disraeli denies Peel's reconstruction of his and the party's political genealogy, insisting instead that the conservative policies that flow from the Tamworth address are a bad-faith revision of conservative principles, full of sound and fury, perhaps, but signifying nothing.

Coningsby affects the world it creates by focusing directly on its competition with political discourse. It subsumes the political into the novelistic, formulating political statements according not only to what can be *politically* voiced but also to what novels can (or cannot) say. The lines between the political and the novelistic are blurred and particular utterances seem to belong to both discourses simultaneously. The result of this synthesis is that the subject matter, *what* is said, ultimately supersedes *how* a statement is made. The text of Tory party statements becomes the subject matter of the novel. Thus the "Tamworth Manifesto" is cast first as an important object of interpretation, as a statement emanating from within the discourse of politics and as having specific institutional impacts on the way the party perceives and presents itself, on the formation of conservative ideology, and on the activities the party undertakes.

However, the Manifesto is disarticulated according to its existence *within* the world of the novel. The coherence of the world of *Coningsby* and the ability of the discourse of the novel to establish the relations of its characters to that world place the text of the Manifesto in dramatic relief. In *Coningsby*, Peel's famous speech cannot explain characters' political subjectivities. As a way of making sense of *Coningsby*'s world it fails utterly. In an ironic *mise-en-abyme*, Peel's real world statement has "only" fictional status in the novel. Its referents are not those of the characters, its justifications are incomprehensible, and the discourse from whence it flows appears to be on the verge of losing its institutional power. Throughout this dismantling of political discourse within the novel, *Coningsby* continues to refer outside itself and the universe it has created, making the history and intertext of Peel's political life and statements as important to this novel as any of its literary forebears.

Since, according to *Coningsby*, the new conservative interpretations of social needs serve no better than the old, new principles of relevance and noticeability must arise and assert themselves if the conservative party is to survive and flourish. This means that the basic tenets of Toryism must be made to extend to a nation that has already begun to bellow for new methods of ordering its changes. As early as the Liverpool ministry, "Commerce requested a code; trade required a currency; the unfranchised subject solicited his equal privilege; suffering labour clamoured for its rights; a new race demanded education" (97). *Coningsby* identifies a veritable babble of tongues crying out for new ways of thinking and speaking that will reinforce the lived relations of the subject to his world and that will constitute those relations as progress, interpreting the world as one moving forward and meeting these social needs.

This novel asserts that the snag in forming a new, more authentic conservative political paradigm that can confront these freshly emergent needs defines Peel's dilemma: how can a discourse of ameliorative change also be one of conservatism? *Coningsby* answers by positing a new telos for political change. Not in spite of Parliamentary reform but because of it, *Coningsby* argues that "the political movements of our time, which seem on the surface to have a tendency to democracy, may have in reality, a monarchical bias" (64). This interpretation of early Victorian political tendencies directly conflicts with the analysis of liberal commentators like John Stuart Mill:

> by the natural growth of civilization, power passes from individuals to masses, and the weight and importance of an individual as compared with the mass, sink into greater and greater insignificance. . . . The triumph of democracy, or, in other words, of the government of public opinion, does not depend upon the opinion of any individual or set of individuals that it ought to triumph, but upon the natural laws of the progress of wealth, upon the diffusion of reading, and the increase of the facilities of human intercourse. ("Civilisation" [1836] 53)

Coningsby does not refute Mill's definitions of civilization, nor does it deny the "natural laws of the progress of wealth," and so forth. Instead, the novel offers an alternative *reading* of the results of those laws. In a passage that assimilates Mill's rhetoric, the character Sidonia makes the point that the "tendency of advanced civilisation is in truth to pure Monarchy." He asserts that monarchy, in order to develop fully, demands "a high degree of civilisation," since it relies upon "the support of free laws and manners, and of a widely-diffused intelligence." He continues:

> Political compromises are not to be tolerated except at periods of rude transition. An educated nation recoils from the imperfect vicariate of what is called a representative government. Your House of Commons, that has absorbed all other powers in the State, will in all probability fall more rapidly than it rose. Public opinion has a more direct, more comprehensive, a more efficient organ for its utterance, than a body of men sectionally chosen. The Printing-press is a political element unknown to classic or feudal times. It absorbs in a great degree the duties of the Sovereign, the Priest, the Parliament; it controls, it educates, it discusses. That public opinion, when it acts, would appear in the form of one who has no class interests. In an enlightened age the Monarch on the throne, free from the vulgar prejudices and the corrupt interests of the subject, becomes again divine! (322–23)

Sidonia's interpretation of society is not far different from Mill's in seeing humanity as progressing; but he attempts to go *beyond* Mill's analysis, positing that the phenomenon Mill describes as a sinking of the "weight and importance" of the individual into "greater and greater insignificance" is actually only a characteristic of political compromise in "an age of rude transition." Ultimately, this transition will culminate in the opposite of Mill's vision. Rather than the masses gaining control of the government, power will be entirely vested in a monarch "free from the vulgar prejudices and corrupt interests of the subject." *Coningsby* implicitly accepts but subsumes Mill's analysis. Representative government, one of those "political compromises" that may be tolerated during periods of "rude transition," is the outgrowth of the natural laws of progress, but it must inevitably be pruned away to ensure the blossoming of a truly civilized state. That the seeds of representative government have sprouted and are flourishing makes its clearing imminent and indicates that greater changes are yet to take place, changes that will *restore* the proper political order.

It is important to note from the comparison of the passages from "Civilisation" and *Coningsby* that while Sidonia coopts Mill's analysis, he frames his speech in quite different terms. For instance, he attacks "repre-

sentative government," equating it with a common usage of "democracy."
Indeed, for most Philosophic Radicals the two concepts were synonymous.
In his *Autobiography* Mill writes that the political opinions of the Bentha-
mites, especially as they were influenced by his father, possessed an "almost
unbounded confidence in the efficacy of two things: representative government, and complete freedom of discussion." He goes on to say that
"democratic suffrage" was the "principal article of his [James Mill's] political creed, not on the ground of liberty, Rights of Man, or any of the
phrases, more or less significant, by which up to that time democracy had
usually been defended, but as the most essential of 'securities for good
government'" (64–65).[4]

Disraeli, unlike the Philosophic Radicals, did not link his conception
of democracy to principles of representation; nor was he hesitant to ground
"democracy" on principles of freedom, as he makes quite clear in his 1835
work, *Vindication of the English Constitution*:

> The Tory party in this country is the national party; it is the really demo-
> cratic party of England. It supports the institutions of the country, because
> they have been established for the common good, and because they secure the
> equality of civil rights, without which, whatever may be its name, no govern-
> ment can be free, and based upon which principle every government, however
> it may be styled is, in fact, a Democracy. (183)

Representative government does not guarantee those freedoms; nor is it
necessarily the most provident way of representing divergent interests.
As Sidonia says to Harry, "People may be represented without periodical elections of neighbours who are incapable to maintain their interests,
and strangers who are unwilling" (246). The result for Disraeli of what
Mill describes as "the natural laws of the progress of wealth. . . the diffu-
sion of reading, and the increase of the facilities of human intercourse" is
representation, but representation in language and thought in the press,
rather than by bodies in the House of Commons. The representation of a
public opinion, which (inexplicably) is free from class interests, expresses
itself in action through the monarch, who is the only true representative of
the nation. Political representation, then, is to be homogeneous, without
conflict, and actualized in the subjectivity (and the symbol) of the monarch. Meanwhile, the political subjectivity of the individual, which Mill
sees being subsumed by the common interests of the masses, no longer
functions according to the limits of parliamentary political discourse, but
through the press, of which the novel is a part.

In her tour de force discussion of *Sybil* in *The Industrial Reformation of English Fiction*, Catherine Gallagher has written at some length on the connections between Disraeli's conceptions of political and literary representation. Gallagher argues that Disraeli inherited the Romantic-Idealistic legacy of Carlyle and Coleridge which attempts to derive a theory of political representation from a larger theory of symbolic representation that includes within it a concept of literary representation (217). By the 1840s, she points out, "the Romantic-Idealistic position had lost its original exclusive commitment to symbolic, tautegorical representation. . . . An ironic potential had been discerned in the symbol itself and had then been located specifically in political symbols" (217). The pressures of this marriage between the ironic and the tautegorical, combined with the exigencies of Disraeli's own political position, lead to a situation in which literary irony and symbolism "become firmly associated with antidescriptive political theory" (217)—a theory that bases political representation on the inherent value of the symbol (representative) rather than on its connection to that which it represents. For Gallagher this culminates in *Sybil*, a "political novel in which politics is always in the process of dissolving into a representation of something else . . . and itself goes unrepresented" (217).

Gallagher's reading of *Sybil* is insightful and useful, but I think we should be cautious about importing it wholesale as a basis for understanding *Coningsby*—a move she suggests when she writes:

> Disraeli cannot, finally, create a mode of representation of his desired politics. Politics and literature tend to exclude rather than complement each other, reminding us of Coningsby's earlier wish to replace Parliament with the press. . . . Here the place of the political institution is altogether usurped by the representative printed word. (218)

In *Coningsby* it is precisely the point that the printed word replaces representative politics, because for Disraeli, the printed word, policed by popular opinion, is more reliably linked to the material conditions of the electorate. And unlike *Sybil*, where politics "itself goes unrepresented," *Coningsby* portrays political discourse as self-contained, self-referential, and unable to represent anything other than its own interests. For *Coningsby* the political is not usurped by the printed word, it *is* the printed word. Politics has exchanged referential affiliations with the novel.

3

The New Generation, the Political Subject, and the Culture of Change

In the exchange of referents between political and novelistic discourse and in the formulation of politics as a hyperreality that is not so much a representation of truth as it is a simulation, we see one of the ways in which politics gets "novelized." Rather than privileging simulation, which "envelops the whole edifice of representation as itself a simulacrum" and which proceeds "from the utopia of [the] principle of . . . *the radical negation of the sign as value*" (Baudrillard 11; original emphasis), *Coningsby*, in good novelistic fashion, insists on "the principle that the sign and the real are equivalent" (11). Parliamentary politics in *Coningsby* may in fact have achieved what Jean Baudrillard calls the fourth successive phase of the image, in which it "bears no relation to any reality whatever: it is its own pure simulacrum" (11). But novelistic discourse and—if I may be forgiven such a totalizing statement—nineteenth-century epistemology are so bound to strategies of representation that "parliamentary politics as simulacrum" is read as the failure of politics. *Coningsby*, in continually referring outside its own simulated world, relies on the concept of representation as "the reflection of a basic reality," even though the equivalence such an assumption asserts may be understood as ideal and unobtainable. Further, for *Coningsby*, the mechanism of the reflection, the medium, the discourse itself, must be an equivalent reflection. By asserting that the novel is the better conduit to reality, Disraeli directs considerable attention to the activity of representation as well as to its product. Increasingly, the printed word demands some sort of self-policing if it is not to devolve into the non-representational status that Parliamentary politics has assumed. The novel then must remain tied to the real, even as it must become increasingly referential. It is at this point, when "the real is no longer what it used to be," that certain reactionary tendencies arise:

Nostalgia assumes its full meaning. There is a proliferation of myths of origin and signs of reality; of second-hand truth, objectivity and authenticity. There is an escalation of the true, of the lived experience; a resurrection of the figurative where the object and substance have disappeared. And there is a panic-stricken production of the real and the referential, above and parallel to the panic of material production. (*Simulations* 12–13)

Perhaps the most important way in which this nostalgia achieves its full articulation in *Coningsby* is in the formation of the political subjectivity of the individual. Sidonia's call for the coalescence of the political subject into the symbol of the monarch certainly is a notable utterance of precisely the sort of resurrection of the figurative that Baudrillard speaks of, but it fails to justify individual, local involvement in politics. This remains an important dilemma for the novel (and for Baudrillard, for that matter), since Harry's very activity depends upon his establishing himself as an individual whose own subjectivity is at least partly constituted by the discourse of party politics.

In the following pages, I will argue that Harry's political subjectivity is directly linked to the ways in which he and the novel theorize political change within a conservative idiom. I will also argue that while such theorizing may provide a political subject position for Harry, his political *agency* is another matter entirely, and for most of the novel is beyond representation, "resonating," as I say below, beyond the limits of the text. Only at the end of the novel, when all the "new generation" are on the threshold of public life, does the possibility of depicting their positive, effective activity arise in earnest. While the upshot of the unrepresentability of Harry's political agency may be to undermine the Romantic politics of Young England, *Coningsby*'s attempt to write Harry's story as a political coming of age has significant ramifications for the status of both the novel and politics as interpretive discourses. For one it establishes the necessity for the movement toward political subjectivity within the novel. As I will discuss near the end of this section, this is in direct contrast to Nancy Armstrong's contention that the subject in the novel is figured as either politically subjugated or apolitical. *Coningsby* also points explicitly to the intersection of the novel and party politics as a discursive space in which certain kinds of resistance and agency are possible and potentially effective.

Early in *Coningsby*, Harry perceives the basic discursive tension in party politics to be one of progress versus stasis. He feels compelled to participate in the change that he sees taking place around him, yet he is never convinced that a politics that advocates utility and progress is without egregious shortcomings. In the first chapter of Book II, *Coningsby's* narrator, echoing Carlyle's "Characteristics," argues that the increase in mechanization and material progress has not been accompanied by a corresponding advance of moral civilization, and concludes that England has outgrown "not the spirit but the organisation of our institutions."[1] In these early pages, Harry's crisis of representation and self-fashioning is emerging, a "panic" that is "above and parallel" to the crises that bedevil English material culture.

Yet despite presentation of itself as an ostensible *bildungsroman*, much of the first portion of the novel is taken up with examples of political subjectivity that serve as models for Harry either to internalize or to reject. The mysterious Sidonia appears, seemingly out of nowhere, to become Harry's political zen master. In their first meeting, on the edge of a midland forest that is suspiciously near Nottingham, Sidonia offers epigrammatic wisdom, Byronic allusions, and historical examples; he calls on the heroic glory of the past (thus the nostalgic setting of Sherwood) and emphasizes the role of the individual in history, all the while exposing what Harry believes is his agency as the product of orthodox habits of mind.

It is in this scene that Harry becomes conscious of his failings, and conscious of the need to *act* in ways he has not yet fully conceived. Sidonia appears to be the example of such action; but ironically, and regardless of his assertions that "the Spirit of the Age is the very thing that a great man changes" and that an individual is "divine" against "a vast public opinion," he is hampered by those social constructs that "heroes" overcome. As the two men part, Harry remarks, "Your mind at least is nurtured with great thoughts . . . Your actions should be heroic." Sidonia replies, "Action is not for me. . . . I am of that faith that the Apostles professed before they followed their master" (147). Sidonia's Jewishness places him outside the realm of the active. He is "and must ever be but a dreamer of dreams" (146). Ethnic identity subverts political agency. Thus, apparently, one must be able to get into the Carlton Club before righting the portrait of Wellington, and the issue of who does and does not get in is not within the realm of the heroic. Such delimiters on who gets to exercise political agency put the onus upon Harry to become the hero that Sidonia can only dream of being.

In direct contrast to the nostalgic and Romantic Sidonia is Harry's distant relative, Lord Everingham. He presents the possibility of another sort of political subject, one who is forward-looking to a fault and whose agency is grounded in the organizational principles of utility. Everingham is "a Whig, and a clear-headed, cold-blooded man, [who] look[s] upon the New Poor Law as another Magna Charta" (158).[2] He is a "master of his subject [the New Poor Law]" and "the Chairman of one of the most considerable Unions in the Kingdom." In argument against him, his father-in-law, the Duke of Beaumanoir, has little chance, for Everingham overwhelms him with "quotations from Commissioners' rules and Subcommissioners' reports, statistical tables, and references to dietaries." When Everingham is at a loss for a reply, "which was very rare," he upbraids the duke "with the abuses of the old system, and frighten[s] him with visions of rates exceeding rentals" (158).

Everingham's new principles of organization offer no evidence for an increase in the moral civilization whose dearth *Coningsby* laments and which Harry sees as requisite to right-reasoned politics. The young Whig's invocation of the "bad old days" strikes to the very heart of Harry's conservative tendencies and his nostalgia for an England that never existed, yet which should be the foundation of politics in the Age of Reform. Utilitarianism, in the body of Everingham, has no room for the expression of moral attributes through popular customs; the utility of ceremony and custom depends on circumstances, and unless useful, the "Spirit of the Age," which is the "Spirit of Utility," is against "such things." For Harry, and more especially for his relative and close friend, Lord Henry Sidney, these popular customs articulate a moral solidarity that extends beyond class boundaries and represents the real spirit of the nation, the "national character." Utilitarianism, conversely, expresses only the desires of the individual, creating undue competition and further alienating the "true estates of the realm" from one another. Since, as Disraeli points out in the *Vindication*, self-interest has so many meanings that it remains essentially meaningless, a moral philosophy based on this principle "only produces a barren and mulish progeny" (10–14).[3]

If utility has indeed become "the Spirit of the Age," it has done so by imposing itself on, radically opposing, and ultimately overthrowing many of the institutions that, radical Tories argued, were informed by immutable principles. *Coningsby*, in the Everingham scene, demonstrates how utilitarianism establishes itself as dominant by relying on its own rhetoric and on texts generated within its discourse to substantiate itself. The logical flaw in Everingham's polemic in favor of utility is subtle but circular; in his discussions with the duke, Everingham depends upon utility to legitimate itself. The evidence for his arguments, his "Commissioners' rules and

Subcommissioners' reports," are produced by—and in—the very political idiom for which he is arguing. Even when the duke does seem to make a point, Everingham continues to rely on Utilitarian rhetoric by abusing the old system—the organization of ancient institutions—and by appealing to the duke's economic self-interest with visions, not realities, of rates exceeding rentals.

Beaumanoir is not without his own political affiliations and ideas. And, notwithstanding the advances of the Whigs and Reformers, he is still a powerful political figure. Yet his political faith has deserted him. Unlike the marquess and Rigby, he is unwilling to continue to subscribe to a politics whose referentiality has become so pointedly divorced from his perceptions of "the state of things." The old Tory standard contains no promise for him, and he tries gamely to meet Everingham on the younger lord's terms; but the duke is out of his depth and thus easy prey for one so well versed in the strengths of his own political philosophy and the failures of the one it has replaced.

In the face of what *Coningsby* portrays as the uncritically self-referential idiom of Everingham's Utilitarianism and the substantial power embodied in his subject position, the duke's political agency deserts him. Although he retains considerable influence and power in his own right, it is evident that in turning a critical eye upon his party affiliations and beliefs, he has found them lacking in force. They are almost chimerical in their relations to current situations. Unsure of his own language of politics, he adopts another. He has abandoned his political subjectivity as high Tory, partly in response to his understanding that to be constituted as such no longer has any potency and in fact denies him agency. In lieu of becoming completely immobilized by his outmoded affiliations, he scrambles for higher discursive ground. Yet by moving toward his adversary Everingham, he merely becomes an easier target, and the affiliations he wished to shed an oversized bulls-eye. His political subject position is so overwhelmed by Everingham's onslaught that it becomes a liability, preventing his activity.

Henry Sidney, the Duke of Beaumanoir's youngest son and Everingham's brother-in-law, is a more formidable opponent, even though, because of his youth and inexperience, his agency is figured as less viable. Unlike his father, "Lord Henry would not listen to statistics, dietary tables, Commissioners' rules, Sub-commissioners' reports"; rather, he returns the focus of the family debate to the issue at hand, namely, what sort of politics serves best to provide for and interpret the needs of the people. He does not make the mistake of adopting Everingham's language. Instead, he points out how centuries of violation and invasion of the distinct rights and privileges of the lower orders, specifically the peasantry, have upset the "parochial constitution" of the country, which "was more important than the political constitution . . . more ancient, more universal in its influence" and which "had already been shaken to its centre by the New Poor Law" (159).

Lord Henry drives home his point against Everingham when his father quite innocently states that he wishes he "could see the labouring classes happy":

> "Oh! pray do not use, my dear father, that phrase, the labouring classes!" said Lord Henry. "What do you think Coningsby, the other day we had a meeting in this neighbourhood to vote an agricultural petition that was to comprise all classes. I went with my father, and I was made chairman of the committee to draw up the petition. Of course, I described it as the petition of the nobility, clergy, yeomanry, and peasantry of the county of —; and could you believe it, they struck out *peasantry* as a word no longer used, and inserted *labourers*."
>
> "What can it signify," said Lord Everingham, "whether a man be called a labourer or a peasant?"
>
> "And what can it signify," said his brother-in-law, "whether a man be called Mr Howard or Lord Everingham?" (160) [4]

The point, of course, is that it signifies considerably what one is called.

When the *language* for thinking about our world and our purposes changes, so does our *way* of thinking about them, and to that extent our world and our purposes also are altered. Neither Harry nor Henry Sidney is willing to accept that sort of change, at least by imposing a discourse they feel to be unfaithful to the origins of the "parochial constitution." For them utility is too radical; it imposes too many changes without proper regard for the original motives of existing institutions.[5] Partly at stake in these institutions is a belief system which utility would replace with reason. But, Sidonia tells Harry:

> an attempt to reconstruct society on a basis of material motives and calculations . . . has failed. It must ultimately have failed under any circumstances. Its failure in an ancient and densely populated kingdom was inevitable. . . . We are not indebted to the Reason of man for any of the great achievements which are the landmarks of human action and human progress. . . . Man is only truly great when he acts from the passions. (262) [6]

Change, especially political change, at the hands of the Utilitarians and any others, such as the "pseudo-Tories," who have forsaken the sanctity of the immutable informing principles of the English Constitution, is to be loathed and actively opposed at every possible juncture. The only truly ameliorative change is that which restores the constitution to its status as a set of rights and privileges transcending the ever-volatile temporal interpretations of political parties and special interests. Harry points this out to his friend Oswald Millbank: "The man who enters public life at this epoch has to choose between Political Infidelity and a Destructive Creed" (372). Those of the destructive creed, the Whigs, "seek a specific for the evils of our social system in the general suffrage of the population" and demand that the principle of political liberalism shall be carried to its extent, "which it appears to them is impossible without getting rid of the fragments of the old constitution that remain" (371). The politically unfaithful, the conservatives, "only embrace as much liberalism as is necessary for the moment; . . . wish to keep things as they find them as long as they can, and will manage things as they find them as well as they can" (372).

The crux of Harry's argument, like Sidonia's earlier in the novel, depends upon his views on the principle of representation. And *what* he can say about how he perceives representation to work is fundamentally linked to *how* he can say it. Although he tells Millbank that he does not "declare against Parliamentary government" and looks upon "political change as the greatest of evils," he is actually advocating a new way of articulating public interests and complaints: a way of speaking, thinking, and writing about politics that essentially undoes the status quo and that includes the very medium in which Harry Coningsby exists—the novel. However indirectly, he is claiming political and social efficacy for fiction. Once again, the novel becomes the realm in which politics is actualized, and the *character* of Harry Coningsby assumes, through his very fictiveness, a subjectivity whose political agency resonates beyond the limits of the text. When he argues that what must be done is to accustom "the public mind to the contemplation of an existing though torpid power in the constitution capable of removing our social grievances, were we to transfer to it those prerogatives which the Parliament has gradually usurped" (374), he is pointing directly to the printed word, the novel, as the way in which such a change in perception may be effected.

Just as Harry finds that the current discourse of Parliamentary politics is unable to represent England's greatest needs, he also finds Parliament to be an ineffective means of political representation, for "representation is not necessarily, or even in a principal sense, Parliamentary." As long as that mistaken idea persists, he says, legislation will be "Class-legislation" regardless of the extension of the franchise. The only capable representatives are the king or queen—unlike the Commons, which is the "house of the few," the individual who sits upon the throne "is the sovereign of all"— and public opinion, which now speaks in print:

> The representation of the Press is far more complete than the representation of Parliament. Parliamentary representation was the happy device of a ruder age, to which it was admirably adapted: an age of semi-civilisation, when there was a leading class in the community; but it exhibits many symptoms of desuetude. It is controlled by a system of representation more vigorous and comprehensive; which absorbs its duties and fulfills them more efficiently, and in which discussion is pursued on fairer terms, and often with more depth and information. (374–75)[7]

For *Coningsby* the power of the word, of language, in its availability to so many cannot be ignored. The extra-parliamentary language of public opinion expressed in the Press has begun to exert its influence on politics in all its articulations, and this newer, more powerful discourse offers the possibility of change without upheaval, since "true wisdom lies in the policy that would effect its ends by the influence of opinion, and yet by the means of existing forms" (375).

Only somewhat paradoxically, Harry's anachronistically "postmodern" justification of his own existence and his emphasis on the constitutive function of language and interpretation is profoundly conservative in its effects. Indeed, the mechanism of the change Harry advocates is similar to the types of changes in interpretive communities that Stanley Fish has described:

> Interpretive communities are no more than sets of institutional practices; and while those practices are continually being transformed by the very work that they do, the transformed practice identifies itself and tells its story in relation to general purposes and goals that have survived and form the basis of continuity. . . . Change is something that does or does not occur in particular institutional situations where this or that set of already-in-place concerns can (but not *must*) lead to the noticing and taking into account of an open-ended, although not infinite range of phenomena. ("Change" 437)[8]

Both Fish's change and the change described and hoped for in *Coningsby* depend on legitimized, in-place ways of thinking and speaking for their instigation.[9] Both rely on breaking down barriers of exclusivity, but not at the expense of the discourse (or paradigm, enterprise, etc.) already functioning. The "something new" that *Coningsby* identifies is what Fish posits as the basis of continuity and not really new at all. Rather, *Coningsby's* "something new" is instead something quite old, in some cases nearly forgotten; it is the relationships between the "estates" or classes as defined by the "parochial" constitution. Even the old guard of the London social and political scene, who speak of "a sort of new set; new ideas and all that sort of thing," recognize that the "new thing" requires "a devilish deal of history" (411), though as I have pointed out this particular "history" is suspect at best. In attaining such a "deuced deal of history," a new generation can confront its elders with the shortcomings of their system, demanding—as *Coningsby* does—that the present political discourse expand to consider the increasingly insistent voice of public opinion, which has found expression in the press.

The conservative and circular qualities of both Fish's and *Coningsby's* explanations of change are immediately apparent. Change occurs only from within the discursive system, the system of interpretation. Even the transformed institutional practices are defined in terms of their continuity. Thus paying "new" attention to something that is not really new at all is merely a reconsideration of the relevancy of an object of interpretation within an empirically verifiable context. Such a shift in relevancy within a discursive system assumes two things: first, that the initial perception of the object as new is due to a different, but synonymous, articulation of the object within the limits of the discourse; second, that some modification of those boundaries has already taken place, allowing the interpreter to take more into account than previously and thus perceive the object as new. In *Coningsby's* case this means that the "new politics" of Harry Coningsby, Henry Sidney, Charles Buckhurst, and the rest of the New Generation could come about because first, the young men were already conversant with Tory politics and, second, because the Tory politics itself had made the perception and articulation of the "parochial" constitution available to them in a way that had previously been inaccessible. But even within this "new" way of seeing the world, political agency itself has been coopted by the functioning of the two "greater" representatives of the public good—the sovereign and the press. The political subject positions of the young men are subsumed by these other discourses; their opinions must have already fallen in line with the assumptions that establish the press and the sovereign *as* representative and thus they have forfeited their political agency; they are no less subjugated than before. The form of the power exerted has not changed—merely its locus.

According to both Fish and Disraeli, changes in the principles of interpretation can (though as Fish says may not always) follow from a new way of seeing; in *Coningsby* it is this new "vision" that constitutes the political subjectivities of the "New Generation." The interpretive practices of a discourse or community can be challenged in terms of those practices' exclusivity only to the extent that those practices are perceived as exclusive; and as I have shown, such a perception is not possible without some modification having occurred already. Thus Harry and his friends could not have challenged the "old" politics without having first interpreted the old politics in a new way. To do this the old politics, the one that informs their interpretation, had to have changed enough to allow them to perceive what had heretofore been hidden, though present. That is, they could never have seen the old politics in a new way if the interpretive conventions of the old politics had not changed to allow their new perception. Yet changes in the paradigm come about from new ways of seeing. According to the logic of Fish and of Disraeli, the old politics changed because these young men began to understand politics differently, and Young England began to understand politics differently because the old politics changed. The conclusion to this syllogism, therefore, is that change depends on change.

Though nearly one hundred and fifty years apart and engaged in different controversies, the similarities in Fish's and Disraeli's arguments highlight a certain characteristic of a type of conservatism that attempts to present itself as "radical." Both men try to come to terms with what they see as monolithic, though internally contestatory, enterprises that constitute "the way things are"; both are bound to account for change; yet both are necessarily dependent on the maintenance of the status quo, or at least their interpretations of the status quo, as the *explanation* for how change takes place. One of the reasons for the circularity of Fish's explanation is that he fails to take into account the importance of competing interpretive systems as possible explanations for change. Disraeli's argument, however, is more complex. *Coningsby* recognizes that other interpretive enterprises, such as the press, could accommodate articulations of change not possible within the existing political discourse. It also recognizes that while the press may be more universal in its articulations of social needs and desires than Parliament, the political system would hardly legitimize the press as the codified means of representation and thus disempower itself. The press and Parliament are competing for the discursive power entailed in the interpretive enterprise of successfully divining and meeting social wants and needs. In this competition, the press is not politicized in the sense that it becomes part of the institution of politics, for politics does not expand to include it. Rather, the press proves itself to be the more flexible enterprise; it subsumes the function of political representation and in so doing controls the nominal representatives who sit in Parliament. The institution of politics and its interpretive endeavors are thus taken over by a more powerful and extensive discursive practice. The usual notion of the press becoming part of the political process is, then, inaccurate. It is really more a matter of politics becoming a part of the process of the press. As Harry says, Parliament "is controlled by a system of representation more vigorous and comprehensive; which absorbs its duties and fulfills them more efficiently."

From this analysis, two related questions arise: what is the extent of the change described in *Coningsby*, and what possibility exists for further change? On the one hand, it is arguable that radical changes have taken place and that even more radical changes can be anticipated, since politics, in confronting its shortcomings, rather tacitly gives over its functions to the competing and increasingly powerful press. Because this new interpretive enterprise operates differently, recognizing different discursive limits and strategies, it is reasonable to assume that principles of noticeability and relevance will be formulated that are unique to it, principles that do not function in political discourse. On the other hand, however, if the press has become the controlling forum for political and social issues simply by subsuming and more efficiently performing the functions once reserved for Parliament (as *Coningsby* states), then it is just a different discursive system attempting to do the same things as the old one, but doing them better. And while the conventions defining this enterprise may *seem* different (for example, more may participate), actually they are only modifications of the rules that govern Parliamentary politics. Special interests are still served; powerful cliques and coalitions emerge to control opinion; statements are still formulated to articulate commonly held interpretive principles; the political agency of the individual is still circumscribed by representation. The criteria of relevance and noticeability in place within the political enterprise are largely transferred to the press, thus subverting the possibility of significant, or at least immediately significant change.

Importantly, I think, the question arises as to how much the press, in this instance the novel *Coningsby* itself, contributes to new ways of perceiving the world and effecting change—even if those new perceptions and effects are essentially restatements of the status quo. Of course, empirical evidence of this sort is difficult to adduce if only because the causal connection between social practice and popular novels must always be suspect. Nevertheless, we see that within this novel and in Disraeli's fifth edition "Preface" there exists the belief that the written word does exert pressure upon the activity of politics and that new ways of thinking about the world and our place in it are possible—if not always immediately apparent.

Just as fiction was becoming one means of thinking alternative political possibilities (or resurrecting mis-remembered old ones), it also had a hand in forming the sorts of individuals who could function in and reproduce those possibilities. This connection between fiction and politics has been specifically addressed by Nancy Armstrong in her *Desire and Domestic Fiction*. She asserts that starting with Rousseau's *Social Contract* and continuing in the English tradition through Hume and Bentham, the concept of the contract came increasingly to rely on the power of fiction. Bentham ultimately maintains that "fiction itself was the only thing that had held people in subjection to one kind of state and could, if properly understood, allow them to take charge over another" (Armstrong 35). Armstrong concludes that given the development of the novel alongside this theory of fiction, "we should be able to read the history of the novel as the formation of the individual who proved fit to inhabit a world based on the twin powers of supervision and information control" (35). Yet, she writes, this is not the case, for the power that fiction "would come to exercise depended entirely on denying the inherently political aim of fictions of personal development: the production of the modern individual required above all else a specific form of political unconscious" (36). Beginning with Rousseau's *Discourse on the Origin of Inequality*, argues Armstrong, the individual needed "a particular form of liberation: a form of self-fulfillment that came with the disappearance of political identity"; the possibilities for human identity are confined between "the poles of political subjection on the one hand and apolitical subjectivity on the other" (36). The result of the cultural imperative as it arose from the concept of the contract was to produce a contradiction necessary for the rise of the novel: a contradiction in which the novel developed "sophisticated strategies for transforming political information into any one of several recognizable psychological conditions" in ways that "concealed the power exercised by this discourse itself in carrying out this transformation on a mass scale" (36). The result for male characters in nineteenth-century novels is that they were "no longer political creatures so much as they were products of desire and producers of domestic life" (4).

Armstrong's complex argument works well in establishing the rise of female authority in the novel and for focusing on subjectivity as an essentially gendered phenomenon in the nineteenth century. It is also a particularly impressive and compelling argument for her contention that "middle-class authority rested in large part upon the authority that novels attributed to women and in this way designated as specifically female" (4), but its presupposition that "the female was the figure, above all else, on whom depended the outcome of the struggle among competing ideologies" proves problematic in helping to read Harry's subjectivity and the issue of political agency in *Coningsby*. Despite the effect of the courtship plot on the events that shape Harry's life, it is too constricting to assume that the political in this novel is always translated into desire and domesticity. Indeed, Harry's political identity has a good deal less to do with heterosexual desire for Edith than with the homosocial bonds he forms with Sidonia, Buckhurst, Vere, Henry Sidney, and the younger Millbank. If Harry is a product of desire and Edith is the object of that desire, the result is not to produce and support the domestic but to solidify the masculinist realm of the political.

To conceive of *Coningsby* existing within Armstrong's extension of the paradigm of the social contract, in which political identity disappears and individuals are confined to the possibilities of either "political subjection" or "apolitical subjectivity" (36), is to deny this novel's foregrounding of the formation of a political subjectivity that attempts to construct an engaged identity outside of simple subjection. Rather than reject or ignore the "inherently political aims of fictions of personal development," *Coningsby* focuses on them. In this novel, political development is ultimately the only kind that matters. And while desire cannot be divorced from political subjectivity, neither is a character's political being merely an expression of desire.

Coningsby is especially clear on this point. At precisely the time that Edith's father forbids any further meeting between the two lovers, the marquess attempts to force Harry to serve as his political lackey by standing for Darlford against Mr. Millbank. Harry must choose his political identity. But unlike the scenario that Armstrong outlines in which one's political subjection seeks retreat and agency in the production of the domestic, Harry chooses political (and romantic) disaffiliation:

> What were the tawdry accidents of vulgar ambition to him? No domestic despot could deprive him of his intellect, his knowledge, the sustaining power

of an unpolluted conscience. If he possessed the intelligence in which he had confidence, the world would recognise his voice even if not placed upon a pedestal. If the principles of his philosophy were true, the great heart of the nation would respond to their expression. Coningsby felt at this moment a profound conviction which never again deserted him, that the conduct which would violate the affections of the heart, or the dictates of the conscience, however it may lead to immediate success, is a fatal error. (435)

We see in this paragraph that Harry is not confined to "political subjection" and "apolitical subjectivity" as his only possible identities. Even if we rightly choose to read the marquess's ultimatum and its result as a form of political subjection, it is also, obviously, empowering. Together with the crisis in Coningsby's love-life, the marquess's bullying forces Harry to articulate his political position as well as shows him the possibilities of resistance.

Significantly, it is near the end of the book that Harry's assertion of his political and moral consciousness takes place, for it is only through this proclamation of his agency that he can fulfill his role as the guiding light of the New Generation. Up to that point he has remained surprisingly inactive in his attempts to realize his potential. In both the education and romance plots, unlike the boy who sets Wellington straight, he is content to be the object of others' actions; and this non-agency also typifies his engagement in politics. Harry refuses the marquess's offer/demand to have him stand for Darlford because he cannot reconcile himself to the marquess's political precepts. When he does enter Parliament, it is because the incumbent, the senior Millbank, has withdrawn from the race and substituted Harry's name for his own. Harry does not even discover he is a candidate until it is too late for him to campaign (or, for that matter, withdraw—which in itself assumes a sort of agency he does not seem to possess). He only appears in Darlford to be chaired and to give his victory speech. But unlike the conditions that would have constrained his political agency had he accepted his uncle's demand, or served at the pleasure of Mr. Millbank, Harry's being "drafted" to the empty Darlford seat allows him to situate himself in the terms he has established for the new generation. According to Disraeli's conservative agenda, of course, Harry's "radical" new ideas can be implemented from within the strictures of Parliament, but Harry nonetheless, at the end of the novel, asserts his own political agency partly in resistance to the subjugation he experienced at the hands of Millbank and the marquess.

In contradistinction to Armstrong's assertion that the modern individual's "particular form of liberation" is one of "self-fulfillment" dependent upon the loss of political identity, we find that Harry, after a time, is fully aware of his inaction and realizes that, for him, self-fulfillment must be a combination of political consciousness and action instigated by that consciousness. Indeed, if we accept Armstrong's thesis, we see that *until* Harry emerges as a political agent at the end of the novel he is figured as what Armstrong calls the "modern individual," liberated from political consciousness by his place in society. As an aristocrat, his life is set for him; he merely has to follow the expected path, do as he is told, give in willingly to political subjection while also (not instead of) assuming an apolitical subject position. Whatever resistance he may employ is always already co-opted by the structures that allow him any subjectivity at all. Seen as such, Harry is in many ways figured as a woman. Like Armstrong's bourgeois women, he is acted upon and is forced to withdraw from public life. His retiring to the Temple Bar is loudly lamented by his New Generation cohort, for it is read by them as a sign of his imminent failure as a public man. As Buckhurst points out,

> And this is the end of Coningsby, the brilliant Coningsby, that we all loved, that was to be our leader! . . . Well, come what may, life has lost something of its bloom.
> . . . I feel my plan about the Austrian service was, after all, the only thing. The Continent offers a career. He might have been prime minister; several strangers have been; as for war look at Brown and Laudon, and half a hundred others. I had a much better chance of being a field-marshal than he has of being Lord Chancellor. (480–81)

This, of course, is not to be Harry's fate. He is not to toil anonymously in the Inns of Court. He will marry into the middle classes (given the narrative's celebration of the abundance of "natural" aristocrats of that class, perhaps a greater longing than any personal desire for Edith); he will enter successfully upon public life as a young man, and apparently as his "own man," despite his debt to Edith's father for his seat in the Commons. Further, he wins by routing the old order and his nemesis Rigby. He has cast off political subjection and simultaneously become a political agent. Finally, he has completed his self-fashioning.

Significantly, the effects of this make-over take place beyond the pages of the narrative, for *Coningsby* can not provide a space for the fully realized political subject. The novel for Disraeli is itself the process of that realization: *nie ist, immer wird*. And despite the usual last chapter round-up of characters, the announcements of Edith and Harry's marriage and the birth of their son, and Harry's finally coming into his inheritance (which, in fairness to Armstrong, he was gratified to present to his wife), the text avoids the usual closure of classic realism, approaching more nearly what Catherine Belsey has labeled the "interrogative text" (91–92, passim). In the end, the narrator will only speculate as to the fate of the New Generation:

> Will they maintain in august assemblies and high places the great truths which, in study and solitude, they have embraced? Or will their courage exhaust itself in the struggle, their enthusiasm evaporate before hollow-hearted ridicule, their generous impulses yield with a vulgar catastrophe to the tawdry temptations of a low ambition? (495)

By refusing to inform the reader of these men's successes or failures as MPs, *Coningsby* maintains its oppositional stance toward party politics as usual and keeps the referents of politics from becoming those of the novel. The truths they are presented as having found in the world of the novel will be challenged by the world of politics. The narrator can only hope that Harry and his friends will assert their newly found agency—the agency discovered in language, the press, ultimately in *fiction*—in the less referentially reliable arena of politics:

> . . . will they remain brave, single, and true; refuse to bow before shadows and worship phrases; sensible of the greatness of their duties; denounce to a perplexed and disheartened world the frigid theories of a generalising age that have destroyed the individuality of man, and restore the happiness of their country by believing in their own energies and daring to be great? (495)

These characters are about to enter into a different, competing, interpretive discourse, one that has been disarticulated in the world in which they have existed and come to agency for 495 closely set pages. On the leash, but "about to be slipped," they are emblematic of the beginning of the fictional reformation of English politics. Even in subsuming the political in the novelistic, *Coningsby* has maintained a tension between the two, has used the novel to interrogate the ideological assumptions and practices of party politics. Such interrogation is inherently resistive, and *Coningsby*'s importance lies in this resistance. For an avowedly conservative novel to be considered in such a light may seem ironic, but it is also indicative of the necessity of oppositionality within any discourse. For while *Coningsby*'s attempt to explain change through the language of nostalgic conservatism often results in vagaries and interpretations of regressive policies as progressive, it also radically empowers fiction and asserts it as the space where alternatives to the way we live in and understand the world are possible. And by opposing itself to one of the most constitutive of Victorian discourses, *Coningsby* helps to push the novel to the center of important discussions of Victorian culture and society. With *Coningsby*, we find that the novel is not only a way to say and think new possibilities of existence, but also the subject matter of those thoughts and utterances. It is difficult for late twentieth-century cultural historians to conceive of Victorian England without the novel, and without novels like *Coningsby* Victorian England could not have conceived itself.

PART II

Observation, Representation,
and *The Report on the
Sanitary Condition of the Labouring
Population of Great Britain*

4

The Novel and the Utilitarian

In *Coningsby*, the novel and the world it describes exchange affiliations with the referents of political discourse. For its readers, especially after Disraeli's politicized asides, *Coningsby* seems more tangible and more immediate, and its claims more persuasive than the world of politics that Disraeli portrays as fraught with unreal expectations and "factitious" representations of itself. In Disraeli's hands, the novel becomes a tool for reworking the world, changing it to meet the material and attitudinal needs that politics no longer perceives. In their constitutive functioning—creating conditions of possibility for thought and action, determining the bounds of agency, and reconceiving the place of the subject in the paradigms their discourses construct—the novel and politics vie for discursive dominance. And in using one discourse, the novel, to call another, politics, to account, find it lacking, and attempt to replace it as the way in which Victorians can order their existences (including their *political* existences), *Coningsby* foregrounds the increasing tension between these two formidable, competing interpretive enterprises. For that reason, if for no other, it deserves to be seen as a formulative moment for the novel and for Victorian epistemology. But we should also remember that *Coningsby* is by no means the only instance of the novel's connection to other, often seemingly incompatible, public languages. By the early 1840s the social force of novels was well remarked; and as the novel established itself as a significant interpretive enterprise, it drew an increasing number of admirers who a few years before would not have admitted to reading novels, to say nothing of acknowledging their potential as instruments of social change.

One of these admirers was the prominent social reformer Edwin Chadwick, co-author of the notorious Poor Law *Report* of 1834, secretary of the Poor Law Commission that was established as a result of that report, and, arguably, Britain's first professional bureaucrat. Upon completing his famous *Report on the Sanitary Condition of the Labouring Population of Great Britain*, Chadwick not surprisingly attempted a communiqué to perhaps the most powerful literary man in England, and certainly the most visible, Charles Dickens. And though his message was sent through Dickens's brother-in-law, reformer and Utilitarian Henry Austin, clearly Chadwick's attempt to reach Dickens and ascertain his state of mind on the issue of sanitation—and the Irish—is a bid to establish a link with one he believes to be like himself—one who sees clearly and represents what he sees in ways calculated to instigate change. Thus in the September 1842 letter to Austin he writes:

> I think Mr Hickson mentioned to me that Mr Dickens is your brother-in-law. I perceive it announced in the newspapers that he has in preparation notes of his tour in North America. . . . I have directed a copy of the [Sanitary Condition] report to be sent to you and I should be obliged to you if you would present it to him as a mark of my respect. . . . Yet I hope he had opportunities of visiting the residencies of the working classes; and observing as in the case of the Irish the effects of habits which seem independent of political motivations, for I am informed they carry with them their wretched and filthy hovels and their pig styes with them into whatever part they settle. (7, September 1842; quoted in Flinn 56)[1]

The *Report* was apparently passed along, since Dickens, while not going on at length about it, mentions Chadwick's work in *American Notes*, remarking that while "much of the disease which does prevail might be avoided if a few common precautions were observed, . . . there is no local legislature in America which may not study Mr Chadwick's excellent Report on the Sanitary Condition of our Labouring Classes with immense advantage" (Dickens, *American Notes* 252).[1]

This brief, somewhat perfunctory reference to the *Report* by the most popular author of the day no doubt thwarted whatever hopes Chadwick might have had for sensationalizing the evidence he had gathered and the conclusions he had formed, but the letter to Austin points up several important presuppositions that inform Chadwick's perception of his own project. In the portion of the letter censuring the Irish for "effects of habits" that perpetuate their squalid existence, he implies an important connection between himself and Dickens as observers of the life of the poor. And while one must not discount Chadwick's probable hopes that Dickens would puff the *Report*, he genuinely endorses the novelist's endeavors, sending his respects as well as material to aid Dickens's preparation of *American Notes*. Additionally, while he seems quite assured in his conclusions about the habits of the working-class Irish, Chadwick's hope that Dickens had an opportunity to visit their homes announces his desire that the novelist's observations correspond to, and thus corroborate, his own.

This corroboration is especially important to Chadwick because, first, it shores up his own assumptions about the world that one sees and experiences and, second, it emphasizes the necessity (and possibility) of *correct* observation. According to Chadwick, it is not so much the seeing as the seeing correctly that leads to proper representation of the problems of the poor, a connection he makes clear only a few lines later in his letter to Austin: "I hope he who has so well exposed parochial administration will do something better than that inaccurate observer and rash generaliser de Tocqueville, and not countenance the mischievous falsehood of mob flatterers that special qualification for administration is unnecessary or that the capacity for it is intuitive" (quoted in Flinn 56–57). The ability to observe accurately, and thus to interpret reliably, is apparently bound up in a perspective that affirms the special training, the professionalism, Chadwick sees as necessary for the proper administration of the measures he proposes in his *Report*. Resolving the problems of the lower classes—both the problems the lower classes possess and the problems they pose for the middle and upper classes—depends on "better and scientific" attention to the mechanisms by which the poor are observed and their destitution alleviated. General, sympathetic notions will no longer serve; there must be a concerted, organized effort to overcome not so much the poverty so many experience, but the *effects* of that poverty. Any means of offering relief must systematically promote "the health and pleasure and moral improvements of the population" (Flinn 57). Observers who would contribute to such an effort must, therefore, look beyond poverty per se to the conditions of existence produced by poverty in order to see how people live their lives in relation to those conditions.

Chadwick's letter suggests that reliable representations of the conditions of the lower classes thus depend on observers' willingness to attend closely to what may be both painful to witness and difficult to describe. Observers must not avert their eyes, nor be satisfied with generalizations that dilute the specifics of the problem at hand, for the effects of their observations will go beyond making the world of the lower classes knowable to readers; their observations will contribute to the remaking of that world, to the promotion of "health and pleasure and moral improvements" of the inhabitants of that world. Their observations will help to police that world.

What is interesting about this letter, in light of this concern over correct observations and "rash generalisations," is that Chadwick is not appealing to another who writes for parliamentary and royal investigative reports, the famous bluebooks; he is trying to reach a *novelist*. He recognizes that for a great many members of the Victorian middle and upper classes, the world of depravity, poverty, and squalor of which they were the self-appointed constabulary existed most vividly in the fiction of popular authors like Harriet Martineau, Elizabeth Gaskell, Benjamin Disraeli, Frances Trollope, Charles Kingsley, and, of course, Dickens, whose novels invariably contain extensive details of the conditions of the poor. As Chadwick notes, the power of his work was far-reaching and could not fail to "produce extensively beneficial results, . . . whatever he may say" regarding the improvement of the conditions of existence for the lower classes (Flinn 57).

There would seem to be little wonder, then, at Chadwick's efforts to win Dickens's approbation and to disseminate his own information through that novelist's pen. Yet a certain contextual irony pervades Chadwick's epistolary remarks, especially since they are written not to Dickens but to Austin, who was himself vigorously involved in the early public health movement. Chadwick's comments on Dickens's exposé of parochial abuse (in *Oliver Twist*) underscore that irony, since Chadwick—or what he represented—was one of that novel's primary targets. Dickens's history of the parish boy critiques and repudiates the values of the "Malthusian" world it describes, but Chadwick—as much as if not more than Malthus—is responsible for that world, or at least the world of *Oliver Twist*. Although Malthus and his more orthodox followers strongly favored abolishing the Poor Law entirely, Chadwick staunchly supported reform, arguing that the evidence he had gathered showed no correlation between poor relief and an increase of population. These theoretical differences between political economists mattered little to the popular press, or to Dickens. Each side was equally "Malthusian"; each side threatened to devastate the poor even further. For those like Dickens whose sympathy for the poor was not based primarily on a system of political economy, the differences seemed inconsequential, a matter of death by degrees.[2] To take the parish work house and "reform" it by placing it under the aegis of a "union" and running it on the "principle of least desireablity" was difficult to interpret as ameliorative. And in large measure these were Chadwick's ideas.

Together with his inability (or refusal) to recognize himself as one of the primary targets of *Oliver Twist*, the context of the Austin letter is shaped by Chadwick's deserved reputation for being as complete a Utilitarian as anyone in the nineteenth century. As a young journalist he caught the eye of James Mill and Francis Place with his 1829 essay, "Preventive Police," in the *London Review*. Soon after, he was presented to the ancient Bentham, who had enthusiastically approved the piece. Within a few weeks of their meeting, Chadwick became Bentham's amanuensis, serving him until the latter's death in 1832, and was given the special duty of writing for Bentham's *Constitutional Code* the sections pertaining to the minister of police and the minister of health. He soon came to be recognized as the old radical's special protegé, the "coming man" in Utilitarian circles. Bentham found his young secretary's companionship and ability indispensable, and in 1831 he invited Chadwick to move into his home, placing him at the very center of radical reformist activity in the heady days just before the passage of the Reform Bill.

Principal architect of the New Poor Laws, Utilitarian *extraordinaire*, and former man Friday for the thinker who gave the nineteenth century the "greatest good for the greatest number" precept, Chadwick did not seem to have the qualifications for winning his way into Dickens's affections (in fact, it was 1849 before Dickens overcame his distrust of the reformer). To top it all off, Chadwick's nearly filial association with Bentham had to have raised doubts about Chadwick's attitudes toward novels. Although John Stuart Mill writes that "much more has been said than there is any foundation for, about [Bentham's] contempt for the pleasures of imagination, and for the fine arts" ("Bentham" 95), he does concede that despite recognizing "music, painting, sculpture, and the other arts addressed to the eye" as "means for important social ends," Bentham believed that words "were perverted from their proper office when they were employed in uttering anything but precise logical truths" (95). The two famous aphorisms, "Quantity of pleasure being equal, push-pin is as good as poetry" and "All poetry is misrepresentation" (95), have come down to us as indicative of his attitudes toward literature. Of course not all Utilitarians felt as Bentham did. John Stuart Mill's experience of literature, especially poetry, was considerably different; even the name "Utilitarian" was taken from a John Galt novel. And whether Chadwick and Bentham were of the same mind in regards to literature is impossible to say. His comments on Dickens's work are no indication, since he is remarking not upon the quality of the imagination that can conceive of an Oliver Twist but upon the *effectiveness* of that imagination: the extent to which it was able to interest others in Oliver's plight. If Chadwick did agree with Bentham as to the essential uselessness and mendacity of "poetry," his letter to Austin makes it obvious that if people *will* choose imaginative literature over push-pin, if they will participate in the "misrepresentations" of fiction, then those misrepresentations should enlighten people to the need for social change.

This lesson was not lost on other philosophic radicals or their supporters. Harriet Martineau's nine-volume *Illustrations of Political Economy* (1832–33) was so enormously popular that over ten thousand copies of *each* book were sold. Because so many of these were bought by libraries of mechanics' institutions, Martineau's publisher estimated that as many as 144,000 people read each tale (Himmelfarb, *Idea* 170). This spectacular success led to a second series of tales, *Poor Laws and Paupers Illustrated* (1833–34), for which Chadwick provided the argument and the information, having sent her an advance copy of the *Extracts* of his *Poor Law Report* together with some of the reports of the assistant commissioners, including his own (Martineau, *Autobiography* 219–22). While Martineau was using her "tales" to instruct the literate working classes on the benefits of political economy and the advantages of Poor Law reform, Chadwick and the economist Nassau Senior completed and published the Poor Law *Report*. Like Martineau's "illustrations," it enjoyed a tremendous reception. In 1834 ten thousand copies of the twelve-volume report with appendices were distributed free of charge to parishes, and another ten thousand were immediately purchased by the interested public (Finer 96). This response could not have been entirely unexpected, for Chadwick had been preparing his potential readers for his work by feeding the press carefully selected extracts well in advance of the publication of the complete report. In 1833 Lord Brougham, after much coaxing, ultimately prevailed on Chadwick and Senior to publish and circulate, with the considerable help of Francis Place, tens of thousands of copies of these extracts (Webb and Webb 95).

Martineau, as a novelist, and Chadwick, as the author of parliamentary reports, were each engaged in important interpretive enterprises; each was attempting to make intelligible a world that was faced almost daily with significant and unprecedented changes in the material conditions of existence. And as the wide dissemination of their respective efforts indicates, these enterprises were reaching across traditional class, economic, and educational distinctions to become available to more people and, consequently, potentially more powerful as means of ordering the world in which those people lived. On the one hand the reports of parliamentary commissions, highlighted by the unflagging efforts of Chadwick to distribute the results of his own investigations, were available to nearly everyone.[3] Once published they were, quite literally, a matter of public record. On the other hand, the novel as a genre was monumentally popular among the middle classes, and—as the sale of *Illustrations of Political Economy* to the libraries of mechanics' institutions makes clear—its reach was extending to the working classes as well.

Each of these enterprises functioned within its own set of interpretive assumptions and discursive conventions—which in turn defined the limits of its language and of its ability to interpret. As I have argued in Part I, however, the material changes that obtained in the Britain of the 1830s and '40s demanded that public interpretive enterprises articulate their observations in ways that previously had been neither necessary nor available. Both the novel and the bluebook were well established as discursive projects, each with its own public language; but as the order of society was challenged by the tumultuous material changes taking place within it, the efficacy of these enterprises' representations and interpretations of their society was also called into question.

Somewhat paradoxically, the order that bluebooks and narrative fiction fashioned was based on observations of a world that, if not in disarray, was at least organizing itself in new and—for many—often confusing ways. The world of these observations was one where men could rise from near penury to become great manufacturers, where concepts of time and distance were being forever altered by the railroads, where an increasing number of people could participate in legally approved political activity, where entire new classes and even cultures were arising from the effects of industrialization. Representing this world as turbulent but coherent posed a particular challenge for the novel. It meant, for instance, that satire— the traditional "antiformal form established from gazing on chaos"—no longer served as a primary mode of narrative. Nostalgic, hoping for restoration rather than innovation, satire could not provide the opportunity for articulating a comprehensive vision of society in which individual cases as well as collective tendencies must be taken into account (Arac, *Spirits* 17–19). And though satire continues as an important element in Victorian novels, it rarely serves as the predominant idiom of a work. For the Victorians, it functions less to emphasize a previous, ideal order than to annihilate notions of the ideal. Unlike eighteenth-century novelistic satire, Victorian satire moves toward comedy in its toleration of folly and human imperfection. In Victorian literary works, irony, which, as Northrop Frye writes, "is consistent both with the complete realism of content and with the suppression of attitude on the part of the author" (224), often replaces satire. As individual fortunes come to be perceived as entwined with "all encompassing public events," the "real" world displaces the "ideal" upon which satire

depends (Arac, *Spirits* 16). Satire "breaks down when its content is too op-
pressively real to permit the maintaining of the fantastic or hypothetical
tone" (Frye 224). And as Jonathan Arac points out, the vices, hypocrisy,
and pretense of the Victorian bourgeois, "once exposed. . . solicited sympathetic understanding rather than the lash of the satirist" (*Spirits* 16). With
the ever increasing insistence on the fragility of the bourgeois subject as a
unified entity and the project of negotiating a position between an idealized subject position and the demands of social totality, the novel—though
significantly informed by the conventions of its eighteenth-century pre-
cursor—broke with and transformed its customary modes of articulation.
Unlike the political discourse of the Tories and the Whigs, which attempted
to reconcile past positions and traditional constituencies with new (or revised) principles for the present and the future, the novel was freer to
innovate, to try new techniques, and to borrow from other interpretive
enterprises such as the parliamentary or royal commission reports.

Such "borrowing" is extremely important for understanding what
informed social- problem novels during the early years of the Victorian
period, and it has been a fruitful area of research for a number of scholars.
Patrick Brantlinger's important essay "Bluebooks, the Social Organism,
and the Victorian Novel," his book, *The Spirit of Reform: British Literature and Politics, 1832–1867*, and Sheila Smith's *The Other Nation: The Poor
in English Novels of the 1840s and 1850s*, are excellent examples of studies that
in part or whole focus on the ways authors like as Disraeli, Dickens, and
other prominent Victorian authors used information from parliamentary
reports.[4] These studies, however, despite their considerable contribution
to our understanding of the connections between Parliamentary reports
and fiction, concentrate primarily on the unilateral influence of the bluebooks on novel writing and, when they do go farther, on the effects of
"industrial" or "political" novels as instigators of social change. Crucial as
these concerns are, they fail to take up the ways in which the novel, as a
dominant cultural form continuing to redefine the boundaries of its discursive practice, exerted an increasingly powerful informative force over
competing interpretive enterprises. As a way of seeing and ordering a world
that seemed desperately to need ordering, the novel exercised subtle authority over other projects that were attempting to establish their own,
viable principles of representation at the same time that they were providing information and discursive possibilities for the novel. By the middle
of the nineteenth century, the affinity between the projects of novelists
and of those we have come to regard as the founders of the social sci-

ences can be easily identified. As Jonathan Arac observes, "The writings of Dickens and Mayhew epitomize the sharing of what went on across the borders of what are now separate domains" (*Spirits* 14). He goes on to point out that although "Mayhew's findings made available material on 'mud-larks,' Thames-side scavengers, for *Our Mutual Friend*," Mayhew's "initial inquiries followed the interest Dickens's early writings had awakened in exploring the life of the poor and outcast, and Dickens's literary methods helped to establish the canons of verisimilitude by which Mayhew's accounts could seem plausible because so fantastic" (14).[5]

In Victorian studies, thanks in large part to the work of scholars like Anne Humpherys, E. P. Thompson, and Eileen Yeo, the "Mayhew" industry is well established. Further, with the availability of *London Labour and the London Poor* in an affordable edition, Mayhew's work is today the most widely known of these early social investigators; but the sharing across interpretive domains starts much earlier than with the beginning of his *Morning Chronicle* project in 1849. Close inspection of parliamentary reports like Chadwick's Poor Law and Sanitation *Reports* and pamphlets such as J. P. Kay's *The Moral and Physical Condition of the Working Classes Employed in the Cotton Manufacture in Manchester* (hereafter *Manchester*) (1832) demonstrates how novelistic discourse helped form non-fictional investigative reports. Faced with a morass of information and following definite agendas, the writers of these reports confronted the prodigious task of presenting, of *representing*, their observations forcefully enough to persuade Parliament and the public to work toward eliminating the causes of the destitution and depravity they had witnessed. At the same time, the social investigators of the 1830s and '40s felt the onus of depicting the conditions they observed as "they really were." The failure of earlier investigative efforts to provide accurate depictions prompted Kay to write that, in England,

> when any emergency demands a special inquiry, information is obtained by means of committees of the Commons, whose labours are so multifarious, as to afford them time for little else than the investigation of general conclusions, derived from the experience of those supposed to be most conversant with the subject. An approximation to truth may thus be made, but the results are never so minutely accurate as those obtained from statistical investigations; and as they are generally deduced from a comparison of opposing testimonies, and sometimes from partial evidence, they frequently utterly fail in one most important respect, namely—in convincing the public of the facts which they proclaim. (19)

Kay and Chadwick's strongly held conviction that complete and accurate investigation and representation are the most vital factors in presenting convincing and compelling evidence to the public highlights the irony of Chadwick's appeal to Dickens. In sending his report to Dickens for use in *American Notes*, Chadwick, the champion of *facts*, is hoping for help from one who makes up stories for a living. Granted, *American Notes* is not a novel, and Dickens was a journalist as well as a fiction writer. But remember that Chadwick refers specifically to *Oliver Twist*'s exposure of the abuses of "parochial administration." Something of the "real," of "facts," of the verifiable had made its way into the novel, and as Arac points out it is the literary methods of writers like Dickens that help to establish the standards of verisimilitude that make representation by Chadwick, Kay, Mayhew (himself a sometime novelist), and others possible. Indeed, we see that the precepts of realism governing the representations of the poor in the works of these social investigators depend, like those underwriting similar novelistic depictions, upon an interpretive scheme that "sets a solid reality on one hand and its mirroring in words on the other" (J. H. Miller 89).

The very words that Miller uses to describe realism point to the difficulties beleaguering that concept. The image of the mirror, though comfortably ensconced in our critical tradition, is troublesome for a number of reasons, not least of which is that it implies accurate reproduction of that "solid reality," when in effect a mirror distorts, turns right to left, and limits vision to the breadth of the glass. The mirror metaphor also invokes a number of other issues concerning not only the question of reflection and the possibility of representing the real, but the very status of a reality that exists outside language. Any theory of representation that utilizes a concept of reflection, however problematized, must ultimately rely on referentiality in a way that proves suspect in its descriptions of "the real." Equally problematic are models of realism that depend upon narrative coherence, or the creation of a world that "seems" real, but is completely fictitious. In each of these explanations of "realism," the status of the referent is privileged— either by its absence or by its "truthful" representation in a text.

The difficulty that thus persists for those who wish to employ some model of empirical realism, as well as for those who wish to call such a model into question, is the extent to which either position can be maintained with any analytical or descriptive usefulness. On the one hand, to return to a reductive empiricism in which texts exist independent of an interpretive paradigm is not only fruitless but potentially hegemonic, since it must depend upon some mutually agreed upon notion of the real. On the other hand, to accept a naïve idealism that privileges language as *the* constitutive element for all objects of interpretation is an equally questionable position. Because language is "socially formed" yet also "socially forming" (Arac and Ritvo 1–2), the interaction between the changes in our representations *of* the material world and our perceptions of the changes *in* the material world attains a non-synthetic dialectical opposition that continually seeks both closure and revision in our discourse about reality.

These issues of the relations of language to "the real" have become central in current theoretical discussions of representation, but as I point out in the introduction, they are by no means new, and concerns over the use of language to mediate reality also vexed the Victorians; they knew full well that language was constitutive and that words could just as easily misrepresent, could "drift away from a strict correspondence to the real" (McGowan 20). As followers of Locke and the empirical tradition, Victorian writers, especially those involved with Utilitarianism, often attempted to mitigate the mediational effects of language by emphasizing observation or experience. As a result, most instances of Victorian realism, whether in novels or non-fiction social writing, do indeed privilege the referent in ways that suggest writers attempted an empirical correspondence as close as possible between the world they perceived and the language of their descriptions. Whether or not they expressly took up the problems of representation, the issue most concerning these writers was how to represent accurately what they saw.

From Kay and Chadwick to Dickens and Mrs. Trollope, writers acceded to their desire for a reality that was seen and known by all, was based on shared perceptions, and was therefore fundamentally the same for everyone. Whatever their mistrust of language's ability to represent the real, they understood that dissemination required that their observations be captured in a language that in its turn becomes universally available. As a result, early social interpreters demanded an unrelenting "fidelity to reality" in their writing, establishing faithfulness of representation as the criterion for evaluating their work. When Kay attacks earlier investigations for producing little more than general conclusions and approximations of truth, he is calling his predecessors to account in the terms of this discourse of realism. Like Chadwick, he is not satisfied with generalizations, and like Chadwick, he insists on corroboration for his observations, corroboration born out by statistical verification: "We have avoided alluding to evidence which is founded on general opinion, or depends *merely* on matters of perception," says Kay of his methodology. "[We] have chiefly availed ourselves of such as admitted of a statistical classification" (72; emphasis added). The evidence must be observable, but also calculable, recordable, and recurring. One observer's perception is not enough for verification just as one instance of a particular behavior does not constitute a trend or a tendency. The "reports" of social investigators like Kay, Chadwick, and Mayhew are actually compilations of similar instances and observations that together discursively solidify a representation of the reality of the poor. Not only do such reports confirm the readers' experiences, but they are internally referential, verifying themselves with repetitions of similar accounts by different contributors. They establish both signifier and signified so that the reality they refer to is always substantiated by their representations of it. This move not only meets the demands for corroboration, it also buttresses the claims of realistic representation that such reports depend upon.

The tradition of realist fiction bases itself on a similar conception of representation, especially when dealing with the poor. As early as Dickens's *Sketches by Boz* (1836), a critical agenda was emerging in which the text is acclaimed for fulfilling its object of presenting "little pictures of life and manners as they really are" (original preface, February 1836). From their appearance, the *Sketches* were praised for their "startling fidelity," for "bringing out the meaning and interest of objects which would altogether escape the observation of ordinary minds," and for presenting "the romance, as it were, of real life" (from contemporary reviews; quoted in Butt and Tillotson 37). This, writes Kathleen Tillotson, "without annotation, give[s] us the world which the young Dickens saw" (37).[6]

If this was the world Dickens saw, it was also the world that others experienced through novels and bluebooks. For a great many, this world is Dickens's "discovery" in that he focuses on "neglected but immediately recognized pockets of urban and suburban society" (Butt and Tillotson 37); and representations of this discovery of what is both literally and figuratively a nether world become important to Dickens's novels soon after the publication of *Sketches*. Often for Dickens this is a place of evil as well as destitution, but even in a work as innately "good" as *Pickwick Papers*, "Dickens's one novel in which wickedness, though it exists, is not a threat" (Marcus *Pickwick to Dombey* 51), Mr. Pickwick nonetheless unearths a world whose existence he could not have conceived. Upon visiting a debtors' prison, Mr Pickwick comments on what he supposes are the tiny cellars where the prisoners keep coal. Looking down upon them from the top of the stairs, he finds them "unpleasant to go down into, but very convenient."

"Yes, I shouldn't wonder if they was convenient," replied the gentleman, "seeing that a few people live there, pretty snug. That's the Fair, that is."

"My friend," said Mr. Pickwick, "you don't really mean to say that human beings live down in those wretched dungeons?"

"Don't I?" replied Mr. Roker, with indignant astonishment; "why shouldn't I?"

"Live! Live down there!" exclaimed Mr. Pickwick.

"Live down there! Yes, and die down there, too, wery often!" replied Mr. Roker; "and what of that? Who's got to say anything agin it? Live down there! Yes, and a wery good place it is to live in, ain't it?" (*Pickwick Papers* 573)

Mr. Pickwick's discovery of the *possibility* of the sort of existence the inmates of the cellars must have led is as important as his actually going down into the cellars to view first-hand the conditions of that existence, for it acts as an analogue to the middle and upper classes' increasing consciousness of the problem of the poor. And while the "unfortunate and the deprived" pass "briefly, almost furtively" through the pages of *Pickwick* (Marcus, *Pickwick to Dombey* 51), that brevity and furtiveness accentuate an important aspect of the middle and upper classes' relations to the poor: the impulse to keep the more abhorrent aspects of lower-class existence out of sight. Mr. Pickwick's failure to go down into the cellars ever so subtly comments on the contradictory impulses that informed an increasing body of writing on the individuals in society about whom most was coming to be known—the lower classes. On the one hand is the surprise and fascination Mr. Pickwick evinces in hearing that people could actually live in such degraded conditions ("Live! Live down there!"). On the other hand is his revulsion by such a life, a revulsion that is indicated both by his failure to go down into the cellars and by the language and emotion in his exchange with Roker.

The "evidence" Dickens adduces in these early works is, as I have noted repeatedly, extremely important to someone like Chadwick, for it supports Chadwick's own perceptions of social reality. And whether describing the dank debtors' prison cellars of *Pickwick Papers* or the squalid Jacob's Island hovels of *Oliver Twist*, Dickens's depictions of the poor and their conditions of life sustain the prevailing concept of realistic representation by "setting a solid reality on the one hand" and by portraying it unflinchingly in words on the other. As the novel begins to establish the standards of verisimilitude that also will govern investigative pamphlets and bluebooks, the perception and representation of the "reality" of the lower classes increasingly cut across discursive boundaries, locating themselves in shared interpretive conventions that, in many ways, "invented" the "wretched proletariat" (Herbert 2).

Rather than a liberating move, however, participation in this consensus of observation is constraining because it presupposes two qualifications to observing and writing about social conditions of the lower classes. First, it posits an audience who, at least in the broadest sense, share the views of the writer and who will grant the observer's interpretations because they do not greatly diverge from their own. Second, and this is really a part of the first qualification, it posits and indeed defines its object of interpretation itself: the poor, their conditions of existence, their "culture," or lack of it, their exclusion from the normative values and perceptions that comprise these observers' own, and to a large degree shared, vision of the world. Thus constrained, observation appears always to reassert currently operative social conventions and to inhibit a re-evaluation of those conventions.

One way of getting off this hermeneutic treadmill is by exploiting the contradictions of the prescribed interpretive standards in such a way that changes in the conventions of interpretation, though perhaps never completely legitimized, can at least be considered. This is precisely how Dickens, Chadwick, and other observers of the life of the poor challenge the limits of the paradigm of observation within which they work. By providing a profusion of unsparing images of the poor, these writers force a confrontation with one of the most insistent of the contradictions abiding in middle-class conventions of representation of the lower classes: the compulsion to view this alien culture, while simultaneously contriving to keep the poor out of sight. In the pages that follow, I will examine a number of the effects resulting from the deconstruction of this particular contradiction of representation.

First, and perhaps most importantly, was the creation of a "literary" poor: that is to say a poor that existed in simulacrum and ultimately became the way in which the "reality" of poverty was understood by many middle- and upper-class readers. This is by no means a suggestion that the lower classes did not exist or that they did not suffer. Rather, I want to demonstrate the force with which a text like Chadwick's *Sanitary Condition Report* created a "culture of poverty"—not for the poor themselves so much (though there was that effect) as for its middle-class readership.

This creation of a textual poor also raises a number of issues about the culture of the "labouring population," as Chadwick calls it, and the positioning of individual subjects within that culture. It would be ludicrous to assume that all working-class poor people were passively constituted by middle-class perceptions, desires, and interests, yet at the same time the *Report* itself, while insistently raising the specter of a revolutionary mob, for the most part depicts members of the lower classes as malleable subjects, easily influenced and made aware that they have "characters" to lose. Thus alongside Chadwick's "writing of the poor" is the question of how poor persons wrote themselves within Chadwick's text. As Chadwick simultaneously "reveals" and interpellates the poor, he walks a difficult line between reform and repression. His exploitation of the contradictions in the paradox of repulsion/fascination that informs middle-class attitudes toward the working classes has ambiguous effects. For while he often hauls the poor into a white hot light of observation they are not prepared to bear, his text is also disruptive enough (sometimes even to its own assumptions) that pockets of resistance often reveal themselves in the *Sanitary Condition Report*. It is these issues of the discursive subjectifying of the working poor, of their being written and of their writing themselves, that are the focus of the next chapter.

5
Mr. Chadwick Writes the Poor

At one point in the *Report*, Chadwick quotes one of his informants, a Dr. J. F. Handley, to express the extremity of the filth many of the Victorian poor lived in:

> When the small-pox was prevalent in this district, I attended a man, woman, and five children, all lying ill with the confluent species of that disorder, in one bed-room, and having only two beds amongst them. The walls of the cottage were black, the sheets were black, and the patients themselves were blacker still; two of the children were absolutely sticking together. I have relished many a biscuit and glass of wine in Mr. Grainger's dissecting-room when ten dead bodies were lying on the tables under dissection, but was entirely deprived of appetite during my attendance upon these cases. The smell on entering the apartments was exceedingly nauseous, and the room would not admit of free ventilation. (316)

Both the description and the commentary in this passage are characteristic of the *Sanitary Condition Report*, and they typify the problem of representation that faced Chadwick as he gathered his evidence. His data indicated that there was a large and almost completely alien world that lay just out of sight for many Victorians. His project was to overcome the observational barriers that shielded this world from view and to offer it to the consumers of novels and bluebooks: a predominantly middle-class readership that was often quite ignorant of the particular hardships of working-class life. But as Handley's description of the family suffering from smallpox indicates, even among Chadwick's associates few were steeled for what he and his investigators found. Handley was a well-trained doctor, a medical officer of the Chipping Norton union. And although the smell in that close room was no doubt difficult for Handley to bear, his perception of the entire scene—of which the odor of the room is a part and for which he was totally unprepared—also must have contributed significantly to his revulsion. In any case, the unfavorable comparison of the physical condition of the people to dissected cadavers is strong stuff and admits of the offense to the very core of middle-class sensibilities that the living conditions of the poor perpetrated. Better, apparently, to be dead than to live in such squalor.[1]

Steven Marcus has asserted that "it was in fact easier to read about such things than it was to experience them directly," reasoning that a "preformed structure" imposed upon "early scenes of industrial life" by written and printed language provided a much needed distance between "the immediate concrete realities of human experience and the reader" (*Engels, Manchester* 44–45). According to Marcus, language, printed language, served at least in part much like the facades on the thoroughfares of Manchester, guarding the affluent classes from too close an inspection of the destitution of their fellow human beings. The dialectical tension at the heart of this circumstance points directly to the relationship between language and representations of reality that vexed the efforts of novelists and bluebook authors alike. On the one hand is the impulse to use language as a shield, to protect the middle class from too direct contact with the poor—in deference to middle-class consciences and constitutions. On the other hand is the desire to represent as fully, completely, and truthfully as possible. Thus even as language functions as a kind of *cordon sanitaire*, defining and broadening the gap between the "two nations," it is also the bridge across that divide.

Yet that bridge is potentially built upon misrepresentations and illusions. After all, if language can be a facade, how is one to know when it is mediating accurately and when it is distorting? Even for committed reformers whose social agendas could benefit the most from the destitution recorded in bluebooks and similar pamphlets, it was often difficult to accept unquestioningly these reports' representations of the working classes. When Francis Place comments on the severity of the lives of the indigent that Kay presents in his *Manchester*, for instance, he reacts in a way that demonstrates how hard it was to separate the wheat from the chaff in these reports. Bound to respond discursively, yet distrustful of the misrepresentations of discourse, Place and others like him who had risen from the working class were themselves caught between believing things were as bad as all that and defending the *English* laboring population as in fact improving their lot. His direct response to Kay's conclusions lucidly identifies his difficult position as well as the pressures the empirical demands of the language of description used by these "new" social observers were placing on accepted ways of thinking and writing about the working poor:

> I believe that what [Kay] says is correct; but he gives the matter as it now
> stands, knowing nothing of former times; his picture is a very deplorable
> one. . . . Many Manchester operatives . . . inform me that his narration relates
> almost entirely to the state of the Irish, but that the condition of a vast num-
> ber of the people was as bad some years ago, as he describes the worst portion
> of them to be now. (*Parliamentary Papers*, 1835, no. 465, VII:838)

Place's attempt to diminish the severity of Kay's claims by making the Irish
a special case and by strongly implying that for a great number of operatives
conditions have improved displays a lack of confidence in the interpretive
norms that were in place for describing the conditions of the poor. Arguing
that Kay paints the worst possible picture and that his conclusions would
have been much milder had he been aware of how much worse things used
to be hardly eases the sufferings of those in the present. Place cannot dis-
agree with Kay's findings; indeed, he says as much. But unlike Kay, who in
deluging his readers with the empirical realities of poverty in Manchester
exploits the contradictory coupling of fascination with and aversion to the
poor, Place defends his interpretive code by both agreeing and disagreeing
with Kay. Even as he takes Kay to task for his representations, insinuating
that Kay's depiction is not entirely reliable, because incomplete, he maintains the very tension he is attempting to address: the poor are visible, but
not too visible, and the vision itself is not nearly as repugnant as Kay claims.

For the new social investigators like Kay, Chadwick, and Dickens
this will not serve. The contradiction is too apparent and another resolution is necessary. According to Chadwick, the forcing of the poor into
"places . . . that are secluded from superior inspection and common observation" contributes to the degradation and vices of the lower classes
(Sanitary Condition *Report* 306–7). The confines to which Chadwick refers
are architectural, to be sure; but as Place's comments demonstrate, linguistic confines also existed: limits to what could—or more properly should—
be said about the life of the lower classes. In seeking to resolve the ambivalence of the middle classes' relations to the poor by urging observation
and inspection from above, these authors actively participate in making
the *socially* peripheral *symbolically* central (Stallybrass and White 5).

Placing the poor at the visual and linguistic center of interpretations of society, however, creates a contradiction similar to the fascination-
revulsion dichotomy. Discursively removing the barriers to inspection and
observation increased the power of the middle classes over the lower: by
creating a panopticon-like program of surveillance, the middle classes aug-
mented their ability to "discipline" the poor.[2] Chadwick's 1833 recommen-

dation of a board of inspectors for enforcing factory regulations was only the beginning of the administrative methods of observation that character- ize innovative social programs of the early Victorian period.[3] For although the inspectors functioned to regulate factory owners, making certain that the particulars of the bill were being followed, Chadwick's bill itself was designed to help factory owners rigorously manage the time of their opera- tives under thirteen years of age (see Finer 64–66).

The problem with this greater exposure to the world of the poor is the increased risk of contamination by that world. In a society increasingly based upon contiguous relationships, where, as Michel Foucault insists in *Discipline and Punish*, the "social body" was sutured together by a "network of mechanisms. . . running through society without interruption" (208– 9), panopticism may indeed have been the means by which middle-class values such as "respectability" or "duty" became the disciplinary mecha- nisms that helped to maintain dominant middle-class representations of its particular interests as those of the whole and that established the norms against which all society could be evaluated. A hegemony fashioned along these lines was not without its Achilles heel, however. The very contiguity that allowed panopticism to function so well also meant that any action no longer had only local consequences, but rather affected every fiber of the social fabric. In such a society it was impossible to escape the touch of the lower classes, despite any amount of observation from above. True enough, panopticism relies on the invisibility of the observer. But the ob- server still exists and is still in proximity to the object of inspection. In a contiguous society, the observer, no matter how invisible, still touches the observed—even if only third- or fourth-hand—and when the interpretive principle connected to such observation focuses squarely on the condi- tions of the poor, forcing a recognition of the "second nation" as culturally distinct (and, usually, inferior), the result is the displacement of the fasci- nation/revulsion dichotomy by observation/contamination, within which both fascination and revulsion may still function, but not at the expense of the new observational imperative of seeing the poor as they "really are."[4]

Because both observation and contamination function, in part, through the propinquity of observer to observed, the novelist or bluebook author is called upon to find ways to articulate these contiguous relations, to represent connections among people and things that might otherwise go unnoticed. Such connections are usually expressed metonymically, sug- gesting relations of similarity or causality between the object (or person) depicted and something adjacent to it (J. H. Miller 94). As the predominant figurative trope in realistic representation, however, metonymy has been most often discussed as constitutive of realistic *fiction*.[5] To return for a moment to Dickens as an example, *Sketches by Boz* has been convincingly described—"in spite of Dickens's well-known use of metaphor"—as a "brilliant and consistent exploitation of . . . 'the metonymical texture of realistic prose'" (J. H. Miller 93). But in a quite different literary realm, Chadwick finds that he too must use metonymy in order to live up to the principles of realism his own interpretive project demands. Indeed, because he opposes a paradigm that would hide the poor from view, and because he espouses an interpretive strategy that depends upon the contiguity of the various strata of social existence, he has little choice but to turn to metonymy, defining people "in terms of their contiguous environment" (J. H. Miller 92), as a means of organizing and presenting his observations.

In *Sketches by Boz*, connections among an odd collection of things found in a pawnshop window, a collection that initially appears to the reader as a list of objects thrown together pell-mell, furnishes Boz with his interpretive text—that seemingly indecipherable set of signs from which a coherent picture of at least a small slice of London life takes shape. Boz himself remarks, "Although the same heterogenous mixture of things will be found at all these places [pawnshops], it is curious to observe how truly and accurately some of the minor articles which are exposed for sale— articles of wearing apparel for instance—mark the character of the neighborhood" (179). In one of the more widely read of the sketches, "Meditations on Monmouth Street," Boz reconstructs the entire history of a man, whose "whole life was written as legibly on these clothes, as if we had his autobiography engrossed on parchment before us" (75). While it would be foolhardy to suggest that the entire representative strategy of this or any of Dickens's sketches is metonymic, I do want to insist that by using metonymy Dickens does not merely reconstruct the history of the man as inscribed upon the clothes, he also moves toward a truly complex narrative structure describing a world that the man of the pawnshop clothes inhabits. In using metonymy to get to this point, Dickens plays upon the connections of the society he represents, connections that extend not only to the writer-observer Boz, but to his readers as well. Beginning with the inanimate particulars of day-to-day life—clothing, shops, streets, writing desks, or dressing cases—the sketches progress to an imagining of the people "of whose lives these objects are the signs, and finally the continuous narrative of their lives, which may be inferred from the traces of themselves they have left behind" (J. H. Miller 96).

For the Chadwick of the *Sanitary Condition Report*, the world is also a set of signs, a text to be deciphered. As he and his sub-commissioners relate their observations, they, like Boz, fix on the artifacts of lower-class life: streets, sewers, privies, dungheaps, attire, cottages, and workshops. Even the people are but objects that signify some important part of the entire picture of the extremity at which the life of the poor was lived. Those who populate the world of the *Report* have no essential meaning, either individually or as an entire class. Rather they take on the meaning prescribed for them by their surroundings. The filth of a cottage or the pestilence of a cellar is embodied in the individual; the connection between individual and surrounding is inseparable. "It appears to be a matter of common observation, in the instance of migrant families of workpeople who are obliged to occupy inferior tenements," writes Chadwick, "that their habits soon become 'of a piece' with the dwelling" (194).

This is a controlling assumption of the *Report*, and articulations of it abound. In the section "Internal Economy and Domestic Habits," one young woman is described as having always attended to her "personal neatness" and as thoroughly schooled in the "habits of neatness, order, and cleanliness most thoroughly as regards household work" (195). She married a servant, and the house they took was in a neighborhood of "cottages of the most wretched kind, mere hovels of rough stone and covered with ragged thatch" (195). After the woman had been married "about two years," Chadwick's informant was surprised to discover the change the woman had undergone:

> Her face was dirty, and her tangled hair hung over her eyes. Her cap, though of good materials, was ill washed and slovenly put on. Her whole dress, though apparently good and serviceable, was very untidy, and looked dirty and slatternly; everything indeed about her seemed wretched and neglected, (except the little child), and she appeared very discontented. She seemed aware of the change there must be in her appearance since I had last seen her, for she immediately began to complain of her house. (195)

Tellingly, the condition of the house, which is such that the woman found it impossible to "keep things in order, so had gradually ceased to make any exertions" (195), becomes the explanation for the woman's lack of personal cleanliness and neatness. There is no escaping the effects of the dwelling to which one is connected. And, of course, these effects extend to the condition of family life. The husband, "dissatisfied with his home and with her," spent less time at home, opting instead to remain at his employer's. Had he been a day-laborer, contends the informant, he would have inevitably preferred a beer shop or public house to his home (196).

To support further the connection between the condition of the dwelling and habits of cleanliness, the informant tells Chadwick that, upon moving to a better constructed house, the woman soon resumed "in a great degree, her former good habits, but still there was a little of the *dawdle* left about her; the remains of the dispiritedness caused by her former very unfavourable circumstances" (196; Chadwick's italics). Not only did the woman take on the characteristics of her surroundings, those surroundings came to constitute her lived relations to all around her. Her habits, like her hovel, are filthy and degraded, but the contamination by the woman's surroundings damages more than the woman's habits, which are but outward signs of her morality. As the informant's comment on the lingering of the "dawdle" indicates, the woman's moral nature, her essence, had been permanently tainted by her wretched conditions of life.

This is the usual conclusion to the tales told in the *Sanitary Condition Report*. And as with the woman with the "dawdle," the material aspects of the metonymies shaping many of Chadwick's description seemingly pertain primarily to dress, cleanliness, neatness of person; that is, his depictions are ostensibly concerned mainly with appearances, the externals of existence. Rhetorically, however, and within Chadwick's logic, these connections establish conditions that allow for an explanation of the deterioration of the morals of the poor. Once members of the lower classes become "of a piece" with their degraded surroundings, it is only by the slimmest of chances that they can escape utter moral degradation. And once an observer identifies this degeneracy, the subsequent representation of the poor changes. Metonymy continues to be the trope for portraying the realities of the poor's material conditions of existence, but it is replaced in importance by metaphor as the means of conveying the essential nature of the poor. As they sink into "demoralization" the poor are characterized as swarms, beasts, savages, wild animals, swine, and feral dogs. Not only is cleanliness next to godliness; in the *Sanitary Condition Report* it is requisite to being human.

Ironically, godliness sometimes leads to the greatest depravity, and also potentially a space of resistance for the working classes. According to Chadwick and his informants, the social determinations of the conditions of the poor often can be traced to misplaced notions (and actions) of philanthropy. A Reverend Whitwell Elwin of Bath writes:

Charity, which when prompted by pure motives, always blesses him that gives, does not always bless him that takes. I am afraid that the indiscriminate adoption of dirt and rags as a test of poverty, especially in a town like Bath, where private charity prevails on an extensive scale, operates as a premium upon ill habits, and as a discouragement to cleanliness, and leads many to affect a vice which was not habitual to them. (*Sanitary Condition Report* 201)

Elwin's explanation of the morals of the poor depends on the associations between dirt and rags and immoral behavior, and also points out the difficulty of addressing the problem of poverty. As long as philanthropists use "dirt and rags as a test of poverty" the poor will be forced to remain dirty and inadequately clothed in order to receive out-of-doors aid. Compounding the effects of misinformed philanthropy is the connection Elwin sees between dirt and poor clothing and immoral conduct. As in Chadwick's own statements, there is nothing essentially immoral in poverty, per se; however, the material circumstances of poverty are so closely associated with profligacy that, though perhaps not naturally drawn to vice, many who are compelled to present themselves as dirty and ragged in order to qualify for charity are moved to acquire "ill habits." To this end, private philanthropy, by using preconceived notions of what poverty must look like, exacerbates rather than alleviates the problems of the poor.

In Elwin's example, we see how the expectations of the middle classes actually inscribe a subject position for the poor. In order to receive aid, they must affect a particular aspect and behavior that is recognizable to the middle classes as characteristic of the needy. It is easy enough to read this as an instance of middle-class hegemony, but we can also see it as a site of potential resistance. Ostensibly, the philanthropy that is being practiced in Bath aims not only to relieve the physical straits of the poor but also to salve their spiritual needs—to help to form their "characters." But at least some poor persons have recognized the internal contradiction of the requirements for out-of-doors relief. If the philanthropy is successful, if indeed the poor become morally uplifted, they will no longer seem to need the aid, for they will no longer be profligate and their presentation of themselves will improve: they will be cleaner, soberer, and better clothed. The poor residents of Bath exploit this logic by subjecting *themselves* to the expectations of the philanthropists, and consequently they continually justify the philanthropists' efforts to improve them both morally and materially. Those providing the aid have indeed inscribed the Other. But at the same time, by assuming agency and fulfilling the role of the Other, the "profligate" poor of Bath have also inscribed the philanthropists. The two groups have become reliant upon each other, and the wealthy need the poor just as much as the poor need the wealthy.

The problem with such an arrangement is that the ill habits and affected vices of which Elwin speaks did indeed often become addictions as they became naturalized characteristics of the poor. Elwin is referring specifically to drunkenness, which ran rampant through the working classes.[6] From the perspective of the bourgeoisie, this was an extreme danger. Chadwick found that intemperance made the poor "prone to passionate excitement" and "apt instruments for political discontents." Their moral perceptions appeared "to have been obliterated, and they might be said to be characterised by a 'ferocious indocility which makes them prompt to wrong and violence, destroys their social nature, and transforms them into something little better than wild beasts'" (199). Part of the "social nature" that Chadwick is referring to is the working classes' willingness to accept their position in a hierarchical society that places them at the bottom, but that depends upon their productivity for its existence. Again, we see the possibility for resistance, especially local resistance in the form of strikes and riots, that is distinctly linked to many middle-class inscriptions of the poor. Not only do Elwin's philanthropists rely upon the poor's "profligacy" to fuel their own beneficent efforts, but the writing of the poor along these lines also is fraught with the danger of revolt, a danger that even Chadwickian observation and containment is unsure it can coopt.

Of course that is not to discount cooptation as an aim of the *Report*. One way it is attempted is by moving once again from metonymic to metaphoric representation. The intemperate poor are no longer human beings. They are indocile, their moral perceptions "obliterated"; they *are* beasts. To drive home this implication, the *Report* depicts the contingencies of the poor's existence metaphorically as well. The very things that link them to each other and to the rest of the social fabric take on wild or inhuman natures. The number of examples is overwhelming. Portrayals of their homes resemble descriptions of uncleaned dens or cages. The floor of a typical dwelling "contains the aggregate filth of years, from the time of its first being used. The refuse and dropping of meals, decayed animal and vegetable matter of all kinds, which has been cast upon it from the mouth and the stomach, these all mix together and exude from it" (96). "Worse off than wild animals, many of which withdraw to a distance and conceal their ordure" (98), the poor are forced to live and die surrounded by their own filth. Like "savages," they go without proper clothing, crowding together to be warm (98). Many of them do not even have proper names. As one Glasgow police superintendent points out when several children hesitate to tell their names to investigators: "The fact is . . . they really have no names. Within this range of buildings I have no doubt I should be able to find a thousand children who have no names whatever, or only nicknames, like dogs" (198–99).

Living like wild animals, these Glasgow children are represented by the policeman, and in turn by Chadwick, as bereft of even the simplest commonplace of human, let alone respectable, society, a proper name. As Chadwick remarks, "the working-classes living in these districts were equally marked by the abandonment of every civil and social regulation" (198). It was as though the concept of respectability, which includes within its rubric notions of cleanliness, thrift, prudence, temperance, and other conventions of behavior that most members of the middle classes felt necessary to civil society, were completely annihilated in (and by) this world of the poor. Yet, like the poor in Bath described by Elwin, many seemed to possess at least the basic economic and cultural rudiments requisite to respectability. As Chadwick observed in Glasgow, a significant portion of the working class were "labourers earning wages undoubtedly sufficient to have paid for comfortable tenements, men and women who were intelligent and so far as could be ascertained, had received the ordinary education which should have given better tastes and led to better habits" (199). Nevertheless, in this world that Chadwick discovers, respectability and civil and social regulation cannot survive, and the reason for this, Chadwick contends, "is, to a large extent attributable to the surrounding physical circumstances" of the poor (199).

Undoubtedly living and working conditions for the lower classes were unsanitary to the point of being dangerous. But that concern is not what appears to drive Chadwick's report. Instead Chadwick uniformly holds out an agenda for moral reform that offers a strategy for containing the poor within the operative moral and political paradigms of the *Report*'s informants. By focusing on the *effects* of the conditions of existence of the working classes, Chadwick implies that a solution to their "demoralization" is possible. Thus when he adduces the working classes' intemperance or their loss of notions of sexual propriety, he can always trace it back to a material cause. If a character can be formed, then it certainly can be re-formed; and when it is, the person who possesses it can become more productive and thus help to eradicate the reproduction of odious living and working conditions. The goal, then, is not only to eliminate the causes of demoralization but to get the working classes to participate in their own moral reform, at least in part, by recognizing the reasons for their wandering from the path of respectability.

This aim of the *Report* announces itself as a representational strategy and a way of presenting the desires and the observations of the informants as the unmediated observations and desires of the working classes. When Chadwick speaks with a tailor, Thomas Brownlow, for instance, he asks him how much of "the habit of drinking was produced by the workplace." Brownlow replies:

> I should say the greater part of it; because when men work by themselves, or only two or three together, in cooler and less close places, there is scarcely any drinking between times. Nearly all this drinking proceeds from the large shops, where the men are crowded together in close rooms; it is the same in the shops in the country as well as those in the town. (168)

This bit of information may help to demonstrate the overcrowded working conditions of tailors, but other evidence in the *Report* is considerably more compelling. It is much more interesting as an illustration of the manner in which the conclusions toward which Chadwick is working are imposed from without, rather than inferred "objectively" from the information he gathered. Chadwick so adroitly manipulates the testimonial evidence of Brownlow, that the tailor readily accepts the connections implicit in Chadwick's question. He is participating, albeit no doubt unconsciously, in Chadwick's narrative of the conditions of the poor and of the middle class's failure to address those conditions. Brownlow, in answering the question in these terms, is playing the role assigned him by Chadwick; and while his (and Chadwick's) conclusions about the causes of drinking may be absolutely correct, the logic of his answer is obviously Chadwick's.

Not every member of the working class who appears in the *Report* is as cooperative as Brownlow, however. Time and again, Chadwick's informants are disgusted and surprised by those who do not share their moral presuppositions. As the recording of such failures on the part of the working classes suggests, however, the poor were not without their own set of moral standards. It was often simply at odds with the moral assumptions of the middle class. Thus when Chadwick submits "a few instances of the extent and prevalence of personal uncleanliness amongst whole classes of working people" (305), his words intimate that something greater than a mere aversion to soap and water is at work among these people, and the examples he cites bear out that assumption. One man expresses "their common feeling" when he states that he considered his being washed " 'equal to robbing him of a great coat which he had for some years' " (316). Another laborer can remember a certain event taking place at Easter because " 'it was then he washed his feet' " (315).

Such statements accent the differences in attitudes toward cleanliness held by the middle and lower classes. The poor in Chadwick's accounts are not ashamed that they are dirty. For them it is a way of life, a part of their identity, and many demonstrate no desire to be clean. For them being dirty is no indication of moral lapse. For some members of the working classes, cleanliness has another association entirely. Asking workers in Glasgow when they had last been washed, Chadwick "more than once" receives the answer, "when I was last in prison" (198). Not discounting the difficulty so many of the working classes would have had in acquiring water suitable for bathing, in their refusal to accept dirt as a comment on their character, and in their figuring of cleanness as a potential violence to the body, connected to confinement or robbery, these workers discursively establish the corporeal presence of the Great Unwashed. Furthermore, that presence, while not so much a threat as a difference, nonetheless announces itself as resistive, stiff-necked in the face of the constitutive power of the "idea of sanitation." For many of these people it is not laziness or demoralization that leads to their dirtiness; it is the work they do. While it was certainly possible to get incredibly filthy by doing nothing at all in Victorian England, the grandly dirty were those who spent their time in coal mines, steel mills, or textile manufactories. As they were being discursively hauled out of these places and prodded to assent to their interrogators' views toward sanitation (and everything it stood for), they often subtly asserted their own presuppositions and subjectivity.

Such instances do demonstrate resistance, but the *Report* busily works to coopt them. By dwelling upon its readers' assumptions about the working classes, and by reinforcing those assumptions, it was simple enough to use the working classes' attempts at self-identification and assertion of agency as demonstrations of moral failure. It is not surprising then that Chadwick's conclusions about cleanliness differ significantly from those of most of the working-class subjects he interviews: "Such conditions of the population, of habitual personal and domestic filth, are not necessary to any occupation; they are not the necessary consequence of poverty, and are the type of neglect and indolence. This is proved by the example of men engaged in the same occupations with improved habits" (316). Chadwick may be right on the mark in his comment on the needlessness of living in the deplorable conditions he describes, but his conclusion that the poor are dirty because they are lazy and uncaring (two attributes that he admits are due to overcrowding and a lack of proper housing and working conditions) suggests as much about Chadwick's own moral presumptions as it does about the moral condition of an unwashed poor. Nor is Chadwick unconscious of the conflicting impulses at work in his depictions. His offer to prove the neglect and indolence of the poor by pointing to other poor members of the working classes who do not live in "habitual personal and domestic filth" indicates the difficulty he confronted in addressing the problem of "uncleanness." Representation of the problem is fraught with an ironic inner logic: the poor are simultaneously the victims *and* the cause of insanitation. If a person's morals are lax, then that person is unclean; if a person is unclean, then that person is (or becomes) immoral. Thus Chadwick's failure to ask of the unwashed poor what seems to be a very pertinent question, "Why do you choose to be dirty?" is offset by his observations that many of the poor *do not* choose to live in filth. When he cites evidence of those whose morals and domestic economy are unimpeachable, yet who make less in wages than their more profligate counterparts, Chadwick can deny that the solution to the problem of insanitation and immorality (for in his mind it is one problem), the solution to what may be called the perpetuation of the "culture of poverty," is the raising of workers' wages.[7]

Neither are the conditions of filth in which so many of the poor live and "for which," says Chadwick, "there is no other necessity than their [the workers'] own habitual indolence" (317), a problem that can be solved simply by demanding that the poor clean themselves up. It has taken root, become part of the "nature" of many of the poor, and "these habits mere admonitions will not always remove from the adult population" (317). How is it, then, that some of the poor escape the moral and physical consequences of insanitation? In part, at least, it is through education of the poorer classes and their initiation into middle-class notions of respectability. This education is successfully effected through the reinforcement of one of the primary connections of the working to the middle classes, a connection that *is* economic and is based in monetary remuneration for labor, which defines the relation of worker to industrialist and the perceived relation of the lower to the middle classes: namely, the employment of members of the lower classes by middle-class owners of factories and businesses.

Chadwick, in demonstrating the determination of many of the poor to keep themselves clean, points out that a great many of the members of the laboring classes (up to 3,000 per day in London and Westminster) do avail themselves of the opportunity to bathe.[8] He cites instances of the building of baths whose hot water is provided by the waste water of factories. Used exclusively by the working classes, these baths were operated at a profit by charging bathers a small fee. Chadwick tells of one manufacturer offering free baths as a reward or holiday, until the workers "had experienced the comfort and formed a habit, when he left them to themselves and they paid out of their own pockets" (317). The irony of course is that the hot water is provided by the mechanism of industrialism that created the filth in the first place. But beyond that, this example demonstrates how complex the seemingly simple issue of cleanliness has become. Even in acquiring the middle-class habit of bathing regularly (and, presumably middle-class attitudes toward cleanliness), the workers remain dependent upon their employers, and relations between the manufacturers and their hands become unrelentingly reified. The factory owners may merely be attempting to improve the health, morale, and ultimately the morals of their workers. For the workers, however, this improvement becomes yet another expense, a commodity purchased from the very people who pay for—and more importantly, profit from—their labor.

As the morality and even the personal habits of the working poor are increasingly figured as a metonymic extension of labor, there is a move toward their being ever more closely observed and constituted by middle-class ideology. In "proving" the social and economic costs and in continually implying the possibility of devastating political costs incurred by all society when the working classes are forced to live in substandard conditions, the *Report* demonstrates that the interests of the poor must be taken up by the middle and upper classes. Indeed, they must become the interests of more economically and politically powerful classes. And as a result these interests are transformed into the interests of society as a whole. The contiguous nature of the society that Chadwick represents is accordingly reinforced, and the substitution of part for whole emphasizes the impossibility of ignoring the strength of the connections between the "two nations."

Despite the potency of these connections, however, a great gap continued to exist "between one set of class attitudes and another, a gap in understanding as well as information" (Briggs, *Essays* 2:136). In the *Sanitary Condition Report* this gap informs the ways in which the poor are represented. As Asa Briggs points out, the investigative reports of the 1840s "were aimed at the reading public, the members, for the most part, of only one of the two nations, who occupied Britain during those years" (*Essays* 2: 132). And while "the stories they told helped to build up an impression of the way the other half lived" (132), it was inevitable that those stories, and consequently the impressions they conveyed, would be coded and interpreted according to the social standards that both investigators and audience upheld. Hence the gap of information and understanding could only be partially bridged, for while information about the plight of the poor might be transmitted to the middle and upper classes, interpretations of how the poor lived were uniformly based on middle-class suppositions about respectability and morality.

This writing of the poor according to middle-class moral suppositions is evident in a number of places in the *Report*, where investigators proclaim their outrage and concern over what they consider to be sexual impropriety and uninhibited conduct in the presence of members of the opposite sex. In an interview in which Chadwick examines one of his investigators, the following exchange takes place:

> In the course of your own inquiry, how many instances, if you were to look over your Notes, of persons of different sexes sleeping promiscuously, do you think you met with?—I think I am speaking within bounds when I say I have amongst my memoranda above 100 cases, including of course, cases of persons of different sexes sleeping in the same room.
>
> Was it so common as to be in nowise deemed extraordinary or culpable amongst that class of persons?—It seemed not to be thought of. As proof of this I may mention one circumstance which just occurs to me:—Early in my visitation of Pendleton, I called at the dwelling of a person whose sons worked with himself in a colliery. It was in the afternoon, when a young man, one of the sons, came down stairs in his shirt and stood before the fire where a very decently dressed young female was sitting. The son asked his mother for a clean shirt, and on its being given to him, very deliberately threw off the shirt he had on, and after warming the clean one, put it on. In another dwelling in Pendleton, a young girl 18 years of age, sat by the fire in her chemise during the whole time of my visit. Both these were houses of working people (colliers) and not by any means of ill-fame. (192–93)

A close look at this passage reveals some interesting details. For instance, included within those one hundred cases are unenumerated instances of adults of each sex sleeping in the same room; of these, there is no indication as to how often such proximity led to what the investigator, Ridall Wood, calls "improper intercourse." Further, it is worth noting that Wood was charged to examine the conditions of overcrowding in Manchester, Liverpool, Ashton-under-Lyne, and Pendleton. Manchester was a sizeable city in 1842, as was Liverpool, and both had a large number of working-class inhabitants. In a working-class population approaching 300,000, one hundred "promiscuous sleeping" arrangements is rather insignificant, especially when there is no indication as to how often illicit liaisons resulted from such arrangements. Nevertheless, Chadwick accepts Wood's assertion that such "promiscuity" characterizes working-class attitudes toward sex, and uses Wood's findings to indicate the general "demoralisation" of the working classes.

Chadwick's comment/question, "Was it so common as to be in nowise deemed extraordinary or culpable amongst that class of persons," like his remarks on the working class's cleanliness, highlights the differences between the two sets of moral attitudes at work here, and Wood's examples further indicate what those differences are. When Wood speaks of the "very decently-dressed young female," he intimates that the offense the young man commits in changing his shirt in front of her is exacerbated because the young woman observes the niceties of middle-class moral convention. Apparently, however, neither she nor the young man nor the mother finds anything shocking, or even notable, in the collier's behavior. As with the attitudes of the unwashed laborers toward bathing, a certain lack of modesty among the working class is indicative less of moral turpitude than of the practicalities of existence. Of course, these practicalities often derive from the conditions of overcrowding that Chadwick and his assistants observed, thus allowing Chadwick to make the connection between overcrowding and lower moral standards. And while Wood's comment that neither house was "by any means of ill-fame" suggests that there may be a considerable difference between what he and members of the working class in Pendleton might consider "ill-fame," it also strongly implies that operating within a different moral discourse does not necessarily mean that one is transgressing some transcendent morality—even when judged by the standards of a different moral code.

Of course, Chadwick's findings on the conditions of the working classes were neither unimportant nor necessarily untrue. Yet Chadwick and his investigators, in the very act of observing the conditions of the poor, were in fact also *creating* the poor, both literarily and actually. By continually calling the morals of the poor to account according to their own class-influenced standards, Chadwick and his investigators extended their moral presuppositions across all society, replacing the moral culture of the poor—whatever it may have been—with their own. As a result, the "reality" they present cannot help but be, at least in part, a reality they create. The relative objectivity of statistics and cost/benefits analysis immediately goes by the boards whenever a personal interview takes place. When the interview is between Chadwick and one of his assistants, such as Wood, both questions and answers conform to the suppositions each participant brings to the meeting. When the interview is between one of the investigators and a member of the lower classes, the investigator, if a sophisticated examiner, implies the proper answer in the questions he asks, as does Chadwick when he asks Brownlow about the drinking habits of the tailors.[9]

Whatever Chadwick and his investigators may have been doing to remake the poor in printed language, their moral discourse often directly affected members of the lower classes, especially when investigators like Wood had difficulty containing their nearly evangelical zeal for demonstrating to the poor the errors of their ways. In one instance Wood reports on his interrogation of a prostitute:

> . . . while I was following out my inquiries in Hull, I found in one room a prostitute, with whom I *remonstrated* on her course of life, and asked her whether she would not be in a better condition if she were an honest servant instead of living in vice and wretchedness. (193; emphasis added)

Obviously Wood's own notions of proper conduct fuel his shock and indignation over the moral condition of the woman, and it is also obvious that the alternative he offers almost by way of exemplum, the life of "an honest servant," is a particular of his idealized conception of a morally upright working class. In part because he putatively subscribes to the standards of social behavior that he and his class sanction, he can assume the role of moral watchdog and upbraid the woman for her conduct. Almost as though he were a parent scolding a child—or perhaps more appropriately a missionary confronting a sinner—Wood points out the woman's failing and then asks if she would make the same mistake again. He holds up to the woman his notion of what a member of the lower classes should properly be, and attempts to convince her that because she does not conform to that conception she has failed herself morally.

The reader is not surprised when Wood reports that the woman agrees with him and—like the other examples of promiscuity Wood cites—that she ascribes her behavior to the overcrowded conditions of her lodging: her proximity to the sexual activity of her sister and her sister's husband (she slept in the couple's bed) ultimately led to her becoming a prostitute. Wood says that he has "good authority for believing" that both women were "common" to the husband and that their "sense of decency was obliterated" (193). A simple reading of the drama enacted between Wood and the prostitute might conclude that their confrontation was, in small, an example of the imposition of middle-class moral conventions upon members of the lower classes, and to a certain degree that analysis would be correct. But Wood's report of the young collier who changed his shirt in front of the "decently dressed young female" indicates that while the working-class discourse of morality may differ from that of the middle class, it too is at work in bringing the young prostitute to agree with Wood that she was indeed living a life of "vice and wretchedness" and that she could be better off. Her perception that there is the possibility, even if it is only an ideal, of a different, better existence suggests that her own moral standards have suffered in her life as a whore.

The encounter between Wood and the woman, then, signifies more than just Wood's foisting his moral standards upon the woman; it is an example of the gap of information and understanding of which Briggs speaks. On one side of the breach is the woman, who understands that her being a prostitute is a moral failing, but whose own moral code allows her to justify it (e.g., she could not help it; it was an economic necessity). On the other side of the chasm stands Wood, who perceives prostitution to be so reprehensible that his moral code can offer no justification. Within the gap itself a discursive conflict between these two moral "systems" is taking place. This clash recalls to the woman the moral convictions she has—to her mind justifiably—abandoned, and it urges Wood to search for explanations, though not a vindication, for the woman's turn to a life of "vice."

This clash is built into the observation/contamination dichotomy that underpins Chadwick's project and its strategies of representing the poor. The contamination half of the binary implies a resistance to observation that must, yet cannot, be overcome, since it is the likelihood of contamination that warrants observation in the first place. Even as the working poor are questioned and watched, their ways of life recorded, they are potentially resistive. The observation/contamination binary may seem to have coopted that resistance by defining a space for it, but in fact contamination often *cannot* be contained. The possibility of a pandemic wildfire of insurgency, which could range in form from violent political upheaval to the perversion of middle-class moral codes, is part of what made the *Report* so compelling. Certainly the impact of the moral discourse of the poor on that of the middle classes could not have been experienced by the members of the middle classes without misgivings, whatever salutary effect they perceived their own moral culture to have on the working classes. When one considers the concern of many over physical (and moral) contamination from the poor's unsavory surroundings, coupled with the traditional view of the moral "failings" of the poor as unavoidable due to the inherent character flaws of members of the lower classes, it is not surprising that the reports of many of Chadwick's investigators are filled with the sort of judgmental commentary that is more in keeping with the ideas about the moral nature of the poor that inform the Poor Law *Report* than with the notions of demoralization that Chadwick propounds in the *Report on the Sanitary Condition*.

Inscribing the poor as possessing inherent moral failings is problematic for the *Report*, since it reconstructs the very sorts of discursive barriers it is attempting to tear down. It keeps the poor at arm's length, keeps them different, and palliates the contamination that is the effect of the form their resistance takes. Chadwick's concept of "demoralisation" attempts to displace the concept of the poor as inherently morally inferior. It emphasizes the contiguity of the poor to sources of uncleanness as the cause of their moral failings. Making dereliction and profligacy contingent and external was apparently not explanatory (or prophylactic) enough for the many investigators who maintained that the poor were not merely more susceptible to moral and physical contamination, which was figured as uncleanness. According to these informants, the poor had a proclivity for such "immorality" and, once infected, their condition was difficult, if not impossible, to correct:

> With the poor . . . no privation is felt as little as that of cleanliness. The propensity to dirtiness is so strong, the steps so few and easy, that nothing but the utmost facilities for water can act as a counterpoise; and such is the love of uncleanliness, when once contracted, that no habit, not even drunkenness, is so difficult to eradicate. (140)

While Chadwick might wrestle with the implication that something in the character of the poor draws them to dirtiness, he would no doubt agree that, like a disease, the habit of insanitation is "contracted" and perpetuated in epidemic proportions throughout the working-class population. I have already argued that because they differed from the middle classes in attitudes toward and information about their conditions of life, many poor persons did not feel the same urgency for sanitation as the middle classes; nevertheless, what Elwin characterizes as a "propensity to dirtiness" and a "love for uncleanness" is more surely an indication of the difficulty so many members of the working class had in getting and remaining clean than evidence of their collective inclination for uncleanness. Also for Elwin and others with similar training, predilections, and affiliations, such portrayals point to all manner of transgressions against middle-class codes of moral behavior. The point I am making here has nothing to do with whether prostitution is immoral or people should wash regularly. These are questions that are decided by social convention. What I do want to stress is how such conventions—anchored in a particular moral consciousness—impose themselves upon a different, less politically and economically powerful class, thus creating that "lesser" class in terms that were familiar not only to members of the middle and upper classes, but also, eventually, to members of the lower classes as well.

Louis Althusser, in his discussion of the formation of the cognizant subject, has argued that "ideology hails or interpellates individuals as subjects" ("State Apparatuses" 175), in much the same way that "can be imagined along the lines of the most commonplace everyday police (or other) hailing: 'Hey, you there!'" (174). As Althusser points out, the person hailed will turn, because he knows "it was *really him* [sic] who was hailed" (174). In discussing this phenomenon, Michel Pêcheux writes, "the interpellation of the individual as subject of his discourse is achieved by the identification (of the subject) with the discursive formation that dominates him (i.e., by which he is constituted as subject)" (114). Both Althusser and Pêcheux indicate that the ideological formation of the subject is attendant in some way upon language. Althusser's metaphor of interpellation suggests a formal request for an explanation of action or policy. Pêcheux, in adopting the term, and thus the metaphor, goes even further by arguing not only that the individual's choices of action are constrained by discursive boundaries that often find expression in social conventions, but that the individual must feel these choices to be the correct ones, the "natural" ones, indeed the only ones available, before being constituted as subject.

For each of these theorists, interpellation is the transformation, or as Althusser says "recruitment," of the individual into a subject of a particular ideology (or discourse). And this transformation takes place by means of discourse. In Chadwick's *Report* we move from the theoretical to see just how such transformations can happen, and how these transformations have their foundation in the material conditions of the lower classes. Using a logic of association that depends on contiguous and metonymic connections, Chadwick demonstrates that the deplorable living conditions of the poor, and not individual choice, are most often the reason for their equally reprehensible morals. He makes quite clear that these people are not born depraved, but are "demoralized," their moral sensibilities affected by their conditions of life. Informing this thesis is the assumption that we all subscribe to the same moral standards, for only then could a falling away from those standards, a demoralization, be possible. Such an assumption does two things: first, by holding out the possibility of including of all members of society in a moral consensus, it helps bolster the middle class's representation of its own interests as the interests of the social whole. Second, it allows the middle class to *exclude* certain members of society from that consensus because they fail to live up to the agreed upon standards of conduct.

Although both the inclusion and exclusion functions of the notion of demoralization situate individuals as subjects, it is with exclusion that I am more concerned here. If some do not belong to the moral consensus, then a category must be devised to identify and describe those individuals. Having already linked moral turpitude with economic deprivation, Chadwick can easily identify members of the lower classes as those who most regularly *exclude themselves* from the larger portion of society that adheres to prescribed norms of conduct. Of course, in order to exclude one's self from anything, one must first understand the requirements of inclusion. As I have shown, such was not always the case with the members of the lower classes; many neither knew nor cared whether they lived up to middle-class standards. The agency that Chadwick imputes to these people did not exist in the terms he suggests. What agency they did possess was directly linked to the contamination they were perceived to effect. It is important for Chadwick, however, to situate their agency in middle-class terms, for the observation/contamination dichotomy through which he inscribes the working poor does not allow him to coopt their resistance safely. By figuring the poor as those who not only understand but actively choose not to engage in his moral discourse, he can appropriate that agency while simultaneously constituting the working class as makers of their own moral fate.

This analysis extends only to some of the poor people that inhabit the pages of the *Report*, however. For as the questioning of certain members of the working class indicates, many *were* learning what those middle-class norms were and were beginning to define themselves in the terms the middle class had provided. This learning, this apparent spanning of the gap of information and understanding, is analogous to Pêcheux's argument that the individual, to become subject, must identify with the dominant discourse. And as a greater number of individuals within the working class came to be aware of *how* the middle class expected them to be, the lower class itself came to be interpellated. Thus the creation of a textual lower class realizes itself in an actual lower class, and the realities of the middle class do indeed become the reality of all society.

Once again it is Chadwick's logic of contiguity that provides the possibility of this identification, and therefore of a sort of moral and economic redemption for the working classes when they are allowed to live in proximity to the middle class and its virtues. Chadwick is able to claim significant benefits from the improvement of sanitation precisely because of the connections he finds between filthy living conditions and decrepit morals. If living in filth leads to vice, then it must follow that living in more "respectable" conditions will lead to higher moral standards. Such improvement can begin at a very basic level. For example, in an examination of one employer upon the effects of the improved appearances of workers, Chadwick asks, "As a general rule, does the advance of his house keep pace with the advance in condition of the person?" The employer replies: "As a general rule, it does. Better personal condition leads to better associates, and commonly to better marriage, on which the improved condition of the house is entirely dependent" (323).

The improved condition of the habitation has "a salutary influence on the moral habits of its inmates," but more importantly "the man who sees his wife and family more comfortable than before . . . is stimulated to industry, and as he rises in respectability of station, he *becomes aware* that he has a character to lose" (323–24; original emphasis). Thus it is that improved material conditions of life do more than enhance moral character; they are requisite to moral consciousness. This awareness is Althusser's policeman hailing the individual. But now instead of saying, "Hey, you there, the dirty (or immoral, or slovenly, or lazy) one," which constitutes the subject as one without middle-class values, though conversant with those values, the policeman simply says, "Hey you." Feeling that he is "somewhat raised in the scale of society" (*Report* 323), the subject sees himself as included within the discourse that identifies and defines the proper way to conduct one's life.

One of the means by which the conditions of the poor are to be improved is through the recognition of the power of adjacent associations. In the section of the report entitled "Employers' Influence on the Health of Workpeople by means of Improved Habitations," Chadwick writes:

> The wife and family generally gain by proximity to the employer or the employer's family, in motives to neatness and cleanliness by their being known and being under observation; as a general rule, the whole economy of the cottages in bye-lanes and out-of-the-way-places appears to be below those exposed to observation. (299)

Here, again, the power of observing acts to discipline the poor, causing them to mimic and finally to assume the values of their masters; and even the assimilation of these values is contingent upon the poor making metonymic connections: "[in an improved cottage] children are trained to labour, to habits and feelings of independence, and taught to connect happiness with industry and to shrink from idleness and immorality" (325). As Chadwick points out, however, the effects of this observation depend upon the proximity of the poor to their employers. And while the middle classes continue to observe, they no longer enjoy the anonymity of the panoptic gaze. The middle classes are now as visible to the poor as the poor are to them. Necessary as this is for setting up middle-class values as the standards by which all society is to be judged, it also places the middle class in a more precarious position. By insisting that the lower classes partake of their values, by placing themselves in proximity to the lower classes so as to be good examples of those values, the middle classes allow the lower to observe them, and thus to judge them according to the standards they have successfully imparted to the working class. Like a classical realist text, the moral discourse of the middle classes becomes internally verifiable and, ultimately, self-reflexive.

Chadwick's suggestions, then, apparently shore up the ideological work of middle-class observation and evaluation of the "Condition of the Labouring Population." The resulting discourse in which both the middle and working classes are interpellated is not as seamless as may first appear, however. Though its participants "consent" to an a priori moral standard by which all activity is evaluated and which, in the process of such evaluation, fortifies and naturalizes its existence, a residue of another, suppressed and muted, moral code is also at work. These leftovers of the "moral culture" of the poor, which we can only just make out as distinct and relatively autonomous in the *Sanitary Condition Report*, remain, subtly marking class and difference and ever so slightly transforming the moral standards by which the poor now evaluate the middle classes. One might well say that by using the power of the gaze to police the moral activities of the poor, middle-class moral hegemony worked almost too well for its own good. For with the observational turnabout that comes from being both the watcher and, as the model for proper conduct, the watched, the paradigm of cleanliness and morality that Chadwick envisions must withstand not only the scrutiny of its own standards but the standards of those who have come to it from without, whose "characters," as Chadwick proposes, have been remade by it. The "dawdle" that remains or the reluctance to losing a hard-earned "greatcoat" of dirt are the places where the moral cultures of the "two nations" clash, the locales of resistance, the places where paradigmatic critique begins.

Such criticism is oppositional in the way Edward Said describes it, functioning "in that potential space inside civil society, acting on behalf of those alternative acts and alternative intentions whose advancement is a fundamental human and intellectual obligation" (30). And, as Said's comments suggest, the place of the subject—between resistance and cooptation—is potentially the most fruitfully empowering. But the material benefits linked to that power may be long in coming, and indeed are likely to require considerable sacrifice. As cultural critics and historians, we are well advised to remember that Chadwick's and others' speaking for the poor, and their attempts at ameliorating the conditions of the working classes came at some cost to the intended beneficiaries of their good works. To inscribe the working classes as failed versions of middle-class aspirations and morals may not go far in clothing, feeding, warming, and—above all for Chadwick—cleaning the poor, but it does strip them of their difference. Even as the *Report on the Sanitary Condition of the Labouring Population of Great Britain* attempted to provide what it perceived as the essentials for human existence, it disregarded its "obligation" to advance "alternative acts and alternative intentions"—a paradox for nineteenth-century liberalism that remains current today.

6
Feminine Hygiene: Women in the
Sanitary Condition Report

Perhaps the most insistent narrative element of the Victorian novel is the marriage plot. Early Victorian novels, especially, achieve closure by having the appropriate characters pair off, read the banns, marry, and—the reader is apparently supposed to assume—live happily ever after. Even *Coningsby*, which as I pointed out in Part I almost ignores the marriage plot as a central narrative device, ultimately has its protagonist marry: the domestic must be managed before that most promising of young politicians can don the mantle of the public trust. Conventionally, eponymous heroes and heroines in particular can either marry, like Nicholas Nickleby and Sybil, or die, like Alton Locke and Helen Fleetwood. Ideologically the marriage plot secures the division of labor and life between the gendered spheres of the public and private, and as a result reasserts already in-place constraints upon the subjectivities of male and female middle-class adults in early Victorian England. A woman's place is in the home and a home is best defined by a wife or, failing that, a daughter or mother. The man's place is in the world, and when he enters his (or another's) home, though it may be "his castle," he should be in a distinctly feminine realm.

The marriage plot, instrumental as it is to Victorian fiction, also finds considerable purchase in the *Sanitary Condition Report*. Although Chadwick is not tracing long portions of the life of any of the many characters that populate the pages of his work, he and his informants often focus on the institution of marriage within working-class culture. Like most political economists, he appears satisfied with "a conventional view of the family as separate from the market and providing a haven from the competitive thrust of the economic world" (Davidoff and Hall 185). This, of course, is a middle-class conception of the world—one in which the male in a companionate marriage is the sole financial supporter of the family and the woman is therefore "free" to attend to domestic matters. Even for "feminist" political economists like Harriet Martineau or John Stuart Mill, this middle-class division of public and private and the labor associated with those spheres dominates discussion of female subjectivity and agency in all classes. In her 1848 work, *Household Education*, for example, Martineau's use of the "artisan household" as the model for the running of a home explicitly relies on a division between private and public. She points out that the artisan's wife, because she cannot afford servants, must be directly involved in the raising of children and in domestic management. The father, who is necessarily absent during the day, earning a living for the family, becomes involved in the domestic scene when he returns home in the evening, but the primary responsibility for the moral education of all the children, and the "practical" education of the daughters, resides with the mother.

Such a depiction of the working-class family is ideal at best and at worst completely divorced from the exigencies of working-class existence. The "artisans" of the early nineteenth century had become the factory hands of the Victorian period, and it would have been relatively rare to find a working-class home of the 1830s and '40s filled with children much older than toddlers. More likely they would be employed at the mill, or, if extremely fortunate, attending a factory school. Daughters and wives as well as sons helped to supplement family incomes by working. This fact of working-class life does not seem to have escaped Martineau completely, for throughout her writing on women she recognized that, whether working-class or single, "a multitude of women have to maintain themselves [economically] who would never have dreamed of such a thing a hundred years ago" (*Martineau on Women* 96). Nevertheless, she writes that "no true woman, married or single, *can* be happy without some sort of domestic life;—without having somebody's happiness dependent on her" (*Autobiography* 2:225; original emphasis).

The social and political forces that converge to allow Martineau to subscribe to such a sentiment—that is to say, the formation of domestic ideology in the industrialized bourgeoisie of late eighteenth- and nineteenth-century England—have been the focus of a number of excellent literary and historical studies, including Nancy Armstrong's *Desire and Domestic Fiction*, Lenore Davidoff and Catherine Hall's *Family Fortunes*, and Hall's *White, Male, and Middle Class*. And as Elizabeth Roberts's *A Woman's Place: An Oral History of Working-Class Women, 1890–1940* points out, at least by the late Victorian or early Edwardian period, working-class women were being taught as girls that their place was in the home; they might work outside it for greater or lesser periods; they could leave it freely for social or charitable excursions; their husbands and children might well help in its care and maintenance; but it was accepted by all that the ultimate responsibility for the home was theirs. (125)

Given the gap that existed between the "two nations" in the 1830s and '40s, the question arises as to how a dominant middle-class ideology crossed class boundaries to interpellate working-class women's subjectivities as well. In the pages that follow, I will argue that at least one way that a class-identified ideology can gain such mobility and power is through the kind of project that Chadwick is undertaking in his *Report*. Not only is he "writing the poor" more or less effectively, but his depictions depended upon gender constructions that were tied to class norms rather than to observation of those living in the "other" nation. But unlike Mary Poovey, who in her article "Domesticity and Class Formation: Chadwick's 1842 *Sanitary Report*" sees the *Report*'s assumptions about domesticity as setting limits upon the working classes' involvement in what she describes as the "newly forming social sphere," I contend that Chadwick's deployment of a domestic ideology *empowers* as well as "controls" the laboring population, for it offers the working classes ways in which to insist upon their difference from the middle classes and from middle-class interests.

It is not very difficult for Poovey to argue that the ideas about domesticity that Chadwick brings to his observation of the condition of the working classes "played a crucial role in the sanitary idea and, through that, in the process of state formation," which she characterizes as "professionalized, bureaucratized apparatuses of inspection, regulation, and enforcement" (66). This is not to say that her argument is trivial or facile; rather its assumptions about state formation as based upon "a dense network of interdependent theories, technologies, and political disputes" are important and intricate. For even casual readers of the "carceral" Foucault, however, her argument has become tried, if not true. Despite the contestation between the various components within this web of discourses Poovey identifies, once Chadwickian styled reports become naturalized as "the conventional genre of government reports," in essence shaping what counted as "authoritative and official" as well as "normal" or "improved," the possibilities of resistance to middle-class hegemony apparently disappear. For Poovey, it seems, the real opposition is not between those who write the poor and the poor themselves, but rather between different philosophies about how the poor will be represented and toward what ends they will be constituted.

In Poovey's depiction, the conception of middle-class domesticity wins. And while there is a good deal of validity to her point that by the 1850s the "divisive issues . . . were not about the right of the working class to vote but about women—their right to own property, to divorce, and to enter the wage-labor force," we should be careful about embracing her assumption that class division itself was fairly resolved into "the struggles of men of all classes for the opportunity to achieve the domestic life normalized by Chadwick's report" (83). Rather than problematizing categories such as class and gender, Poovey's argument reifies and hierachizes them. If the class-based political struggles of the 1830s and '40s were "displaced" by gender issues in the '50s, as Poovey insists, then the constitutive effects of class on individual subjectivities is negligible; what really counts is gender identification. The implication of her conclusion is that by the final Chartist fizzle in 1848, the working classes had become so thoroughly constituted by middle-class norms that class difference is effectively obliterated, or at least is no longer important, and that gender difference becomes the nearly exclusive ground for political engagement.

As a model of "strategic essentialism," Poovey's position is useful. And in suggesting the complex links between concepts of domesticity, social organization, and the making of the working class, it is provocative and valuable. But if we move away from macro-level considerations of state formation (as if the state were a non-contradictory, unified apparatus) to examinations of how particular subject positions are constituted and represented both in Chadwick's report and after, separating class and gender into hierachized discourses becomes more difficult. Furthermore, the concept of domesticity itself should be examined as it gains ideological force among the working classes. Catherine Hall and Lenore Davidoff have persuasively demonstrated that the domestic model was broadly contested and was by no means an internally coherent discourse (see Davidoff and Hall 180, passim). Nor should we assume that, even if it were *perceived* to be a unified discourse, it would be adopted without modification by the working classes. The differences within the working class alone, differences in regions, education, occupations, material means, religion, and political culture, not to mention the differences *between* the middle and working classes, would result in significantly diverse instances of domestic ideology contributing to the formation of individual subject positions.

Catherine Hall has commented on that diversity, pointing out that "working-class men and women did not adopt wholesale the middle-class view of a proper way of life" as much as they *adapted* it to "make sense of some experience and appeal to some needs" (*White, Male* 144). Using the examples of temperance movements and of female mine workers, she argues that when these issues emerged—in part as articulations of the discourse of domesticity—the cross-class alliances that empowered temperance leagues and helped pass legislation making it illegal for women to work in mines were solidified by class-specific interests. When temperance supporters, for instance, typically maintained that abstinence and sobriety are linked to the happiness of the hearth, a happiness dependent upon "female relatives and friends," they spoke to both middle and working class, but in different ways. The woman's responsibilities in the middle-class home were moral guidance and the management of the household, especially the servants. The proper working-class woman, while still the guardian of the home's moral rectitude, was also responsible for teaching (and performing) the practical skills that Martineau alludes to: cleaning, cooking, and raising children. Further, she was often solely responsible for managing the family finances (see *White, Male* 145). In the case of the Mines and Collieries Act of 1842, which banned women from working below ground, we see at root in the middle classes' championing of such legislation the affront to their own notions of femininity: because of the conditions in the mines, women miners, like their male counterparts, often worked naked to the waist. Such a spectacle and the fears it generated about public morality and "the imminent collapse of the working-class family" helped galvanize middle-class Evangelical support for the Act. In contradistinction, working men were in favor of getting women out of the mines partly as means of wresting control over their own culture ("if the wives of the owners could stay at home, then so should theirs"); but more importantly, to them, they wished to keep wages high. Women worked for considerably less than men and when employed in large numbers in the mines they drove wages down (*White, Male* 146).

The different effects from the promulgation of middle-class ideology, on the one hand, and its function within the working classes, on the other, need to be foregrounded in examining a text like Chadwick's report. Further, as Poovey and others such as Joan Scott have argued, it is equally important to maintain a particular focus on the confluence of gender and class in ways that recognize their "uneven developments" as analytical categories. The middle-class male hegemony that Poovey identifies in the *Re-*

port is undoubtedly there, in spades. But it is by no means seamless, nor is its efficacy absolute. Even as Chadwick and his informants struggle to maintain an indestructible link between domestic efficiency and morality, particular cases crop up, that insist upon the tenuousness of that connection and suggest (though not necessarily to Chadwick) that other ways of figuring working-class home life might give us a better idea of the demands upon working-class women.

A good example of an exception to the *Report*'s assumptions about the connections between domesticity and morality immediately follows the report of the case I discussed above of the young woman with "a little of the *dawdle* left about her." Upon completing the faithful transcription of his informant's story, Chadwick breaks into the narrative in his own voice to tell the story of a different woman, who dwelt "not far from the one above described." Before her marriage, this woman had been known for her fine singing voice and for her knowledge of the Bible and her church's doctrines. Chadwick now finds that

> Her personal condition had become "of a piece" with the wretched stone undrained hovel, with a pigsty before it, in which she had been taken. We found her with rings of dirt about her neck, and turning over with dirty hands Brown's Dictionary, to determine whether the newly elected minister was "sound" in his doctrine. In this case no moral lapse was apparent, but the children were apparently brought up under great disadvantages. (196)

As with the dawdling woman, the reasons for her physical appearance are directly attributable to the state of her abode. Also, like the dawdling woman's, her children are apparently not neglected. Nor can Chadwick find any moral failings on the part of the woman. She has managed a place for herself that defies Chadwick's figure of domesticity and morality. She is outside the marriage plot that ends all things with the promise of living "happily ever after," but she is also uncontainable in its conventional alternatives: complete moral depravity or death, or both.

Another of the *Report*'s examples of the home life of the working classes pits domestic management *against* moral policing as the responsibility of wives. Edwin Hill, owner of two large Birmingham metal stamping mills, reports that in contrast to the workmen in the silver mill, the copperworkers "were much addicted to drinking and feasting in the public alehouse." And though they earned nearly as much as the silverworkers, who kept their families well provided and had even become men of property, the copperworkers' "families were in wretchedness, and the wives obliged to eke out a slender pittance by washing and other laborious occupations." Hill learned that these men knew exactly how much their wives needed to manage the household and contrived to deceive their wives as to the amount of their wages. The result, says Hill, was that the "wives actually desired that their husbands might get drunk on Saturday night, because they could the more easily abstract the money from their persons" (310).

Hardly a model of the domestic ideal, this example demonstrates that good, or at least prudent, homemaking does not equal what Hill, Chadwick, and other middle-class observers of the working orders would classify as a good home life. Unlike those women who "drive" their husbands out of their homes and into the pubs because they are such poor housekeepers, these women drive their husbands into the pubs so that they can be *better* homemakers. Like the woman with Brown's Dictionary, these women occupy a place at odds with the domestic ideology that informs the *Report*. The limits of that ideology cannot accommodate women who encourage drunkenness in order to be better housewives. Thus they exist only as exceptions both ideologically and in terms of the position of their narrative within the *Report*. Their story is not meant to illustrate some point about appropriate domesticity; nor is it found in the sections on domestic economy. Rather Chadwick records it in section VI, "The Effects of Preventive Measures," and uses it to emphasize employers' responsibility to pay workers in ways that promote the very domestic ideology that cannot contain them—or more importantly, cannot contain their wives.

The location of this anecdote in the *Report* is important to note because it stresses the dual role women play in the concept of domesticity Chadwick brings to his observations. Women are figured as the moral force of the home and family. To this end they are the locus of considerable power—power that can enable working-class militancy or middle-class hegemony, depending on how it is exercised. Yet women are also marginalized, repeatedly, throughout the *Report*. Their economic contributions to the family in terms of paid labor are hardly ever recognized by Chadwick and his fact- gatherers. Their unpaid, domestic labor is taken for granted when performed "properly" and singled out as a moral failing when it is not. As Poovey says, women in Chadwick's political schema are important, but clearly "auxiliary" (82). Thus it is not particularly surprising to find the story of the coppersmiths' wives in a section several hundred pages from the portions on domestic economy. Similarly, it is not surprising to find that the mill owner solved the problem of his profligate copperworkers by informing each worker's wife of exactly how much her husband received in wages. "From the day the plan commenced," writes Hill, "a most decided and permanent improvement took place in the habits of the men, and in the appearance and general comforts of their families" (310). The women become an extension of middle-class propriety when they are taken into the capitalist's confidence. As a result, they relieve him of his own duties as moral policeman. No longer is it necessary for him to "manage" his workers; their wives do it for him.

It is in such ways that narratives that resist the strategies of containment employed by the domestic ideology of the *Report* are coopted. But it is also in such ways that we can begin to see how gender and class formation are imbricated. Relative to their middle-class counterparts, working-class women on the whole exerted considerably more influence in their households. As moral guides, as contributors to and keepers of the family coffer, and as teachers of important practical skills, these women reached below the layer of ethical culture that defined their own and their families' subject positions; their actions extended to the material base of working-class life. Thus, while continually being pushed into an ancillary position, they were also the link between the contingencies of working-class daily life and various middle-classes's attempts to impose moral culture on the lower orders. Working-class women are often represented as both the cause and the effect of lower-class moral failings. They, more than their male relatives, are constituted by their surroundings. They are the individuals whose essences are tainted by substandard living conditions, and it is through them, then, that others—men and children—are led into depravity.

This representation of the working-class woman, one common in the *Report*, is ambiguous at best. It creates a space for a specific kind of gendered power much akin to the sort of subject position that Nancy Armstrong identifies when she argues that the first "modern" subject is woman. But unlike Armstrong's constructions, which are the direct product of middle-class domestic norms and linked to middle-class participation in activities such as parliamentary politics or the acquisition of capital, the possibilities of female subjectivity that emerge in Chadwick's *Report* are specific to working-class conditions of life. Thus in one sense they are politically and economically marginal: the working classes have little realized political and economic power, and women of that class, *because* they are women, have even less.

Paradoxically, however, those possibilities of female subjectivity are simultaneously politically and economically central. The link that continually emerges between working-class domesticity and the incentive to engage in socially disruptive acts moves women, their roles, and their potential agency to the forefront of representations of the working classes. And by figuring working-class collective power as essentially female, the *Report* offers a palliative to its middle-class readers. If working-class collectivity can be perceived as feminized, then fears of the "masculine" activities of armed revolt, Chartism, and trade unionism can be significantly assuaged.

This discursive move is supported by the declining role of women in radical politics during the early Victorian period. Though some women had been quite active in working-class political movements, in the 1700s especially, as radical politics became more formal, women were increasingly pushed to its margins.[1] Yet even as women were losing what centrality they had held in radical working-class politics, their constitutive force was being insisted upon by middle-class observers. By ascribing to a "hand that rocks the cradle" representation of working-class political power, Chadwick and his informants provide the spectre of a potentially depraved, but also potentially tractable, working class. In such a representation and despite the always present hint of revolt, the crises afflicting the working classes and of primary concern to the middle orders are fundamentally moral rather than political. The practical solution was to attempt to impose a normalized code of moral conduct upon the working classes, and according to what I have labeled a feminized depiction of working-class power, the best way to set this code in place was through the promulgation of the various forms of domestic ideology that abounded within the middle classes. At bottom, it made little difference whether the domestic model was based in religion or political economy, since in either case the desired effect was to smooth over the differences in moral culture that separated the "two nations."

But here, again, I want to emphasize my differences with Poovey. Rather than clearing the way for gender issues to displace class issues, and presumably, for many class issues to be relatively resolved in comparison to the "women questions" that were to arise over the next half-century, domesticity in fact perpetuated class difference and contributed to the class-conflict of the 1850s and 1860s. As concepts of domestic propriety took firm hold among the working classes, the moral cultures of the "two nations," on the surface at least, appeared to become increasingly similar. But as we have seen, the *activity* of domesticity varied significantly from middle to working class as well as within the working class itself. Consequently, the cultural moral norms that were established were impossible to maintain; the working classes simply did not have the means. The *Report* itself is clear on this. Even when members of the working classes ideologically took part in what was becoming the dominant moral code, they were usually unable to participate materially.

The innumerable accounts in the *Report* of families being unable to segregate themselves into "appropriate" age and gender groups for sleeping because they lacked enough rooms attest to the material requirements for preserving such moral attitudes. A particularly good example of the disparity between holding "correct" moral precepts and being able to act upon them is supplied by one of Chadwick's informants, a Dr. Gilly, the canon of Durham. He describes a local farm worker, "a fine, tall man of about 45, a fair specimen of the frank, sensible, well-spoken, well-informed Northumbrian peasantry." This man and his family of a wife and nine children were about to move into a worker's cottage, "whose narrow dimensions were less that 24 feet by 15" and which provided the family of eleven only three beds to sleep on. The worker told Gilly that he, his wife, a daughter of 6, and a boy of 4 years old would sleep in one bed; that a daughter of 18, a son of 12, a son of 10, and a daughter of 8 would have a second bed; and a third would receive his three sons of the age of 20, 16, and 14 (192) When Gilly asked the man if he agreed that this was "a very improper way of disposing of [his] family," the man replied, "Yes, certainly . . . it is very improper in a Christian point of view; but what can we do until they build us better houses?" (192).

As Poovey has correctly pointed out, this "Christian point of view" of propriety was primarily middle-class and promulgated by the assumptions of Chadwick and his informants. But simply because it was increasingly adopted by the poor, it did not do away with the material marks of difference between the classes, as the farm worker was well aware. The fact that the farmer and his family identified with the moral discourse of Dr. Gilly and other respectable members of the middle classes does seem to indicate that commonly held notions of domesticity may indeed have been responsible for disseminating these moral norms. But the very existence of the anecdote also indicates that domestic ideology had certain material requirements that some could not meet. In those cases, however powerfully subjects were constituted by the discourse of domesticity, they could not completely identify with it, for they could not put its dictates into action.

For Poovey, this similarity in moral codes, the effect of domesticity, brings the working classes, in a limited way, into the newly forming public sphere. But this similarity does not equal identity. The working classes were still aware of their difference; as I have demonstrated in a number of places in Part II, they were often proud of that difference. For those who aspired to middle-class identity, the promise held out by domesticity became a kind of bait and switch. Whatever a working-class person perceived the middle-class domestic ideal to be, it almost certainly could not be enacted: the means just were not there; the responsibilities were different. But it could be transformed to become an integral part of working-class culture, where women washed their own curtains, scrubbed their own floors, cooked the family meals, and did the family marketing themselves. And even when incorporated in this way it could still inform a space of opposition: beating the middle classes at their own game, so to speak, but without all the benefits of servants and discretionary income.

Ultimately the "marriage plot" that Chadwick would impose on his working-class characters has bourgeois antecedents. When the worker "sees his wife and family more comfortable than formerly," and he "rises in respectability of station," when he "*becomes aware* that he has a character to lose," that worker is being written by Chadwick according to the middle-class norms of morality and domesticity that govern Chadwick's own notions of propriety. This worker is the provider for a family; he seems bound to live happily ever after. But the character that emerges, reconstituted according to middle-class desires and fears, rewritten by middle-class representations, is, nevertheless, working class and identifies with working-class culture. The difficulty for the happy ending is that, even in having the possibilities of the worker's subject position reshaped by the new and powerful discourses of the middle classes, enough of working-class culture endures, both discursively and materially, that the working-class subject remains "other" in the class-based system of difference that informed all Victorian public utterances, from reform writing to the novel. When Chadwick introduces issues of gender, the effect is not, finally, the making of a manageable working class as much as it is yet another example of the difficulties that must arise when one speaks for/of the Other. In attempting to construct both working-class and female subject positions, Chadwick's *Report* may indeed preempt some opposition, but it also strains so hard in its coverage, that fires of resistance arise in precisely the places it strives to extinguish them.

Chadwick's text belongs squarely within the disciplinary "tradition" that D. A. Miller eloquently describes in *The Novel and the Police*. Except, of course, that it is not a novel. Nonetheless, much of its most effective policing is directly linked to its understanding of, competition with, and finally cooptation of novelistic practices. As it vies for interpretive space with novels that are also discovering and uncovering the poor, the *Report on the Sanitary Condition* lacerates itself on the double edge of middle-class observation, a hazard that novels and their reviewers had already recognized. That is, in setting up the middle classes as both observers of the poor and the models for working-class conduct, the *Report* effectively produces a cultural straightjacket that despite its "progressive" intentions is profoundly conservative. In somewhat Dickensian fashion, the *Report* is always taking itself "into custody," becoming prisoner as well as constable. Social norms, individual identity, even, one might argue as Dickens does in *Our Mutual Friend*, national identity become the domain of the middle classes, generated, affirmed, and reproduced by them. Change in these terms no longer means the kind of epistemological shift ushered in by thinkers like Bentham; rather it means extending and imposing more of the same, even where material conditions cannot support it. Thus even as it offers practical solutions to the problem of insanitation, the *Report* is unable to move beyond its assumptions to articulate why or how such a problem could arise in the first place.

PART III
Washed in the Blood of the Lamb: Religion, Radical Politics, and the Industrial Novel

7

Religion, the Novel, and Speaking for/of the Other

Edwin Chadwick's *Report on the Sanitary Condition of the Labouring Population of Great Britain* reveals to its primarily middle-class audience how far apart economically and socially the middle and lower classes had grown by the end of the 1830s. The differences between the two classes were seemingly irreconcilable. Yet one of the most notable features of the *Report* is its impulse to smooth over those differences by having all acknowledge and participate in a common moral culture. Reform, the *Report* implies, can only work if all affected (i.e., all society) share the same (or at least very similar) aspirations, standards of moral judgment, and beliefs—a premise that partially explains the impetus of several of Chadwick's informants to challenge the moral standards of their working-class subjects with a zeal that is nearly Pauline in form and content. As I argue in Part II, the informers' questions often gave way to remonstrance, and lessons on proper thought and conduct frequently replaced the "objective" collection of data.

For Chadwick himself the issue of ethical conduct occupied a prominent place in his recapitulation of "the extent and operation of the evils which are the subject of [his] inquiry" (422). He concludes the *Report* by arguing that

> the removal of noxious physical circumstances, and the promotion of civic, household, and personal cleanliness, are necessary to the improvement of the moral condition of the population; for that sound morality and refinement in manners and health are not long found co-existent with filthy habits amongst any class of the community. (425)

Because uncleanness was seen as leading to *systemic* demoralization—to which no class is immune—much more is at stake than the health of individual members of the working classes; the soundness of an entire society is in jeopardy, and concern for its well-being often looked beyond the material world for ways to treat society's ailments. When Chadwick writes of the inability of "sound morality" and a "refinement in manners" to coexist "with filthy habits," the immediate context of his remark denotes the physical conditions adduced in the *Report*: overcrowding, inadequate clothing, the lack of clean water, poor ventilation and drainage, and the like. Most of Chadwick's readers, however, were members of "respectable" society, and to them "filthy habits" have meant more than lapses in personal and civic hygiene. For these readers "filthy habits" referred to intellectual and—more importantly for many—spiritual failings as well.

That so non-religious a document as the *Sanitary Condition Report* could be so thoroughly permeated by the practices and discourse of religion, however secularized, is but one instance substantiating George Kitson Clark's claim that the revival of religion in Victorian England "pervaded all of society, challenged men and women of every level of society or of education, and became fused with the objectives of most political parties and the hopes of every class" (*Making* 147). Similarly, J. F. C. Harrison has labeled the Victorian period "essentially a religious age," for "religious values and allegiances coloured most social issues" (122). Certainly Chadwick's heritage, if not his actions, support the validity of such claims, for as little use as he may have had for organized religion, he could not deny his antecedents: his paternal grandfather, Andrew, a friend of John Wesley himself, had been an important local Methodist and was responsible for establishing the first four Sunday schools in Lancashire (Finer 6).

Paradoxically, Victorian participation in organized religious activity was statistically lower than one might expect, given the ubiquity and influence of religion. According to the famous religious census taken on Sunday, March 30, 1851, only a fraction more than 7 million of the nearly 18 million inhabitants of England and Wales attended church. About 30 percent of the population was prevented by age, employment, or infirmity from going to services, leaving a total of some 12.5 million possible worshipers. 60 percent of this number attended some form of recognized church service; 40 percent did not (see Harrison 122–23; O. Chadwick 1:363–69). These figures do not repudiate Kitson Clark's and Harrison's conclusions, however, for as the two historians clearly indicate, the social power of religion had far less to do with the number of people in church each week than with its existence as an informing discourse and its ability to combine with other such discourses, like those of parliamentary politics, reform, or the novel, in ways that helped give meaning and order to the world. Also, one should remember that just as sitting in Parliament or writing a novel is not requisite to involvement in the public utterances and idioms connected with those enterprises, immersion in the discourse of religion or espousal of the values expressed in it is not contingent upon one's occupying a pew each (or any) Sunday.[1]

But what were those values? What did religion stand for? Few could say for certain; the idioms of religion were too numerous and various, their doctrines too diverse. From the Tractarians to the Society of Friends, Protestantism was a veritable grab bag of beliefs.[2] For many of the poor, like Mayhew's costermongers, religion was "a regular puzzle":

> They see people come out of church and chapels, and as they're mostly well dressed, and there's very few of their own sort among the churchgoers, the costers somehow mix up being religious with being respectable, and so they have a queer sort of feeling about it. It's a mystery to them. (*London Labour* 1:21)

Perhaps the costers were much nearer understanding religion than they or Mayhew knew. Asa Briggs, quoting from the 1849 *Congregational Yearbook*, points out that many mid-century Evangelicals "were content to note the part their religion had played in improving English morals while admitting at the same time, however reluctantly, that by that 'we do not mean that great masses are converted to God but . . . that great numbers are under the indirect influence of the Christian religion'" (*Improvement* 467). If religion did not produce good Christians, then at least there was hope for a generous crop of respectable infidels.

Yet it was difficult, if not impossible, to be a respectable infidel as well as a member of the working classes, and by the late 1830s infidelity was perceived by many to be a serious problem among the lower orders. In 1840 in a piece in the *British Critic*, Tom Mozley calculated that "three-fourths or nine-tenths" of the poorer classes practiced no religion whatsoever, and of those who did attend services most were working-class women and children who were "never or rarely" accompanied by working-class men (337, 346). In the eyes of the middle classes, this boded ill for society, not simply as a sign of Chadwick's "demoralisation," but as a harbinger of possible violent social upheaval.

Thus, by the 1830s, representations of lower-class agitations for relief or reform, or both, were constructed in such a way as to dispossess them of "legitimate or comprehensible goals" and to cast laboring-class movements as "working toward the complete unravelling of society" (Storch, "Plague"

62). The lower classes had become a force to be regulated and controlled, and religion seemed one obvious means of such control. Increasingly, however, and especially in urban areas, members of the working classes were falling away from the Church of England and often from religion entirely. The Tory politics of the majority of the Anglican clergy, the abuses within the church that allowed well-connected clergymen to hold several lucrative livings at once, the Erastianism of the Church, and the latitudinarian tradition—which made the Church appear more concerned with keeping wealthy tithers and procuring good livings for its vicars and curates than with ministering to the needs of its less fortunate parishioners—combined to make working people believe that they and the established Church had few common interests.[3] Even the early appeal of the Evangelical wing of the Church, which had won many adherents during the second and third decades of the century, waned by the 1830s when Evangelicalism had become fashionable and respectable.

Indisputably, dissenting groups, especially the Primitive Methodists (originators of the camp meeting), did secure a following among the working classes; for example, according to Horace Mann's census figures, in Manchester only 39.9 per cent of the seatings were provided by the Church of England; the remaining 60.1 per cent were furnished by dissenting chapels.[4] Despite such figures, however, it was becoming clear by mid-century that "British Christianity [was] essentially the Christianity developed by a middle-class soil" (Miall 151), addressed middle-class needs and interests, and confirmed middle-class values. These interests extended well beyond the walls of the established Church, infiltrating important dissenting sects such as the Wesleyan Methodists. As Harold Faulkner has asserted in his landmark study, *Chartism and the Churches*, "by the beginning of the Chartist period, the Methodist church had become 'respectable' and had lost the confidence of the intelligent workingman because of the conservatism of its political policy, the Tory affiliations of its leading ministers, and the undemocratic form of its government" (12). Thus discussions of what was perceived as infidelity but what is more accurately described as religious apathy among the working classes took on a political coloration that underscored middle-class fears of the effects of precisely the kinds of "immorality" that followed from a lack of religious training and that, as Chadwick and others had found, festered dangerously among the lower orders. A decade before the *Sanitary Condition Report*, W. R. Greg had expressed those fears, stating that, unless the morals of the working classes are altered "and that speedily, there are silent but mighty instruments at work . . . which ere long, will undermine the system of social union and burst asunder the silken bonds of amity which unite men to their kind" (39–40).

Though religion was to be the means of altering the working class's morals and thus preserving amity's "silken bonds," the economic ties between workers and employers (which were decidedly cotton and which often chafed) also needed safeguarding; and if religion was to fulfill this portion of its charge, it had to appeal to the working classes with more than a promise of becoming "rich in spirit" and "laying up treasures in heaven." No longer defensible were claims that the doctrine of spiritual equality softened the differences of conditions in this life and made them comparatively unimportant (see Hart 112). Religion's public face, whether presented as established church or dissent, needed to make itself over, if not in the image of then at least in response to the rapidly changing world in which it existed and that it was attempting to interpret and to order.

Like other interpretive discourses of the period that confronted their own hermeneutic limits in the face of unprecedented material and social change, religion looked to other ways of seeing the world for the means of shoring up its own enterprise. It is less precise, therefore, to speak of the "influence" of religion on other discursive activities of the Victorian era than of a confluence of distinct but related groups of public utterances, each contributing to the others' attempts to interpret and organize the world in which they existed. A description of the Victorian period as an "essentially religious period" grants an undoubtedly deserved priority to religion but fails to consider how the values, the traditions, or the use of religion was affected by its interactions with other discourses that perhaps shared the same interpretive goals but started from very different presuppositions.

A particularly useful place to examine the effects of this confluence is in what has come to be labeled the "industrial novel." Unknown as a subgenre before the late 1830s, the industrial novel reaches its apex with such works as Dickens's *Hard Times* (1854) and George Eliot's *Felix Holt* (1866). In large measure, however, these texts rehearse the themes and the issues of their precursors—works like Elizabeth Gaskell's *Mary Barton* (1848), Frances Trollope's *Michael Armstrong* (1840), *Helen Fleetwood* (1839) by Charlotte Elizabeth Tonna, and Charles Kingsley's *Alton Locke* (1850). The following discussion focuses on two of these earlier novels, *Alton Locke* and *Mary Barton*, as instances of spaces in which several discourses are taken up and in their interaction come to reshape their own assumptions and responses to the world they are attempting to interpret. Often presuppositions, such as those governing attitudes toward respectability and social responsibility, are reaffirmed, but just as often assumptions are re-fashioned in light of the contradictory impulses and utterances that must arise from the convergence of several discursive enterprises.

Consider, for example, the way in which these novels increasingly problematized the subject position and consciousness of certain members of the working classes. Especially important to evaluating works like *Alton Locke* and *Mary Barton* is an understanding of the difficulties of describing and placing that individual who falls somewhere between the "savage" de-bauchery characteristic of representations of the "literarily created" working classes such as those depicted by Mayhew, Chadwick, Kay, or Engels and the "embourgeoisment" of the laboring classes, such as one often finds in novels of the period. *Mary Barton* and *Alton Locke*, though often guilty of idealizing the poor, do create the possibility of accessing knowable com-munities—the communities of the working classes—that were also alien to most of their readers.

In their creations of these knowable communities—and by extension the possibility of agency for those who inhabit them—works like *Mary Barton* and *Alton Locke* share a good deal with a work like *Coningsby*. For each of these novels, at issue is the ability of either parliamentary politics or religion and radical politics to interpret effectively and, thus, help to order the world.[5] One would hardly call *Coningsby* a "realistic" novel, at least in the way we speak of realism today; however, as I argue in Part I, a portion of the project of *Coningsby* is to establish the novel (specifically Disraeli's novel) as more veraciously descriptive of the political realities of early Vic-torian Britain than is (or could be) politics itself. To this end there is a realistic element that informs *Coningsby* inasmuch as there is an appeal to a referential world that can be "better" represented in one discourse than another. As I will argue in Chapter 8, *Alton Locke* also attempts to estab-lish one discourse—that of the metaphysical, the ineffable—as better able to meet the interpretive needs of individuals than a discourse that is con-cerned primarily with the political and material. Kingsley's novel posits the metaphysical as the more "real" of these two discourses. Likewise Gaskell's own attempt to "tell the truth" duplicates the narrative's attempts at estab-lishing a community, open to all and therefore the basis of both making and understanding the world.

Even in those social-problem novels that ostensibly concentrate on the activities of one character, the role of community should not be underesti-mated. The concept of community, of shared goals and ideas, provides the characters populating the pages of these novels with norms, standards of conduct, rules that place them as subjects and that also grant them a certain amount of agency within the community. The role of religious discourse for the working classes functions somewhat paradoxically in these novels. On the one hand, it supports community by proposing an ethical system necessary to the cohesion and functioning of the group; indeed, it is a system that often defines personal relationships in *Alton Locke* and *Mary Barton*. On the other hand, Christianity, especially in the forms it takes in English dissent, demands agency and action from the individual. Consequently, religion has force in both public and intensely private circumstances. The resulting discursive confluence of religion, radical politics, and the novel leads to the *creation* of a referent, a world in which some individuals do exist in the interstices between the strict confines of their class boundaries. And while the mediators (and creators) of this world are themselves still significantly informed by the middle-class moral discourse that literally and literarily contributed to the creation of the Great Unwashed, their works push against the confines of that morality in their attempts to know the "Other" and to make it understandable in its own terms. Consequently, in these early industrial novels, we see an effort to evaluate analytically more than just the effects of Victorian culture; we see attempts at assessing the very foundations of that culture. The novel, in providing the place and the paradigm for such critique, re-evaluates religion and politics; it formulates these discourses as narrative and inserts them as narrative into the web of actions, utterances, and beliefs we call culture. In so doing, the novel participates in nineteenth-century culture's representation of itself to itself and to us, its heirs.

8

Alton Locke and the Religion of Chartism

Charles Kingsley's *Alton Locke* is not a "typical" industrial novel.[1] In it tailors' sweatshops are depicted with some attention to detail and accuracy, but the novel contains no unsettling descriptions of factories—inside or out. The novel's action takes place primarily in London, not in one of the great manufacturing towns of the north. Alton is not a factory operative like John Barton, or Helen Fleetwood, or Stephen Blackpool; he is apprenticed to a tailor. Nor, like other characters in industrial novels, is Alton forced to rely on the factory system as his means of subsistence. When his shop is taken over by a "sweater," Alton quits, preferring not to become a slave to his trade. A man of literary aspirations and skill, if not outright talent, he is self-taught and able to use his pen to pay his way. Despite such differences, however, *Alton Locke*—like the other social-problem novels of this period—finds the "system" of industrialization with its doctrines of individualism and competition to be the culprit in the demoralization and degradation of the underclasses. And like these other novels, the solutions *Alton Locke* offers to the problems of the lower classes are informed by middle-class notions of moral rectitude, civic prudence, and social respectability, even while it attempts to criticize those notions.

Alton Locke's life story is written in the first person as a sort of autobiography and seeks to present itself as the true account of the life of a "redeemed" Chartist. In its first two editions the novel was even published anonymously. Of course, few were fooled into believing that the Latin-reading, well-spoken Alton was a real person. The technique of a first-person, autobiographical account was common to many Victorian novels, and in this work, that technique attempts to create the illusion of a truly working-class perspective. The opening pages of *Alton Locke*, however, subvert that perspective by Alton's distancing himself from the class of which he is a part, and they illustrate the difficulty so many middle-class novelists of the nineteenth century had in reconstructing a working-class point of view that necessarily both accepts and opposes certain values and beliefs that are often represented by the middle classes as universal and beneficial to the advancement of all society.

Alton begins his narrative by stating that God made him a "Cockney among cockneys" so that he "might learn to feel for poor wretches who sit stifled in reeking garrets and workrooms, drinking in disease with every breath—bound in their prisonhouse of brick and iron" (6). As we see in the course of the novel, he has indeed experienced such conditions himself; yet rather than becoming the sort of human being that such circumstances would seem to produce, one who would give into uncleanliness, drunkenness, and sexual promiscuity, Alton strives for a certain intellectual and moral respectability that allows him to understand and identify vice and filth *as* vice and filth. His sensibilities are much more closely affiliated with those of his middle-class readers than with those of the members of his own class, and his narrative self-consciously calls attention to that connection. He apologizes to his readers for introducing the "ribaldry" of working-class culture, remarking, "God knows it is as little to my taste as it can be to theirs [his readers'], but the thing exists; and those who live, if not by, yet still beside such a state of things, ought to know what the men are like to whose labour, ay, life-blood, they owe their luxuries" (27).

Little did he suspect, he writes, that he was different from his fellow workers, that he "possessed powers above the mass" (35). Yet it is those "powers," his intellect, especially his creative, poetic abilities, that distinguish Alton. Though ostensibly a member of the working classes, he is really a man without a class and to a great extent a man without a clearly defined identity, or for that matter a subjectivity. His desires, his affiliations, his being continually vacillate between the two possible and opposing subject positions, defined primarily by class, that the narrative holds out to him.[2] Throughout the novel, he wavers between aspiring to the middle classes and fervid political involvement with Chartists. The incongruity of the occupations he claims in the title of his autobiography—tailor and poet—underscores Alton's uncertainty about his own place in society. He scorns the man who "will desert his own class" and try to become "a sham gentleman, a parasite . . . and a Mammonite," whom the world will compliment on "his noble desire to '*rise in life*'" (53; original emphasis), even as he accepts the literary patronage of Dean Winnstay. And although Alton writes poetry about the plight of the working classes, in order to print his poems, he accedes to the dean's advice to expunge the more inflammatory pieces.

Representing Alton as existing in a sort of limbo between clearly identified social groups problematizes the very concept of class and its workings within Victorian society. Like Carlyle, by whom he was heavily influenced and who "appears" caricatured as Alton's intellectual mentor Sandy Mackaye, Kingsley advocates a society based upon an aristocracy of talent, a society that would ignore (or at least minimize) the external trappings of the order into which one is born. Of course this idea was by no means new in 1850, when *Alton Locke* was published. Carlyle had been arguing for such a social order at least since the 1843 publication of *Past and Present* and in a less specified way since "Signs of the Times" (1829). Even John Stuart Mill, in his 1831 series of essays, "The Spirit of the Age," writes that the "natural state" is the one in which "worldly power and moral influence are habitually and undisputably exercised by the fittest persons whom the state of society affords" (17).

While such ideas were in the air, they were not necessarily in the novels of the period, at least not until *Alton Locke*. Even Disraeli's *Sybil* stops well short of promoting an "aristocracy of talent," preferring instead to argue for an "enlightened aristocracy" that can reunite the two nations and redefine England as a community rather than a "dissociative aggregation." Later, Kingsley's own view comes very close to this, especially in the expurgated "Cambridge Edition" of *Alton Locke* (1862). After his appointment to the Regius Professorship of Modern History at Cambridge, Kingsley revised and partly rewrote the novel to exclude the often unflattering scenes of Cambridge life that had given the early version part of its edge, and arguably part of its popularity. In the preface to the new edition Kingsley writes:

> As long, I believe, as the Throne, the House of Lords, and the Press, are what, thank God they are, so long will each enlargement of the suffrage be a fresh source not of danger, but of safety; for it will bind the masses to the established order of things by that loyalty which springs from content; from the sense of being appreciated, trusted, dealt with not as children, but as men. (9)

That is, by enfranchising ever more members of the populace, one guarantees that the institutions one (such as Kingsley) holds most dear will be forever protected. Through carefully guided and controlled change is permanence and stability assured.

In 1850, and the first version of the novel, however, Kingsley's position appears much less conservative. Yet advocating an "aristocracy of talent" makes it no easier for Alton to find his own place in society, nor does such advocacy create any sort of vision of community for Alton; rather it often turns him into a bit of a prig toward his own class and self-righteous toward the middle and upper classes. The scene that takes place during Alton's visit with his cousin, George, at Cambridge, when he is questioned by the college servant about his preference for dinner, bears out his attitudes and the difficulty of his situation particularly well:

> "What would you like, sir? Ox-tail soup, sir or gravy soup, sir? Stilton cheese, sir, or Cheshire, sir? Old Stilton, sir, just now."
>
> Fearing lest many words might betray my rank—and, strange to say, though I should not have been afraid of confessing myself an artisan before the "gentlemen" who had just left the room, I was ashamed to have my low estate discovered, and talked over with his compeers, by the flunkey who waited on them. (130)

Not only does this passage indicate Alton's ambivalence toward his status as a member of a "low estate," but it suggests a certain preoccupation with language as a way of establishing one's place in society. Alton is wary of speaking too many words, lest they "betray" his rank. Of course, his shame at having the college servants discover and discuss his "low estate" connects directly with betrayal of his rank in another sense—that of denying it, or at least of not accepting it before those of his own class. In fearing to betray his rank, he betrays his class.

The link between language, especially spoken language, and social rank is well represented in this passage, and Alton is fully aware of the constitutive power of language, seeking to control others' language *about him* by controlling his own and thus seeking power over the interpellation of his own subjectivity. If the college servants are to discuss him, it should not be as one of their own rank, a sentiment he makes quite clear by referring to the servant as a flunkey. On the other hand, he is perfectly willing to have himself discussed as a member of the working class by the Cambridge "gentlemen." But why "confess" unless at one level Alton's membership in the lower classes is a sort of social transgression? The word implies not only disclosure of information on Alton's part but either forgiveness or punishment on the part of the "gentlemen." If one examines "confession" in the context of Alton's upbringing and a tradition of dissent with which Kingsley would have been familiar, the allusion is to the Baptist practice of the Invitational, during which members of the congregation are urged to come forward and publicly profess their sinfulness and their acceptance of Christ as their savior. This act is prerequisite to becoming a member of the church, an equal with those "saved" members of the congregation. For Alton, it is as though confessing himself a member of the working class will wash away the sin of his poverty and allow him to be accepted as an equal—at least an intellectual equal—among his cousin's friends. The servants, however, have little to offer Alton except their contempt (or so Alton imagines), thus he is loath to expose himself as one of their rank. Further, because they are of the lower orders he must be concerned to distance himself. In a variation of the contamination trope that governs a good deal of mid-Victorian writing, Alton tries to conceal the metonymic connection he has to the servant. In this case it is as though contiguity, association, with the lower class is as potentially contaminating as the typhus that ultimately kills his cousin.

All of this, as Alton points out, is "strange to say," but the fact that it is said at all indicates the difficulties that educated members of the working class had in finding a place for themselves in a rapidly changing social structure. Literacy, thanks to working men's associations and to Sunday schools, was rising dramatically throughout the 1830s and '40s.[3] Yet the ability to read and write well does not in itself make one "respectable" nor does it transform laborers into middle-class ladies and gentlemen. At the same time, as many of all classes were beginning to see, doing physical labor for a living does not make one inherently depraved or stupid. Is it any wonder then that Alton, as one of the educated lower class, at times wears his social rank like a badge of honor, especially when he is among his middle- and upper-class patrons, and at other times carefully conceals his class identity to protect himself from exactly the sort of scorn he heaps on "sham gentlemen" and "parasites"? In either case, whether he is participating in the tumult of a riot or the lively patter at the dean's dinner table, Alton is always a detached, if not a disinterested, observer; he is always outside looking in. The circumstance of his having been born into the working class only intensifies his feelings that he is different from his fellows, whatever their rank.

Alton's "otherness" operates to the advantage of one of the strategies of the novel—its protagonist's conversion into what Raymond Williams has called Kingsley's version of a Chartist (*Culture and Society* 100). The intensity of Alton's longings for beauty and truth, which he equates with knowledge and poetry, and later in the novel with a love of God as well, impel him toward a sympathetic union with oppressed members of his own class, while permitting him to advocate individual moral reform rather than the more general political reform demanded by the Charter. In the strange and provocative chapter, "Dream Land," Alton, in a vision brought on by the delirium of fever, sees that only after many ages, "gradually and painfully, by hunger and pestilence, by superstitions and tyrannies, by need and blank despair, shall [humankind] be driven back to the All-Father's home." Going forth "selfish savages," all shall return to paradise as "brothers of the Son of God" (350). In his dream, Alton experiences the beginning of his conversion and comes to understand the necessity of suffering as a sort of purification of the intellect and the soul.

Catherine Gallagher has astutely observed that Kingsley—like other authors of industrial fiction—is torn between two explanations of the causes of suffering and poverty among the lower classes (*Industrial Reformation* 92). On the one hand, as the sentiments in the "Dream Land" chapter indicate, he depicts such suffering as expressly providential and necessary for an increased awareness of moral responsibility, or at least for an increased receptivity to the word of God. On the other hand, Kingsley recognizes the force of social conditions not only in determining the suffering of members of the working classes but also in circumscribing the ways the lower orders may attempt to alleviate their misery.

An important scene in the chapter "Light in a Dark Place" lucidly portrays the tightness of the grip in which members of the working classes were held by prevailing social and economic conditions. Led by Sandy Mackaye "through Clare Market to St. Giles's" (87)—two of London's poorest and most vice-ridden districts—Alton is introduced to a family of four: an old, demented woman and her three seamstress companions, presumably her daughters, one of whom is dying of consumption and is too sick to work. Unable to provide for the family by their needle work, the two healthy daughters have turned to prostitution. When the consumptive daughter tells Mackaye that she had hoped that at least her youngest sister, Lizzy, would repent, Lizzy responds "passionately, almost fiercely"; " 'Repent—I have repented—I repent of it every hour—I hate myself, and hate all the world because of it; but I must—I must; I cannot see her starve, and I cannot starve myself. . . . there's four of us with the old lady, to keep off two's work that couldn't keep themselves alone' " (92). Here, as in Chadwick's representations of the poor, poverty itself breeds sin, and the moral awareness of the girl, Lizzy, is not enough to prevent her committing the sin; it merely makes her more acutely conscious of her moral dilemma: either she prostitutes herself in order to keep her sister and mother from starving, or she keeps her body and soul pure and, in effect, kills two of her family members.

The problem for Alton, and for Kingsley, is to determine what suffering is intended by God and what is brought about by "the will of the world and the devil, of man's avarice and laziness and ignorance" (6). For instance, Alton believes that his being a Cockney is the will of God; his sickness, however, he blames on the city where he "was born and nursed, with its little garrets reeking with human breath, its kitchens and areas with noisome sewers" (6). This difficulty of distinguishing between the will of God and the malice or thoughtlessness of humankind also is the problem facing the working classes in their attempts to instigate social and political reform, for according to *Alton Locke*, if suffering is the will of God, it must be endured; if it is attributable to the behavior of humankind, it should be reformed.

In order to distinguish between human-induced and providential suffering, members of the working classes must first free themselves of their "slavery" to their own stomachs, their own pockets, their own tempers;[4] that is, they must somehow transcend the demands of the physical world and undergo the same sort of spiritual and moral awakening that Alton experiences in the "Dream Land" chapter. In order to do that they must see and order differently, through a discourse that emphasizes the metaphysical over the material. For Alton such a move signals a return to an interpretive paradigm strikingly similar to the fundamentalist dissent that informed his childhood. "The eye only sees what it brings with it, the power of seeing" (13), and Alton was taught by his strict Calvinist mother to avert his eyes from those things that do not glorify God. Only then could he keep his sight clear, his view unobstructed, and thus actively seek redemption, all the while waiting passively for the grace of God to fill him like an empty vessel so that he might, once converted, "understand the things of God" (10).

Such an interpretive model may make for "gentle and obedient children" (9), but it operates upon preconceived notions of what the world is and what the world should be rather than upon gathering new information that must be understood both in terms of the paradigm one brings to such information and in accordance with the properties peculiar to that information. Interpretations that reduce all possibilities to black and white, good and evil, fail to consider the moral ambiguity that often defines a working-class individual's relations to his or her social conditions of existence. If there is no place for moral uncertainty within this interpretive scheme, the effect of its application is to dissolve community by excluding those who do not subscribe to its doctrines. In such cases, religion does not reconcile social difference; rather, it magnifies those differences and creates isolated groups that (often correctly) perceive themselves to be at odds with the ethical norms of society. As the example of Susan's and Alton's "cloistered" youth shows, such an inflexible interpretive model has little need for observation as a means of expanding knowledge or questioning its own cognitive and descriptive efficacy. Because the world is already interpreted, divided between sin and redemption, observation is unnecessary and can even destroy the effect of the religious interpretive scheme, which is the protection of its participant from those things it has already determined to be harmful.

This interpretive scheme of *Alton Locke* is directly at odds with the narrative design of the "typical" industrial novel of mid-nineteenth-century Britain, which depends upon observation and upon making apparent what before had been hidden. If, as D. A. Miller has argued, the novel of this period fulfills its policing function through surveillance, then in the industrial novel such surveillance takes the form of discovery, indeed of detection, of a way of life that disregards and also calls into question many of the assumptions middle-class, literate Britain may have had about the poor working populace.[5] Unlike the social interpretation undertaken by many of the stricter Protestant religious sects that sought to shield their members from exposure to sin and degradation, the industrial or social-problem novel actually focuses on the moral and intellectual "failings" of the lower orders as it attempts to move the differences between classes to the center of its discourse.

The reader of *Alton Locke* immediately recognizes the power of religion as a discursive formation in nineteenth-century Britain, yet the utterances from within it tend away from social concerns and toward questions of the individual. As a result Calvinism becomes a sort of metaphysical Malthusianism. The state of one's soul is more important than the conditions of one's class. Because of this emphasis, for Alton (as a boy) religion makes no demands on his seeing the depravity of those around him; consequently, he has no notion of the power of observation or of the necessity of observing as a means of understanding the world in which he lives. Accordingly, when Sandy Mackaye takes Alton on the tour of the streets and back alleys of Clare Market and St. Giles, the young tailor-poet is nearly overwhelmed by the filth, poverty, and vice he sees there. Growing up in a strict Baptist home shielded him from the wretched conditions of the poor, his religion—or the effects rather of his mother's religion—serving as a façade much like the Manchester storefronts Engels describes.[6] Likewise,

Mackaye's introduction of Alton to the scenes of destitution and despair surrounding him suspends and challenges any associations the young man may claim with working-class men and women. Though one of the working class, Alton must seek out the conditions of his own order as though he were Chadwick, Engels, Mayhew, Kay, or any middle-class observer of the poor, and like Chadwick and the others he is struck by a way of life that is so alien to his own.[7]

At this point a question arises both for novels in general and for Alton as poet. To Alton, whose notions of literature are based upon his wide though uneven reading of classical and popular literature, it is not immediately evident that the subject of his poetry should be the poorer classes' circumstances of life and work and their political impotence—conditions he is either unable or unwilling to see until Mackaye lifts the veil from his eyes. Beautiful, tropical islands and naked native girls are Alton's idea of the proper subjects of poetry, but Mackaye remonstrates, "Coral Islands? Pacific? What do ye ken anent Pacifics? Are ye a cockney or a Cannibal Islander? . . . Why, if God had meant ye to write anent Pacifics, He'd ha put ye there—and because He meant ye to write aboot London town, He's put ye there—and gien ye an unco taste o' the ways o't" (86–87). For Mackaye poetry is born of experience, not of fantasy.

This too becomes a main point of the novel, which draws on Kingsley's own London experiences as well as on Mayhew's *Morning Chronicle* pieces as the raw material for its narrative.[8] But when scenes and information as shocking as those in *Alton Locke* are presented in fiction—a presentation that Kingsley apparently was not completely comfortable with given the publication of the novel as "autobiography"—then it becomes evident that whatever literary norms of decorum and taste such novels might challenge are as restrictive as young Alton's religious education, that they *obstruct* the observation and representation of the experiences of a significant portion of the population—the poor. And once those experiences that until the mid nineteenth century had been routinely ignored—or at best romanticized—in literature move to the heart of a narrative, the result must be a politicizing of the aesthetic. Observation invites commentary, *critical* commentary, which before the social-problem novels often was not considered a legitimate aspect of the novelistic enterprise and which even with the popularity of works like *Mary Barton*, *Yeast*, and *Alton Locke* was still not always favorably received by all readers. As one critic in *Fraser's* wrote of *Alton Locke*: "To open a book under the expectation of deriving from it a certain sort of pleasure, with perhaps a few wholesome truths scattered amongst the leaves, and to find ourselves entrapped into an essay upon labour and capital, is by no means agreeable" (Nov. 1850, 575).

Of course, that is part of the point. Reading a social-problem novel should not be "agreeable"; quite to the contrary, if the novel is a success as social criticism, reading it should have been one of the most disagreeable of occupations for the Victorian reader. Despite the Victorian fascination with the plight of the poor, being told that one is in some way responsible, however indirectly, not only for their destitution but also—if those conditions are not ameliorated—for the violent social unrest that could ensue brings the political and social ramifications of novel writing and of the conditions of the poor directly to bear upon the reader. Thus the aesthetic experience of reading a novel becomes a political and social experience as well, for in the social-problem novel, seeing, understanding, and attempting to solve the "two Nations" issue are intertwined activities, and their representation in literature questions the function of literary creation itself.

This unsettling of the function of writing confronts Alton with both political and aesthetic difficulties as he attempts to come to terms in his poetry with the predicament of the poor. And, working outward from the novel, Alton's problem as Mackaye sets it for him is in small the same as the one Kingsley has set for the working classes: to find the sublime in the everyday, even in the vulgar; to find a language of exaltation among the din of cries of those suffering from pestilence, hunger, and filth. Once Alton begins working toward solving this problem, he can see the possibility of turning those cries into poetry. Using what he calls Tennyson's ability to find "a world of true sublimity—a minute infinite," in hedgerows and sandbanks as well as in alpine peaks and "the ocean waste" as a model, Alton expands his conception of poetry to include the empirical as well as the metaphysical and begins to look for poetic images whose "roots are in the unfathomable and the eternal," in the common things that surround him (97–98).

For Alton, and for Kingsley, poetry has the power to make the transcendent qualities of an object or an event more real than the same object's or event's tangible properties. For both author and character this is the value of the aesthetic. In a world poetically interpreted, the *essence* of a tattered worker is far more real than the worker himself, for after the worker has perished from long hours of toil, or gin, or malnourishment, that which is undying—and ultimately unnameable—in him remains. Alton believes poetry to focus on the truly real, the "unfathomable and eternal," and in an almost Carlylean sense, to strip away the layers of superficial signification that attach to all things. For Alton, as for many within the Romantic tradition, the language of poetry enables the poet to see through appearances to the "truth" of what he is observing. It is in literature that understanding, and one assumes change, can begin.

But such understanding is only a beginning. For all this novel's emphasis on an individual, literary, and metaphysical understanding of the empirical world, that alone is not sufficient. Even Alton's transformation into a poet is not an end in itself, but a means toward the "realignment of social organization with Christian values" (Gallagher, *Industrial Reformation* 91). This realignment presents a considerable problem in establishing a social or communal enterprise, however, for among the working classes religion had fallen into widening disrepute. The "literature of the working man was violently anti-clerical, antichurch, antimethodist, antichapel. It rollicked in abuse of the establishment" (O. Chadwick 1:333).[9] And while few of even the most jaded members of the working classes would have described themselves as heathens or as anti-Christian, throughout the '40s an increasing number would have agreed with Chartist leader William Lovett when he declared himself "of that religion which Christ taught and which very few in authority practise—if one might judge by their conduct" (229).

Lovett's brief statement of his own religious convictions serves as an analogue to prevalent Chartist attitudes toward established religion and moral conduct, which were rightly perceived by many Chartist leaders as complementary but separate issues. Indicating that he has divorced himself from the religious practices of the majority of society, Lovett nonetheless implies that his own moral standards are irreproachable. In the little Chartist churches that sprang up in Scotland and the Midlands during the 1830s and 40s this seems to have been a common position. In 1840, for example, the *Chartist Circular*, the official publication of the Scottish Chartists, printed an extract from the first Chartist sermon preached in Scotland, the text: "Beware of false prophets" (1:129).

The independence of these churches was notable, and in May 1841, J. R. Stephens, editor of *The People's Magazine*, describes them as coming into being

> in the absence of any previously arranged plan for their formation, and without the assistance of any missionary or proselyte-maker acting as the agent of some distant "parent society." They are not "branches" or "auxiliaries" worked from a center but separate fellowships of the weighty and strong-minded people, who now begin in good earnest to ask what is the will of God in these things that belong as well to their earthly as their heavenly weal. (159)

Their usual method of "worship" was to choose an appropriate text from the Bible "after the manner of a sermon, and with that as a starting point launch into a discussion of political and economic problems, attempting to find the solution in the teachings of Christianity" (Faulkner 44). Attracting some dissenters and for the most part holding their meetings in schools, halls, or houses (Faulkner 42–43), these small congregations were hostile to other churches though they professed Christianity and condemned lapses in moral uprightness.[10] And while they were almost invariably led by lay preachers or Chartist "missionaries," these churches nonetheless administered the rites of baptism and the Lord's supper, and in Scotland, marriage (see *Chartist Circular* 1:110, 222, 226, 374 [1840]).

In other instances, "communist churches" were established that were patently non-Christian, though sometimes eccentrically religious. Goodwyn Barmby, founded just such a chapel at Bow Lane in Bromley in 1841. The meeting house walls were whitewashed, and the room was furnished with white deal pews and chairs. The liturgy consisted of "lessons-business-epistles-discourses-conversation" (*Reasoner* 1:13, 109 [1846]; quoted in O. Chadwick 1:334). Barmby later edited the *Communist Chronicle* and insisted that he was a prophet sent from God and had even been directly commanded by God to change his place of abode (O. Chadwick 1:334).

These colorful examples of the existence of Chartist and "communist" churches, even as Chartist leaders repudiated established religion, accentuate the equivocal status of religious discourse for the Chartist movement. This ambivalence of the Chartists toward religion is perhaps best noted in their affiliations with certain Methodist sects that had disassociated themselves from the increasingly respectable Wesleyan Methodism—headed by Jabez Bunting—and its disinclination toward political activism. The officers of the Wesleyan Conference moved steadily from political quietism to become genuinely conservative in their political opinions, often voting Tory.[11] Not all Methodists' material fortunes rose during the second quarter of the nineteenth century, however, and during the 1830s and '40s Primitive Methodism, which ministered almost exclusively to the lower classes and which practiced "ranting" or street revivals and camp meetings, grew more quickly than any other seceded Methodist group. By 1850 they were "strong in the Potteries, among Durham and Northumberland miners, in the West Riding and Hull and southward into Lincolnshire, where they were especially strong in remote villages" (O. Chadwick 1:387). In 1851 their numbers were nearly one third that of the Wesleyans, and on census Sunday almost 230,000 worshippers were counted.

Many of the most virulent anti-clerical, radical statements were uttered by men who were (or had been) Primitive Methodist or radical Wesleyan Methodist preachers.[12] At the Chartist convention at Peep Green in 1839, a local preacher named Hanson passionately declared that the clergy

> preached Christ and a crust, passive obedience and non-resistance. Let the people keep from those churches and chapels (We will!). Let them go to those men who preached Christ and a full belly, Christ and a well-clothed back— Christ and a good house to live in—Christ and Universal Suffrage. (reported in *Halifax Guardian*, May 25, 1839)

At the same convention, the important Chartist leader Ben Rushton, who had been a New Connexion Methodist preacher until about 1821, seconded a motion to prohibit those at the meeting from attending "any place of worship where the administration of services is inimical to civil liberty" by declaring that "for himself he had given nothing to the parsons since 1821, and the next penny they had from him would do them good" (quoted in Thompson, *Making*, 398). And there is the often repeated account of Feargus O'Connor's responding to local preacher William Thornton's convention-opening prayer that "the wickedness of the wicked may come to an end" by clapping Thornton on the back and proclaiming, "Well done Thornton; when we get the People's Charter, I will see that you are made Archbishop of York" (quoted in Harrison 130 and E. P. Thompson *Making* 398).

Despite the moral fervor and the religious rhetoric that men like Thornton, Hanson, and Rushton brought to marginalized political discourse, what in this context we might call the rhetoric of Chartism,[13] by no means were they all supporters of the "moral force" party within Chartism. E.P. Thompson points out that men like Rushton were of the "physical force" party and that they "served a God of Battles whom the men of the New Model Army would have understood; and more than a few lay preachers were willing to speak to the text, 'He that hath no sword let him sell his garment and buy one'" (*Making* 400). After 1839 the character of Chartism changed dramatically, the machinations of Feargus O'Connor overshadowing the efforts of the London Working Man's Association and the Birmingham Political Union. Partly because of O'Connor's blustery style and his rather confused notions as to what sort of society and economy Chartism should seek, the threat of physical violence—usually in the form of destruction of property—remained an important aspect of Chartist strategies throughout the '40s.

An entire intellectual industry has grown up around Chartist studies, and one of the most fecund of many topics closely associated with the study of Chartism has been whether Methodism, as Elie Halévy has argued, prevented revolution in England during the formative years of industrialization. Given the number of diverse and often competing idioms within Methodism, not to mention dissent in general, as well as within radical politics (both legitimate and marginal) during this era, it is extremely difficult to draw any conclusive *causal* connections either to disprove or to support Halévy's thesis.[14] Nevertheless, it remains irrefutable that the discourses of religious dissent and of radical politics, in all their various incarnations, often were employed by the same voices and for the same causes. As interpretive enterprises, each repeatedly found the other indispensable as a paradigm for expanding the limits of its own interpretive scheme and for rethinking and restating its place in culture and society.

Within this flurry of competing and, paradoxically, complementary discourses *Alton Locke* attempts to make its way. Kingsley himself was by no means a dissenter; indeed as his letters to Newman show, he was an energetic, if overmatched, apologist of the Church of England.[15] Yet *Alton Locke* is pointedly concerned with examining the failures of the Church and with making it useful to the working classes. And in making Alton a lapsed Baptist, Kingsley demonstrates that strict Calvinism does not move one any closer to "truth" than does Church of England "orthodoxy" as practiced in the professionalism of a young, social-climbing clergyman like George Locke, Alton's cousin and rival. In the scene in which Alton confronts his mother and "the pent-up scepticism of years burst[s] forth," Alton says:

> Religion? Nobody believes in it. The rich don't; or they wouldn't fill their churches up with pews, and shut the poor out, all the time they are calling them brothers. They believe the gospel? Then why do they leave the men who make their clothes to starve in such hells on earth as our workroom? No more do the tradespeople believe in it; or they wouldn't go home from sermon to sand the sugar and put sloe-leaves in the tea, and send out lying puffs of their vamped-up goods, and grind the last farthing out of the poor creatures who rent their wretched stinking houses. And as for the workmen—they laugh at it all, I can tell you. Much good religion is doing for them! You may see it's fit only for women and children—for go where you will, church or chapel, you see hardly anything but bonnets and babies! I don't believe a word of it,—once and for all . . . I will . . . believe nothing but what I know and understand. (56)[16]

Alton's tirade should not be mistaken for an impugning of God. It is the dicta of organized religion that Alton refuses to accept, not the existence or even the benevolence of God. As Alton makes clear in this passage and throughout the novel, a religion that either restricts human activity, as do the doctrines of many dissenting sects, or that rewards sophistry, insincerity, and avarice as the Church of England seems to (at least in George's case), has little to offer the working classes. It is only natural then, especially under the influence of his friends Crossthwaite and Mackaye, both of whom he later discovers are Chartists, that Alton would turn to radical politics as a way of demonstrating his belief in what he knows and understands.

It is never quite clear, however, what exactly Alton does know and understand. Even after his second "conversion" (from poet to Christian Chartist), he is able to offer little more than lofty sentiments and hopes for community. In response to his benefactress Eleanor's question of whether he is "a Chartist still," he replies:

> If by a Chartist you mean one who fancies that a change in mere political circumstances will bring about a millennium, I am no longer one. That dream is gone—with others. But if to be a Chartist is to love my brothers with every faculty of my soul—to wish to live and die struggling for their rights, endeavouring to make them, not electors merely, but fit to be electors, senators, kings and priests to God and to His Christ—if that be the Chartism of the future, then am I seven-fold a Chartist, and ready to confess it before men, though I were thrust forth from the very door of England. (383)

Bereft of plan or program, and indeed soon to be "thrust forth from the very door of England" never to return, Alton adopts a rhetoric as evangelical as any Victorian missionary's. And like most who go forth to spread the word of God, or of Chartism, or of Christian Socialism, Alton presumes to have not only privileged knowledge to reveal to his fellow workers, but the authority to impart it as well. These two presumptions, however, work against any notions of equality that might inform what Alton, at the end of the novel, sees as his political and religious purpose. His statement to Eleanor is filled with metaphors of elevation, of making working men what they are not, of raising them beyond the material and political circumstances that would allow them to be electors; Alton would re-make them into men who *deserve* to be electors.[17] These are the "rights" for which Alton is willing to continue to struggle. Working men do not inherently merit enfranchisement, but they should be raised to the moral state that makes them fit to vote, to hold office, or to serve God.

This "Chartism of the future" is the discourse of community for which

Alton searches throughout the novel; in it morality and righteousness take precedence over the "merely political." Yet this is not a discourse of leveling and rebuilding but of attempting to raise up those who have been oppressed. But raise them to what, precisely? And by what standards does one evaluate the moral culture of either the working or the middle classes? In reflecting upon these questions that beg the interpretive and prescriptive project of *Alton Locke*, one can see how inextricably entangled religion, radical politics, and even reformist literature become in Victorian culture and society, and how the novel shapes these different enterprises (and often provides temporary resolutions to the paradoxes they pose).

Examples of how the novel acts with and upon religion and politics can be seen in the material and political moves Alton makes as he progresses toward a moral consciousness that allows him to sympathize with those whose problems may be blamed upon a class system but that is itself ostensibly uninformed by class prejudices,[18] moves that are ultimately bound to the possibilities of thought and articulation available to him within Evangelicalism and strict Calvinist Protestantism. As a young boy, Alton for a short time is consumed with the desire to become a missionary. And although he confesses that in his fantasies of Tahiti and New Zealand, "my spiritual eyes were, just as my physical eyes would have been, far more busy with the scenery than with the souls of my audience" (13–14), he nonetheless concludes that he has found his vocation, and even expresses his wishes to his mother. Upon meeting a missionary, however, Alton recoils from the man in revulsion. "He talked of the natives," says Alton,

> not as St. Paul might of his converts, but as a planter might of his slaves; overlaying all his unintentional confessions of his own greed and prosperity, with cant, flimsy enough for even a boy to see through, while his eyes were not blinded with the superstition that a man must be pious who sufficiently interlards his speech with a jumble of old English picked out of our translation of the New Testament. Such was the man I saw. (15–16)

Or, more appropriately, such was the man he heard, for in this passage Alton is not objecting to the missionary's appearance, but his words. What Alton hears is the rhetoric of Evangelicalism—even though he immediately sees how un-Pauline it is. This missionary's monologue, which as Alton says rings false even to a boy, persuades Alton that rather than being men of principle and conviction, it is "the rule that many of those who go abroad as missionaries, go simply because they are men of such inferior powers and attainments that if they stayed in England they would starve" (16).

Despite the hollowness Alton perceives in the missionary's speech, Evangelicalism is considerably more powerful in Alton's home than inquiry. Whatever they may truly think of the missionary, Alton's mother and the two local ministers who are also present appear to be in complete agreement with the opinions of the colporteur. When Alton asks why "in old times the heathens used to crucify the missionaries and burn them, and now they give them beautiful farms, and build them houses, and carry them on their backs" no one present will offer an answer (16). Alton attempts to answer his own question by suggesting that "perhaps the heathens are grown better than they used to be" or that they are not as angry with the missionaries' message because it "is not quite the same as what the missionaries used to preach in St. Paul's time" (17), but he is met with angry looks and a stock answer that is, appropriately, a conflation of Ecclesiastes and St. Paul: "The heart of man . . . is, and ever was, equally at enmity with God" (17).[19] Alton's questions are legitimate, and the kindly Mr. Bowyer suggests that "It may be that the child's words come from God" (17), making the scene a contorted allusion to the child Jesus conversing with the rabbis in the temple (Luke 2:46–50). Jesus' discussion with the teachers was the beginning of his being "about his Father's business." Alton's "discussion," is also a sort of evangelical beginning for him, even though it thoroughly explodes his dream of becoming a missionary in the usual sense.

In Alton's general conclusion that nonconformist Evangelicals are characteristically impious, greedy men of "inferior powers and attainments," and that their rhetoric is substanceless, the novel directly confronts an enterprise with which it is competing as an interpreter of material, social, and political change. It is important, then, that the failure of Evangelicalism's presentation of itself as interpretive paradigm is part of the reason for Alton's disillusionment. Evangelicalism cannot answer the questions it poses; apparently, to Alton, it has no way of accounting for change or for differences between now and then. If humankind is ever and always at enmity with God, then Evangelicalism has very little to tell and interpretation is at an end. In opposition to this, the novel, by way of Alton's question about the difference between the actions of heathens in St. Paul's time and now, offers a new way of seeing the world, a way that not only perceives the world as dynamic, changing, but also interrogates the consequences of such change. Alton suggests that the heathens are not essentially depraved, that they have changed for the "better" even without the intercession of the missionaries, and that the missionaries themselves have responded to this change by altering their message to accommodate the heathens' more receptive attitude.

As we see, however, Alton's suggestion is not kindly taken. Evangelicalism cannot admit the possibility of the heathens being "better than they were," for such a condition undercuts one of its fundamental presuppositions. Evangelicalism's understanding of its own purpose insists that non-Christians be inherently opposed to the doctrines Evangelicals espouse. The business of saving souls is based on this opposition, on replacing one set of beliefs with another. But Alton and the novel imply that the opposition of former years has waned, that heathens now readily embrace Christianity. The result of this has been to make the missionaries themselves rich and greedy and masters over the heathens. Whatever austerity was once a part of Evangelicalism is no longer shared by the missionary, but is experienced solely by the converts, who in earlier times seemed to have viewed Christianity as threatening and coercive and now, oddly enough, willingly consent to Christianity.

As minor a narrative event as Alton's meeting the missionary may seem, in fact we see two important discourses of the Victorian period converging in this scene and the effects they have on one another. While the novel offers Evangelicalism a way to view itself as developing and transforming to meet its goals more effectively, it also offers Evangelicalism a view of human nature as progressive, improving, moving toward a kind of moral consciousness: an evolution of the moral mind, much as Kingsley paints it in the "Dream Land" chapter, where Alton sees himself developing physically and spiritually from tree-sloth to moral, self-reflective human being. Further, the novel provides a critique of Evangelicalism that acts as a model of the sort of questions the Evangelicals must ask of themselves: how is it that they become rich and self-satisfied? Why is it that non-Christians now appear so willing to adopt Christianity? To what extent do non-Christians *actually* adopt Christian values? How effective are missionaries in disseminating the "Word of God?" [20]

The discourse of Evangelicalism permeates the novel, informing many of Alton's actions even after he purportedly repudiates it, for, paradoxically, Alton's true vocation *is* that of missionary. He publishes his poems to express the plight of the London poor; he joins the Chartists as a means of furthering the causes of laborers; he writes for a Chartist paper; he makes a disastrous journey to the countryside to urge agricultural laborers to join the working-class "brotherhood." Alton may be ambivalent about his own place in society, and even, ultimately, about the aims of Chartism, but he is true to his calling and never flinches from what he perceives to be his duty to make the poor aware of their power and other classes aware of the poor.

Of course, Alton does not equate himself with those of "inferior powers and attainments." Rather, he believes quite the opposite. A few pages after he gives up his childish dream of becoming a missionary and starts dreaming of becoming a writer, he demonstrates how well his special abilities might accommodate his proselytizing impulses when he conceives of his first poem, a *Childe Harold*—like romance in which the hero was "not to be a pirate, but a pious sea rover, who with a crew of saints, or at least uncommonly fine fellows, who could be very manly and jolly, and yet all be good Christians of a somewhat vague and latitudinarian cast of doctrine (for my own was becoming rapidly so), set forth under the red-cross flag to colonise and convert one of my paradises, a South Sea Island" (84). Alton recalls the poem with a certain humorous nostalgia, describing it as "probably great trash" and terms the combining of his two inspirational materials—*Childe Harold* and old missionary records—a "spiritual wedding in my brain, of which anomalous marriage came a proportionately anomalous offspring" (84). As Alton matures he forgoes the more overt gestures toward Evangelicalism, and he gives up writing about south sea islands for writing about the world around him. Nevertheless, the poem indicates how deeply inculcated the project of Evangelicalism is in Alton. Even though he criticizes its practitioners as inept and selfish, he cannot completely reject it. He works to eliminate in his own work those aspects of Evangelicalism he finds most objectionable—namely, its implicitly effeminate manner and its promulgation of master-slave relationships.

Just as the south sea island poem provides a necessary linguistic space in which Alton temporarily resolves the conflict between discourses that significantly inform his view of the world by making them, as he says, "anomalously" complementary, so too does this novel call to account unenfranchised radical politics according to the interests and presuppositions of religious discourse and, concurrently, evaluates religion in light of many of the commonly held principles underlying Chartism. As a result we see in *Alton Locke* that neither Chartism nor religion escapes censure, and that both are at work in a composite discourse, which in its synthesis is reminiscent of Disraeli's combining of the political and the novelistic in *Coningsby*. This synthesis fails for Kingsley, and Alton ultimately returns to religion and individual enlightenment as the only way of understanding and resolving the social problems that beset mid-century Britain. But he first tests the viability of his politicized view of society by going among those who have been completely "blinded" by their physical needs, the rural poor, only to find a gap of understanding between himself and his potential "converts" that he cannot bridge.

To order the world on the basis of a Chartist interpretation, one must be prepared for a considerable amount of physical violence first, as Alton discovers when he goes to "D***" to "spread the principles of the Charter." Despite being warned by Mackaye not to "talk magniloquently" and not to cast his pearls "before swine . . . lest they trample them under their feet, an' turn again an' rend ye" (254), Alton cannot control himself or his sympathy with the starving poor. His speech on their political rights, on the fact that they are unrepresented in the legislative body, and on the Poor Laws as recognition by the wealthy that the poor are insufficiently remunerated, is answered by the crowd's cry for bread and their declaration, "And bread we will have!" (267–268). To this Alton responds, "Go . . . and get bread! After all, you have a right to it. No man is bound to starve. There are rights above all laws, and the right to live is one" (268).

This is the language of militant Chartism, the language of the "physical force party." These words are the pearls that enrage the swinish inhabitants of D*** and are the cause of Alton's imprisonment. Alton sees his mistake immediately, and shouts himself hoarse "about the duty of honesty," warning the mob against "pillage and violence," and entreating them "to take nothing but the corn which they actually needed" (269). Alton finds, however, that in such dire circumstances the proclivity for violence is like tinder before a flame, ready to burst into a blaze with only the slightest exposure to the smallest spark. The moral impulse Alton counts upon to dampen the wildfire of the mob's violence is consumed by the demands of the god of their bellies. As he might have guessed from the reports in his own narrative, the moral impulse Alton relies upon to check their violent reactions is lacking among the agricultural poor.

The moral culture of the rural poor is much degraded in comparison to the moral assumptions acted upon by Alton and his London associates. Although one widow says that she would sooner starve (and see her children starve too) than enter the workhouse, where she would be parted from her children and where they would "live with they offscourings" [sic] and would "keep the company as they will there, and learn all sorts o' sins that they never heard on" (264), others within the rural community have a much bleaker view of the moral choices they have made or that they can make. One old, blind man, a sort of Victorian Jeremiah, proclaims that because of their sins God has turned his face from them. Meetings will do no good, "nothing won't do us no good, unless we all repent of our wicked ways, our drinking, and our dirt, and our love-children, and our picking and stealing, and gets the Lord to turn our hearts, and to come back again, and have mercy on us" (266). Yet another speaker at this meeting of the rural poor argues that, practically speaking, theft and violence are a much better alternative than suffering in silence, since being caught means going to prison, and prison is far superior to the conditions they now endure, for in prison, "it's a darned deal warmer, and better victuals too, than ever a one of you gets at home, let alone the Union" (266).

Except for the last speaker, religion strongly informs the moral choices of these rural poor. As the ensuing riot demonstrates, however, the church can offer little to those who are dying of hunger. For Alton as for Kingsley, morality that depends upon dogma without a concomitant dependence on a personal understanding of one's moral responsibilities to self and to others cannot supply useful choices to those it has failed to educate. In a situation such as the one described in this chapter of *Alton Locke*, violence will win out over the useless rhetoric of the Church. The interpretive enterprise of the Church, religion in general, has failed to establish itself as more (or even equally) "real" in comparison to radical politics that leads to violence. This chapter of *Alton Locke* itself acts much as the old blind man's warning speech about God's turning away from the plight of the poor. It shows how imperfectly religion has shaped the moral presuppositions of the poor and how easily those morals are discarded (or reinterpreted) in the face of oppression and want. To assume then that religion can meet the moral *and* physical needs of the poor is to court the possibility, indeed the probability, of violence and to exacerbate already strained relations between the classes. It is, in effect, to invite revolt.

In comparison with the moral culture of the poor as a whole, the morals of the London Chartists, ironically, are much closer to the middle-class norms that are the standard of moral judgments in *Alton Locke*. At one point, for instance, Crossthwaite and Alton are walking past the Victoria Theater, debating the principles of political representation currently at work in England, when "a herd of ragged boys, vomiting forth slang, filth, and blasphemy" pushes past the two men, causing them to "take good care" of their pockets. Crossthwaite is morally outraged, but his affront takes the form of political cause and effect:

> Look there! look at the amusements, the training, the civilisation, which the government permits to the children of the people!—These licensed pits of darkness, traps of temptation, profligacy, and ruin, triumphantly yawning night after night—and then tell me that the people who see their children thus kidnapped into hell, are represented by a government who licenses such things. (108–9)

When Alton asks if a "change in the franchise would cure that," Crossthwaite replies:

> Household suffrage mightn't—but give us the Charter, and we'll see about it! Give us the Charter, and we'll send workmen into parliament that shall soon find out whether something better can't be put in the way of the ten thousand boys and girls in London who live by theft and prostitution, than the tender mercies of the Victoria. (109)

Crossthwaite's own moral presumptions, at least as they contribute to his ideas of the "thing most needful" in the foregoing passage, have more in common with representations of middle-class notions of moral conduct than with popular and powerful representations of the moral culture of the lower classes.[21] Likewise, when Alton balks at attending his first Chartist meeting for fear of being involved in treason and violence, Crossthwaite exclaims:

> Conspiracy? Bloodshed? What has that to do with the Charter? It suits the venal Mammonite press well enough to jumble them together, and cry "Murder, rape, and robbery," whenever the six points are mentioned; but they know, and any man of common sense ought to know, that the Charter is just as much an open political question as the Reform Bill, and ten times as much as Magna Charta was, when it got passed. What have the six points, right or wrong, to do with the question whether they can be obtained by moral force, and the pressure of opinion alone, or require what we call ulterior measures to get them carried? (107).

Through such speeches by Chartists and through representations of Chartists as the moral exemplars and the intellectual elite of the working classes, the connection between Chartism and violence is diminished; and the analogy of the middle classes, who had received the vote only sixteen years earlier, to the literate working classes who are committed to gaining the franchise is fortified: after attending his first Chartist meeting Alton remarks to Crossthwaite that he was struck by hearing men of his own class "and lower still, perhaps, some of them—speak with such fluency and eloquence. Such a fund of information—such excellent English" (108).

Despite his surprise at finding Chartists to be something other than a band of ruffians, Alton's own narrative has prepared him for finding exactly the earnest, yet well-behaved, group he describes. For instance, when Crossthwaite first appears in the novel, he is represented as the most morally upright of all the tailors in Alton's shop: "He alone had shown me any kindness; and he, too, alone was untainted with the sin around him. . . . His eye always cowed the ribald and the blasphemer. . . . He was not only, I soon discovered, a water-drinker [teetotaler], but a strict 'vegetarian' also; to which perhaps, he owed a great deal of the almost preternatural clearness, volubility, and sensitiveness of his mind" (29). He is also the only Chartist (until Alton becomes one as well) in the shop, which almost by association makes him moral. When Alton says that though still bad, the morals of the working classes are improving, he states:

> But nine-tenths of the improvement has been owing, not to the masters, but to the men themselves; and who among them, my aristocratic readers, do you think, have been the great preachers and practisers of temperance, thrift, chastity, self-respect, and education? Who?—shriek not in your Belgravian saloons—the Chartists; the communist Chartists; upon whom you and your venal press heap every kind of cowardly execration and ribald slander. (27)

Such representations of Chartism and Chartists effectively show the middle classes to be their own worst enemies in attacking Chartism or opposing Chartist activities. Curiously, Chartism becomes a way of controlling the poor, of spreading middle-class values such as "temperance, thrift, chastity, self-respect, and education." By depicting Chartism as an ideological ideal for the working classes *because* it is so similar to bourgeois ideology, *Alton Locke* offers the workers' movement an oppositional status while simultaneously demonstrating that the only reason it is oppositional is because middle-class interests have failed to coopt it formally. For Kingsley, Chartist discourse has already been significantly informed by middle-class values, and the best sort of working-class individual is one whose subjectivity is shaped by the values and desires that were so informative of the Victorian "bourgeois subject."

Chartism seems to be the answer to Alton's search for an interpretive paradigm that can be both politically and morally effective for the working classes. It can absorb religious discourse while still attending to the here-and-now needs of the working classes. As Alton states, the difficulty the Chartists have with the Church is not so much in religion itself but with systematizing religion. According to him, the Chartists—"as paradoxical as it may seem"—would gladly work toward regenerating the world by helping it "become more a Church." But "being dosed somewhat more with a certain'Church system,' circumstance, or 'dodge'" (111) does not serve the interests of the working people so much as it benefits those who would help to put in place and to maintain such a system.

It would be wrong-headed, however, to maintain that the narrative completely eradicates what seem to be the inherent connections between Chartism and the fear of violence it elicited in many of *Alton Locke*'s middle-class readers. Although the Chartists Alton knows adhere to middle-class moral and intellectual standards, standards that would appear to suppress violence as a means of compelling political change, the language of Crossthwaite and even of Alton is suffused with incipient violence. Though "moral force" may win out, Crossthwaite does not overrule the possibility of riotous upheaval (his "ulterior measures"). Similarly, when Alton is commending the Chartists (to his aristocratic readers) for their high morals and their untiring activity in raising the moral consciousness of the lower classes, he states, "You [upper class readers] have found out many things since Peterloo" (27). Though the reference is to past violence perpetrated upon the lower classes by the cavalry and yeomanry, the implication of possible chaos and rioting on the part of the oppressed portion of the populace is quite clear. Certainly the rural poor whom Alton addresses perceive the rhetoric of Chartism to contain an appeal to violence, as do the middle and upper classes who called out the aged Wellington to defend London on April 10, 1848 when the Chartists, under a divided leadership, presented their petition to Parliament.

Thus says Alton of the miscarried plans of April 10, "We had arrayed against us, by our own folly, the very physical force to which we had appealed" (323). As he realizes, too late, the Charter had become "an end, an idol in itself." Like many others, explains Alton,

> I had so made up my mind that it was the only method of getting what I wanted, that I neglected, alas! but too often, to try the methods which lay already by me. "If we had but the Charter"—was the excuse for a thousand lazinesses, procrastinations, "If we had but the Charter"—I should be good, and free, and happy. Fool that I was! It was within, rather than without, that I needed reform. (110)

As Alton makes clear, it is only through reform of the self, of the soul, through a spiritual and moral awakening that a remaking of either the noumenal or phenomenal world can take place. To be swept up in the evangelicalism that constitutes the faulty institution of the Church or in the equally evangelical and equally misguided discourse of the Charter is, effectively, to turn from God and to participate in the worship of images. Toward the end of the novel, when Crossthwaite perceives his spiritual mistakes, he virtually admits to idolatry, crying out, "I see it—I see it all now. Oh, my God! my God! What infidels we have been!" (365).

Alton Locke portrays both religion and radical politics as too closely tied to institutions, whether legitimated—like the Church—or marginalized—like the organization of Chartists—actually to have the power to instigate reform. As an interpretive enterprise religion lacks a necessary self-reflexive quality: it cannot call itself to account; it is bound to follow certain practices that circumvent the critical and constitutive power it may possess. Similarly, the Chartists in criticizing the society in which they live have adopted certain non-discursive measures, like violence, toward which their interpretations must eventually lead. In and of themselves, Chartism and religion offer ways to begin to rethink and reorder society, but only from without can their assumptions be rethought. Thus Alton is able to question the religion of his mother and the missionaries. He is also able to criticize the presuppositions of radical politics by removing himself from that discourse, that is, by considering it from the perspective of a constitutive, interpretive undertaking: of personal reform.

Alton's personal discourse of politics *and* religion is truly synthetic inasmuch as it partakes of the two it appraises. Yet it also discards certain aspects of each that might impede the change that it is trying to impel. For instance, there is no place for the violence that attends the public discourse of radical politics, for a large component of Alton's attempts to situate himself within his new interpretive paradigm is constituted by a morality that is primarily middle-class and *reformist* rather than revolutionary. Unlike radical politics, which sanctions violence as a possible and quite practical solution when discourse fails, Alton's new discourse of spiritual reform denies any legitimacy to violence as a means of creating a new, more equitable social order. At the same time, as Eleanor's nursing of Alton and as George's death by fever make clear, this new discourse also opposes the sorts of economic class distinctions that the church has helped to maintain and which, as E. P. Thompson—among others—has shown, went far toward informing (and indeed toward making respectable) nineteenth-century dissent. This is not to say that Alton, or Kingsley, denied any distinctions among what one might call classes. However, Alton's declarations of his then unrealized abilities as well as his rising to a position of some authority within his own Chartist local indicate that class distinctions should be drawn along intellectual and spiritual rather than economic lines.

Alton Locke's discourse of spiritual reform, its "religion of Chartism," then, assuages middle-class fears of revolt born of immorality (or rather the participation of a large portion of the population in a moral code of conduct that differs significantly from that of the middle classes) or of up-rising rooted in infidelity, since its rhetoric is explicitly bound up with the rhetoric of Christianity. Yet this discourse is of little social value as long as it remains only a private interpretive paradigm and is used primarily to con-stitute Alton's own subjectivity. If it is to instigate change, it must become public; indeed it must take on the very Pauline characteristics it repudiates in its own narrative.

Interestingly, it is at this point that *Alton Locke* becomes both most self-reflexive and most blind to its own status as a novel. On the one hand, how better to disseminate a new interpretive paradigm than through the most public of Victorian media, the novel? Yet in attempting to offer a Christian Socialist message that posits essence or ideal as the ultimate reality, *Alton Locke* undermines its own, assumed, authority. As any good Platonist knows, if indeed the world experienced by working and middle classes alike is but a poor copy of transcendent reality, then novels, which are both "invented" and simulations of the empirical world, are even fur-ther removed from the "truth" that *Alton Locke* ostensibly conveys.

Alton Locke implodes, unable to live up to the very standards it estab-lishes for critically engaging with other interpretive enterprises. But in its own way it attempts to buttress the strength of the novel as a constitutive discourse. Like *Coningsby* it offers a representation of lived experience that is at odds with competing interpretations of the world, and for Victorians as tired of the loud, if feeble, threats of Chartism and the seeming impo-tence of religion as they were of reading about the plight of the working classes, *Alton Locke*'s notions of how the world works, may have seemed reasonable, even true for a moment. Inasmuch as *Coningsby* is a document of the Young England Movement, so too might *Alton Locke* be read as a manifesto for Christian Socialism. Both texts do their ideological work, and to that extent they contribute to the ways Victorians made—as well as made sense of—their world.

9

Mary Barton and the
Community of Suffering

Those readers familiar with Friedrich Engels's *The Condition of the Working Class in England* as well as with Elizabeth Gaskell's *Mary Barton* may be immediately struck by a peculiar similarity in the opening pages of these two important social texts of the middle nineteenth century. Engels begins with a "Historical Introduction" in which he recalls the intellectual and moral state of workers in the years before the advent "of the steam engine and of machines for spinning and weaving cotton" (9).[1] In those years, writes Engels, workers were "righteous, God-fearing, and honest. . . . Most of them were strong, well-built people" (10). The children grew up "in the open air." Workers were uninterested "in politics, never formed secret societies, never concerned themselves about the problems of the day, but rejoiced in healthy outdoor sports and listened devoutly when the Bible was read to them" (10–11). They had "no intellectual life and were interested solely in their petty private affairs" (12). These people, explains Engels, "vegetated happily" in their idyllic life, yet "they remained in some respects little better than the beasts of the field. They were not human beings at all, but little more than human machines in the service of a small aristocratic class" (12). The Industrial Revolution "carried this development to its logical conclusion," turning the workers "completely into machines" and depriving them "of the last remnants of independent activity" (12). Paradoxically, however, it was also the Industrial Revolution that "forced the workers to think for themselves and to demand a fuller life in human society" (12). According to Engels, political and economic changes that are tied directly to the Industrial Revolution brought the middle and working classes into the "vortex of world affairs" (12).[2]

The opening of *Mary Barton* also alludes to a simpler, idyllic past. One April day in the early or mid 1830s, the operatives from Manchester spend "a holiday granted by the masters, or a holiday seized in right of nature and her beautiful springtime" (40) in Green Heys Fields.[3] Scattered about these fields, which are within a half-hour's walk from the busy manufacturing town, one can see "here and there an old black and white farm-house," which speaks of "other times and other occupations than those which now absorb the population of the neighborhood" (39). And like Engels, Gaskell comments on the physical appearance of some of the operatives, a group of factory girls, whose "faces were not remarkable for beauty; indeed they were below the average, with one or two exceptions" (41). Yet just as Engels remarks on the increased intellectual activity of urban workers, activity that distinguishes them from their rural counterparts, Gaskell also comments on these plain working girls' "acuteness and intelligence of countenance, which has often been noticed in a manufacturing population" (41). A few sentences later, the narrator describes Mary Barton's mother, also named Mary, as a woman who has "the fresh beauty of the agricultural districts; and somewhat of the deficiency of sense in her countenance, which is likewise characteristic of the rural inhabitants in comparison with the natives of the manufacturing towns" (41–42).

Gaskell and Engels observe the same changes in the English lower classes that have come about as a result of the Industrial Revolution. Whereas Engels's workers are thrown into the vortex of world affairs by industrialization, Gaskell's factory operatives are "absorbed" by occupations other than farming. In each text, the lower classes are passive; they are acted upon by the conditions in which they live, conditions they had historically done little to change. But as they have collected together in large masses in towns like Manchester, they have made the most of their compelled socialization. This new type of workers, the urban workers, have become keen and intelligent; they have begun to think for themselves; they have begun to participate in the making of their world.

It is important, I think, to recognize how significant the similarities in these two texts are. In each case the observer is an outsider to the world of the working class, and in each case it is up to the observer to make sense of that alien world. Likewise, in both *Mary Barton* and *The Condition of the Working Class in England* there is an insistence on a continuity with a past that has become mythologized as a simpler, less physically and intellectually demanding time. Further, this past is only recoverable as history or memory, whether it be in Engels's comparisons of pastoral to urban life or in Alice Wilson's anecdotes (or delirium). For both Engels and Gaskell the change that was transforming nineteenth-century life was inexorable and ultimately "progressive" inasmuch as it held within it the potential for amelioration of the laboring classes' conditions of life as well as the promise of a vital intellectual and spiritual life for the working orders. But in each text, the workers are represented as partly responsible for their lot, no matter the oppression they experience at the hands of more economically and politically powerful classes. Further, just as industrialism has thrown both laborers and the middle class into the vortex of world affairs in Engels's description of the effects of the Industrial Revolution, in *Mary Barton* we find that the working classes and middle classes are inextricably bound to one another. In Gaskell's novel, the interests of either are the interests of both, and it is only through understanding this interdependence that their mutual concerns can be served.

The difficulty of making this linkage clear to members of both classes becomes apparent in the John Barton portion of Gaskell's 1848 "Tale of Manchester Life," which is bifurcated into his story and the story of Mary Barton and Jem Wilson's romance. The one-time titular hero of the novel, John Barton has found that he can expect very little comfort from his economic and educational betters. As he says to his friend of many years, George Wilson,

> I tell you, it's the poor, and the poor only, as does such things [as give aid in time of sickness or death] for the poor. Don't think to come over me with the old tale, that the rich know nothing of the trials of the poor. I say, if they don't know, they ought to know. We are their slaves as long as we can work; we pile up their fortunes with the sweat of our brows; and yet we are to live as separate as if we were in two worlds; ay, as separate as Dives and Lazarus, with a great gulf betwixt us; but I know who was best off then. (45)

John Barton ends this, the first and perhaps most famous of his many speeches on the enslavement of the lower classes by the manufacturers, "with a low chuckle that had no mirth in it" (45). One critic has argued that "this closing reference to heavenly justice is a gloomy prophecy of revenge, not a joyful anticipation of saintly rewards" (Gallagher, *Industrial Reformation* 71). While Barton's character certainly lends some credence to this interpretation and while such a closing does emphasize the "polarized social vision, and the determinism that informs [John Barton's] thinking" (70), it is important to consider this statement within the context of the scene in Green Heys Fields and within the rhetoric of suffering that even in the first few pages of this novel is being established as the work's interpretive filter.[4] With such considerations in mind, the similarities of *Mary Barton*'s opening pages to the "Historical Introduction" of Engels's book take on added significance, and John Barton's punctuating the parable of Dives and Lazarus with his mirthless laugh becomes more than an indication of his character or a foreshadowing of later violence; it also indicates the humorless irony of the situation in which the poor find themselves.

The industrial poor are the natural consequence of the very "system" that made some, such as Barton's employer Mr. Carson, rich. Yet whatever such men may have learned in their success, they have refused knowledge of an existence even more deplorable than that out of which they rose and which they now exploit. As the narrator says, "in the days of his childhood and his youth, Mr. Carson had been accustomed to poverty: but it was honest decent poverty; not the grinding squalid misery he had remarked in every part of John Barton's house, and which contrasted strangely with the pompous sumptuousness of the room in which he now sat" (439). The refusal to know this aspect of the factory system is compounded in the younger Carson when at one point he states his intentions toward Mary Barton: "my father would have forgiven any temporary connexion, far sooner than my marrying one so far beneath me." When confronted with the fact that his mother was a factory girl he replies, "Yes, yes!—but then my father was in much such a station; at any rate there was not the disparity there is between Mary and me" (184). This offhand repudiation of his own working-class antecedents highlights not only the lack of knowledge that the middle classes have about the lower but a lack of desire to know. It is not for nothing, then, that Barton's "explanation" for killing Harry Carson rings like a refrain in the elder Carson's ears: "I did not know what I was doing" (436).

Barton's use of the parable also illustrates the kinds of explanations and thus the understanding available to the workers as they attempt to interpret and, to an extent, to order their world. This world, as both Engels and Gaskell point out, is one the working classes had very little say in making. It is a world into which they are thrown or absorbed, yet one which they must make some sense of if they are to survive; in this world that seems so hostile to their existence, they must create a space for themselves that they can at least partially control. Barton's reference to the parable of Dives and Lazarus indicates the perspective of opposition and oppression that informs the workers' view of this world and thus provides them with some measure of containing this world within an interpretive paradigm of their own. Oddly enough, however, despite Barton's gloomy understanding of the world and his place in it, the reference to Dives and Lazarus rather incongruously offers the workers some hope for amelioration. It goes far in indicating how profoundly Christian eschatology constitutes the lower classes' comprehension of the industrialized world; or at the very least, Barton's reference demonstrates Gaskell's perception of the working poor's attitudes toward their lots in life.

In the introduction to his *Lectures on the Philosophy of World History*, Hegel speaks of the "cunning" of reason in history, those events, figures, circumstances that seem to quell the progress of mind and humanity, but which, upon closer examination, reveal themselves as *necessary* for that progress. In the opening pages of Engels's *Condition*, we see exactly how such cunning functions, for in the very deprivation suffered by the laboring classes, historical progression is at work. It is precisely because they suffer that the working classes begin to create and to demand for themselves "a fuller life in human society."

The "principal and most potent Hegelian category and instrument of analysis—the negative" (Marcus, *Engels, Manchester* 137) primarily informs Engels's logic of representation of the history of the working classes. The working classes are for Engels "the universally negated," who had "been deprived of everything except their humanity, and even that existed for them in an estranged and unachieved form" (Marcus, *Engels, Manchester* 138). As universally negated, however, they also represent the "power of universal negation" and prefigure an "immense and dreadful convulsion" (138) that will produce, finally, a positive result. For Hegel, and later for Engels and his famous associate, this result is freedom. In Hegel it is a freedom of the mind; for Marx and Engels it becomes a freedom from the manipulations of capitalism—a social and material freedom.

Importantly, Engels sees the negativity of the working class as that class's impetus for the reinterpretation of itself and its place in the world, and he provides the structure for this new narrative of the working class: the result of the working classes being placed "at the vortex of world affairs" is revolutionary. The workers are no longer at the periphery of the social "machine"; they now are the means by which industrialization thrives. No longer need they be content to be acted upon by history; the urban, industrial workers can *make* history; they can—if they will—destroy the institutions that continually enslave the lower orders and that persist in debasing their humanity. Thus deprivation and the deplorable conditions of life for the lower orders comprise a vital component both in the way the working classes can interpret and thus redefine and reorder their world, and also in how they can materially change their fate.

Mary Barton's use of the negative, though by no means Hegelian in its derivation, also influences interpretation and understanding, at least for the main characters. Through their suffering they create a world of meaning and thereby a community that is inaccessible and unintelligible to their employers. Suffering is the linchpin of the society of the poor in *Mary Barton*; all experience it and, as with death, the fact that one will experience it can be foretold with certainty. Suffering is also the impetus to positive change, even when it appears to stifle all possibility of amelioration. Yet unlike *The Condition of the Working Class*, and much more akin to other social-problem novels of the period, *Mary Barton* promotes reform rather than revolution, and the ways in which such reform can take place are connected, finally, to those with whom power resides and will continue to reside—the middle classes. In contrast to works such as *Helen Fleetwood* or *Alton Locke*, which focus on the importance of individual spiritual purity or regeneration, *Mary Barton* concerns itself with the problem of communication between the two nations of England, characterizing the gulf between the two classes as a sea of silence, an absence of discourse. According to *Mary Barton* if communication is established, the middle classes will be able to understand their obligation to the lower orders and to proceed apace with material reform, which Gaskell represents as more immediately necessary than spiritual or moral reform.

At one point early in *Alton Locke*, Alton is struggling with his conscience about whether his duty to himself and to the attainment of knowledge should outweigh his duty to his inherited religion and his mother. As he says to the reader, "I was not likely to get any very positive ground of comfort from Crossthwaite; and from within myself there was daily less and less hope of any" (53). Out of his discomfort, his suffering, he is able to come to a decision about which course of action he will take. Reform, let alone revolution, is not undertaken by a sated or complacent subject. For Alton, the interpretative paradigm bequeathed to him by his mother no longer satisfactorily orders his world or answers his inquiries. Thus he begins to search for new ways to come to terms with his world and eventually underwrite changes in that world. This too is happening in *Mary Barton*; from the opening pages of the novel, characters are moved to action through their suffering. And as in *Alton Locke*, one of the first aspects of the characters' lives to be examined are the discourses that constitute them and their understanding of and relations to their surroundings.

These examinations are particularly interesting, because in *Mary Barton* the constitutive discourses of the lower classes are predominantly informed by middle-class presuppositions. For example, when John Barton speaks of the "great gulf" between rich and poor, he asks, "does the rich man share his plenty with me, as he ought to do, if his religion was not a humbug?" (45). Barton is questioning the value of a moral system that has no more force than middle-class religion seems to have, but his query is followed by the famous Dives and Lazarus reference, an indication that middle-class Christianity, the religion that Barton is interrogating, has found its way, however mediated, to the lower classes and lies ready to hand for those who will follow it or will employ it. Barton turns this discourse on itself in defining his and his family's place vis à vis the middle classes. Only a few sentences before commenting on middle-class religion as "humbug," Barton tells of warning his sister-in-law, Esther, about filling Mary's head with notions of becoming a lady:

> I'd rather see her earning her bread by the sweat of her brow, as the Bible tells her she should do, ay, though she never got ay butter to her bread, than be like a do-nothing lady, worrying shopmen all morning, and screeching at her pianny all afternoon, and going to bed without having done a good turn to any one of God's creatures but herself. (44)

Note the ideological and moral alignment in the foregoing examples of Barton's words. Both in his assertion that it is only the poor who look after the poor and in his determination that Mary shall earn her living through honest work, as the Bible instructs, Barton strongly insinuates that the lower orders conform more closely than the middle classes to the middle classes's own code of moral conduct—a code that for Gaskell follows almost exclusively from the precepts of Christianity. Second, the moral rectitude of the poor is represented as all the more remarkable for the debilitating material conditions of life they are forced to endure. When the poor do for the poor, as John Barton says they must, the important biblical analogy is no longer that of Dives and Lazarus but of the scene in Matthew's depiction of the Last Judgment in which the "Son of Man" bids the righteous to come forward to "inherit the kingdom" prepared for them: "For I was hungered, and ye gave me meat; I was thirsty and ye gave me drink: I was a stranger and ye took me in: Naked, and ye clothed me; I was sick, and ye visited me: I was in prison and ye came unto me" (Matt. 25:34–36). And when the righteous ask how it is that they have done these things for Christ, he answers: "Inasmuch as ye have done *it* unto one of the least of these my brethren, ye have done *it* unto me" (Matt. 25:40).

Certainly this or a comparable text (such as the parable of the Good

Samaritan) determines, in part, Barton and Wilson's errand of mercy to the Davenport household; and as the novel points out of the poor in general: in times of distress, though there were "desperate fathers . . . , bitter-tongued mothers . . . ," and "reckless children," there was "Faith such as the rich can never imagine on earth; there was 'Love strong as death'; and self-denial, among rude, coarse men" (96). Writes Gaskell, "The vices of the poor sometimes astound us *here*; but when the secrets of all hearts shall be made known, their virtues will astound us in far greater degree" (96).

This sort of moral consciousness is a part of all the working-class main characters of *Mary Barton* and even contributes to some of the actions of the pandering Sally Leadbitter (132–33). From Gaskell's middle-class per-spective, the perspective shared by most of her readers, this must have been in some degree comforting. Despite well-known attacks by those such W.R. Greg in the *Edinburgh Review* (1849) in which the novel is criticized for its overly sympathetic portrayal of factory operatives and for Gaskell's failure in understanding the principles of political economy, *Mary Barton*'s representations of a moral segment of the working class escaped serious challenge by its contemporary critics. And though there is little time for church attendance (or at least there is very little discussion of it) in the novel, the fact that the lower classes' moral code is so often *exemplary* in many ways diminishes the fears of violence and infidelity that so many observers of the working classes, and of Manchester in particular, had ex-pressed.

Thus, unlike *Alton Locke*, which attempts a reform of public religion and politics by offering a personal spiritual awakening, *Mary Barton* does not perceive the need to fortify or remake working-class morality as a means of achieving political goals. Indeed, the novel's aim, according to Gaskell, is far from political—even on a tertiary level. As she says in the preface to *Mary Barton*, "I bethought me how deep might be the romance in the lives of some of those who elbowed me daily in the busy streets of the town in which I resided" (37). The novel's stated goal is dramatic and rep-resentational. As Gaskell writes at the end of the preface, "I know nothing of Political Economy, or the theories of trade. I have tried to write truth-fully; and if my accounts agree or clash with any system, the agreement or disagreement is unintentional" (38).

Unintentional perhaps, but unavoidable nonetheless. Like Kingsley, Chadwick, or any other observer of the lower classes, Gaskell could not completely repudiate a perception of reality formed by experiences and their interpretations that could only be very different from the experiences and interpretations of most members of the working classes. Thus while John Lucas validly asserts that *Mary Barton* is an important corrective to *The Condition of the Working Class in England* because Gaskell was able to represent important variations in attitude and conditions of life among different groups within the lower classes, he errs in his argument that Gaskell's representation is more "truthful" because it is formed out of a more complete "experience" (see Lucas, *Literature of Change* 39, 56). As subtle as Lucas's definition of "truth" is and despite his denial of any sort of empirical basis to his thesis, ultimately his argument must revert to one of observation and representation. That is, Gaskell, according to Lucas, saw things as they really were. But things "as they really were" to Gaskell differs considerably from the reality experienced by those who had first-hand experience of living in cellars below the water line, or of the gnawing hunger of going days without eating, or of relief at the death of a child because there is one less mouth to feed and because burial society funds might even make such a death profitable.

Moreover, Gaskell never purports to be representing the reality of the situation she observes; she knows this is a claim she cannot make. She writes of *Mary Barton* in an undated letter of 1848, "I can only say I wanted to represent the subject in the light in which some of the workmen certainly consider to be true, not that I dare to say it is the abstract absolute truth" (*Letters* 67). She is always aware of the limits on what she can see, and thus the limits on what she can (or should) say.[5] It comes as no surprise therefore, that she should write to Mary Ewart late in 1848 that "no one can feel more deeply than I how *wicked* it is to do anything to excite class against class" (*Letters* 67; original emphasis). For her, to incite revolt would indeed be wicked, for it would be to encourage the destruction of an order that, given her Unitarian theology, must be ordained by God. Yet in the same letter to Ewart she writes:

> I do think that we must all acknowledge that there are duties connected with the manufacturing system not fully understood as yet, and evils existing in relation to it which may be remedied in some degree, although we as yet do not see how; but surely there is no harm in directing the attention to the existence of such evils. (67)

Mary Barton exists between what Gaskell construed as the "wickedness" of inciting class against class and the duty of acknowledging and remedying the evils inherent to the factory system. The problem for this novel, much like the problem for *Alton Locke* or other novels written by members of the middle classes who were sympathetic to the plight of the poor, is how to devise interpretations and representations that can successfully depict the conditions (and for Gaskell, the emotions) of the workers without upsetting the order of society. Also, like Chadwick, Engels, Mayhew, or Kingsley, Elizabeth Gaskell is an observer of the poor and their lives, and she is sharing her discovery with a world of readers that otherwise would have only limited access to it. Winifred Gérin remarks that "the setting of the tale is, unrelievedly, Manchester" and that "except to the commercial travellers of England, Manchester was virtually unknown in the south" (87).⁶ Speaking of *North and South* (1855), Gérin writes, "Her descriptions of the back-to-back insanitary dwellings of her dramatis personae, of the stationary pall of smoke polluting the air, well removed though the mills were from the residential areas where the prosperous cotton-spinners and calico-printers lived, had in themselves the power to shock" (87). As with other observers of the lower orders, Gaskell must conceive a strategy of representation that can provide the fullest possible depiction of this alien, unfathomable world yet still be accessible to her readers in terms they can understand.

As an interpretive trope, suffering provides those terms, for it reaches across class boundaries, affecting even those who, John Barton believes, easily weather the storms of bad economic times.⁷ This is the discourse of John Barton's resentment and bewilderment at seeing "that all goes on just as usual with the mill owners. Large houses are still occupied, while spinners' and weavers' cottages stand empty, because the families that once occupied them are obliged to live in rooms or cellars" (59). As far as Barton is concerned the worker alone suffers through bad times at the mill. The narrator of *Mary Barton* tells the reader, "I know that this is not really the case; and I know what is the truth in such matters: but what I wish to impress is what the workman feels and thinks" (60). The workers, then, are creating their own reality, understanding their world through interpretations that describe the material circumstances that bind them together— and that apparently situate them as adversaries of the manufacturers.

As the reader sees with the murder of Harry Carson, it is not only the operatives who can be affected by loss, nor does suffering lie exclusively in the domain of the laborer. Urged to action by the murder of his son, the senior Carson arranges for a speedy trial and construes the available evidence, circumstantial though it is, as conclusive proof of Jem Wilson's guilt. Carson's loss provides him with the interpretive imperative to create a reality in which the only explanation for his son's death is linked to the rivalry between Harry and Jem for Mary's affections. And after Jem's acquittal and Barton's deathbed confession to Carson, it is mutual suffering, ironically, that heals the breach between laborer and manufacturer, that makes a community of the two nations much as it creates community among the poor:

> The eyes of John Barton grew dim with tears. Rich and poor, masters and men, were then brothers in the deep suffering of the heart; for was not this the very anguish he had felt for little Tom, in years so long gone by that they seemed like another life! (435)

The poor's suffering and the utterances that arise from it seem to be tied directly only to their material conditions of life. Yet in its interpretive functions, that suffering and its articulation is inextricably linked to their religious perceptions and utterances as well. Alice Wilson's "optimistic determinism" is a case in point. For Alice, all bad things ultimately are for the good. Rather than grieving immoderately over the loss of a friend or relative, Alice prefers to believe every misfortune is "sent" and falls "to trying to find out what good it were to do. Every sorrow in her mind is sent for good" (84). This can only be described as a way of articulating suffering that gives vent to the experience of loss or deprivation, yet which also provides comfort. This means of interpreting the world, argues the narrator of *Mary Barton*, depends upon the strength of one's faith. Thus when Mary strives "to deny the correctness" of her friend Margaret Jennings' fear that she is going blind and thus will be unable to support herself and her grandfather, she offers false comfort, primarily because she refuses to interpret the event of Margaret's blindness as an event of loss, yet one also of gain. As the narrator says, Mary should have helped Margaret to "meet and overcome the evil" (85).

Not all characters find suffering informed by religious faith an adequate discourse for interpreting the world in which they live. Once again, one need only think of John Barton's many attacks on religion. Because the rhetoric of suffering is tied to religious discourse, even in Barton's own speech, this does not mean that religion cannot be or is not called to account. For Barton, religion as a means of understanding the lot of the worker fails miserably. When he and Wilson are in the appalling cellar ministering to the dying Ben Davenport, Wilson tells how while sitting alone with the dying man and his family and bitterly musing on his having to "sponge off" his son Jem, he reads a letter the dying man had written to his wife, which was "as good as Bible-words; ne'er a word o' repining; a' about God being our father, and that we mun bear patiently whate'er he sends" (104).

For George Wilson these are words of comfort, but Barton immediately scoffs: "Don ye think he's the masters' father too? I'd be loath to have 'em for brothers" (104). Such a statement notably denies the community between master and man that Gaskell presents as the only solution to the problems of the poor. In every case such community depends upon communication between the classes, and to an extent an identification of one class with another. As Gaskell demonstrates, however, such identification is impossible when the factory operatives see their employer "removing from house to house, each one grander than the last" until finally the manufacturer withdraws his money "from the concern, or sells his mill to buy an estate in the country" (59). Gaskell goes on to point out that it is not only the actions of the employers but their unwillingness to communicate with the operatives that contributes so greatly to the alienation of classes:

> And when he [the worker] knows trade is bad, and could understand (at least partially) that there are not buyers enough in the market to purchase the goods already made, and consequently that there is no demand for more; when he would bear and endure much without complaining, could he also see that his employers were bearing their share. (59)

Of course, remarks like Barton's indicate that the refusal to identify with another class is not solely a characteristic of the monied orders; indeed, his stated aversion to claiming his employers as "brothers" only contributes to the gap separating master and man so that finally there can be no communication at all, as Gaskell's description of the confrontation between the factory owners and the striking workers bears out:

> So class distrusted class, and their want of mutual confidence wrought sorrow to both. The masters would not be bullied, and *compelled to reveal why they felt it wisest and best to offer only such low wages; they would not be made to tell that they were even sacrificing capital to obtain a decisive victory over the continental manufacturers.* And the workmen *sat silent and stern* with folded hands refusing to work for such pay. There was a strike in Manchester. (221–22; emphasis added)

The novel itself steps into the space created by the refusal of the representatives of each class to speak. As with the riots in *Alton Locke*, the strike is indicative of the breakdown of discourse, the inability (or refusal) of either side to understand its adversary's position. The strike, however, also demonstrates the unwillingness of each group to make known the reasons for its position. The novel interrupts this silence and provides intercourse between these opposing positions, not only as a way of offering a possible solution to the impasse the confrontation between employer and operative has reached but also in order to provide knowledge about the convictions held by those involved. In this way, the novel—both *Mary Barton* specifically and the novel as a genre in nineteenth-century Britain—presents as well as evaluates social practices that may have been completely alien to a large number of its readers. This function is not only cognitive but constitutive; Manchester, Chartists, fallen women, and working-class naturalists exist for many of *Mary Barton*'s readers according to their textual representation. Knowledge provided, we should remember, is also knowledge made. Possibilities of meaning and understanding are both broadened and circumscribed by the limits of representation.

Whatever readers may not have known about the lives and attitudes of the laboring population, they were quite familiar with the significance of a strike in a manufacturing town. As one historian has asserted, for a Victorian reader the sentence, "There was a strike in Manchester" was "ominous, a signal of violence to come" (Himmelfarb, *Idea* 506). Violence does indeed follow the declaration of the strike in the form of the operatives' attacks on the "knob-sticks" (scabs) and of course Barton's murder of Harry Carson. But the strike is also preparatory to another act of violence in the parallel plot of the romance of Jem Wilson and Mary Barton. Having learned from Mary's "fallen" aunt Esther that young Carson has been somewhat successfully wooing Mary, Jem seeks out and confronts the manufacturer's son to ascertain Harry's intentions. Harry divulges nothing, and when Jem refuses to let him pass until he gets Harry's word that his intentions are honorable, the verbal confrontation quickly becomes a physical altercation:

> The young man raised his slight cane, and smote the artizan across the face with a stinging stroke. An instant afterwards he lay stretched in the muddy road, Jem standing over him, panting with rage. (230)

This happens after the strike has seized Manchester and has seen Carson and Son emerge as the "most energetic of the masters" in fortifying the resolve of the manufacturers not to give in to the demands of the operatives

(222). The encounter between Jem and Harry takes place at a time when communication between master and man is at its least fluent and when violence is most likely. The narrator even attributes young Carson's exuberant involvement in the masters' strategies to "the excitement of the affair. He liked the attitude of resistance. He was brave, and he liked the idea of personal danger, with which some of the more cautious tried to intimidate the violent among the masters" (222).

In light of the more general social context of John Barton's story and the Manchester strike, the confrontation between Jem and Harry may seem trivial and coincidental; but its novelistic function, aside from helping to tie together two disparate plot lines, emphasizes the connections that reach across class boundaries to bind together master and worker in a community that must operate with open communication and mutual respect. Harry's attitude toward Jem is one of suspicion; he is not intent upon "attending very particularly to the purpose [Jem] had in addressing him" but upon "trying to gather . . . what was the real state of the case" (228). For Harry, any interest Jem may have in Mary's affairs must be selfish and must be ulterior to Jem's reasons for stopping him, though Jem avers that he will tell his reasons in "plain words." Likewise, Jem distrusts Harry's motives in courting Mary and feels justified in accosting, striking, and even threatening the young manufacturer. Of course, this scene is part of the romance plot of the novel and as in most romances there is a hero and a villain. To be sure, Jem is cast in the former role, and Harry (except perhaps in refusing to press charges when Jem flattens him) is portrayed as contemptible. Nevertheless, the short scene between these characters corresponds in its precepts to the social drama that Gaskell is representing in *Mary Barton*. Unwilling to acknowledge the claims of its counterpart, each class contributes to the violence that threatens to destroy completely communicative relations between the classes.

Although it is individuals that *Mary Barton* is most concerned with, as the novel makes clear when the narrator states, "So much for generalities. Let us now return to individuals" (223), it is the generalities that contribute so significantly to relations among individuals and in some measure constitute the conditions of individual existence. And it is through the individuals that generalities are articulated and made apparent. More than forty years after the publication of *Mary Barton*, Charles Booth in his *Life and Labour of the People of London* comments on the difficulty of recognizing the individual relations that bind together an urban populace:

> It is not in country but in town that "terra incognita" needs to be written on our social map. In the country the machinery of human life is plainly to be seen and easily recognized: personal relations bind the whole together. The equipoise on which existing order rests, whether satisfactory or not, is palpable and evident. It is far otherwise with cities, where as to these questions we live in darkness, with doubting hearts and ignorant unnecessary fears. (18)

Admittedly, Booth is writing about "deepest darkest London" in 1889, but there is much in his observation that is at the very center of Gaskell's novel. For in Manchester, a town that had grown from 75,000 residents in 1800 to 300,000 in 1840 (and more than 400,000 by 1848), the whole had become an aggregate, a collection of individuals and interests whose relations to each other were no longer "palpable and evident" except that they were informed by certain economic considerations. The human and the humane often were obscured by the layer of sooty misery that blanketed lower-class existence, creating a cover of darkness that materially and imaginatively separated the two nations. *Mary Barton* is specifically concerned with piercing that darkness, with promoting understanding and eradicating at least some of those "ignorant unnecessary fears." Certainly this informs the work's narrative, for it is a novel of secrets and misunderstanding, of attempting to discern the unsaid and construe the silences that exist within and between communities. Simultaneously, *Mary Barton* is a novel about communication and disrupting those silences in order to make things known.

The failure to communicate, to share across class boundaries in the common discourse of suffering, specifically contributes to the very form the narrative takes, for it ultimately is one of the causes of Harry Carson's death. His inability to conceive of the suffering of the workers and his mockery of their condition singles him out as the manufacturer who must die and is foreshadowed early in the novel when George Wilson goes to the Carsons' to beg an infirmary order for Davenport. The contrast between the two homes is striking and fraught with irony. Mrs. Carson's mood is "very black this morning. She's got a bad headache." To assuage her suffering she orders her breakfast carried upstairs to her chambers, where she will have "the cold partridge as was left yesterday, . . . plenty of cream in her coffee . . . and . . . a roll . . . well buttered" (107). Amy, the youngest Carson daughter, pooh-poohs the cost of a small rose (half a guinea), saying that her father will not begrudge her the money, knowing full well that she cannot "live without flowers and scents" (108). The amount and types of "suffering" in the Carson household are farcical in comparison to the dire conditions of the Davenport cellar. When Wilson enters with his request, it is almost as though the Carsons cannot conceive of the distress Davenport and his family must be experiencing. Mr. Carson can do no more than give the man an out-patient's order for the infirmary, and young Harry, who is extravagant in all things pertaining to his own person, presses five shillings into Wilson's hand for "the poor fellow"—the same sum Barton, who had no money about him whatsoever, was able to contribute to the Davenports after pawning his better coat and his silk handkerchief—"his jewels, his plate his valuables, these were" (99).

While the failure of the Carsons to acknowledge or participate in suffering until Harry's murder demonstrates the discursive responsibilities of living in a society organized according to Christian values, Barton's withdrawal from the community that has always supported him emotionally and spiritually, if not economically, indicates that the internal dissolution of the community of the poor is not only possible, but a substantive threat to society as a whole. After the death of his wife and of George Wilson, the two influences in his life who mitigate his hatred toward the middle and upper classes and who are the conduits, along with Mary, of his relations with his own class, Barton effectively refuses to participate in the community of which he has so long been a part. The sympathetic ties he has always had to those of his own class who are less fortunate than he are transformed into political bonds. Barton's ambivalence toward the religious basis of the rhetoric of suffering, which for the poor is the discursive basis of community, turns to outright denial of religion as a solution to the problems of the working classes. Instead, he opts for Chartism.

At first, Barton has great hopes for Chartism, though, as Gaskell points out, not all who were involved with the 1839 petition were Chartists and the idea that men "could voluntarily assume the office of legislators for a nation, ignorant of its real state," while originating with the Chartists, "came at last to be cherished as a darling child by many and many a one" (127). In the beginning, *Mary Barton* depicts Chartism as positive in many ways and sharing many qualities with religion: it too recognizes the discursive power of suffering; it too attempts to form a community committed to common goals. Ultimately, however, John Barton's turning from religion as the basis of community is as personally and socially devastating as his sister-in-law Esther's turning from the religious teachings of her youth.

Unlike *Alton Locke* in which Chartists are the most moral and the most highly educated of the working classes, *Mary Barton* represents individual Chartists as haggard, forlorn, desperate men, and Chartism, despite its good intentions, becomes the most dangerous of activities. Consequently, it is when Barton can no longer interpret his or other workers' distress in the religious discourse of patience, of suffering silently, that *Mary Barton* is at its most "revolutionary" and most at odds with commonly accepted middle-class values and perceptions of the poor.[8] This is not to say that the novel ever completely abandons its social and moral presuppositions, but in John Barton's attempt to formulate his social existence discursively through politics instead of religion, *Mary Barton* examines those presuppositions and presents the alternative to Christian society—violence.

The move from religion to radical politics, as in *Alton Locke*, is far less difficult for the laborer than one might at first imagine. And, as in *Alton Locke*, Chartism is described in religious terms: "John Barton became a Chartist, a Communist, all that is commonly called wild and visionary. Ay! but being visionary is something. It shows a soul, a being not altogether sensual; a creature who looks forward for others, if not for himself" (220). Such a description portrays the *activity* of becoming a Chartist as an attempt at creating oneself in social and non-material terms. It represents the consequences of the increased intellectual activity of the urban factory operative as Engels describes him. Barton is partially propelled toward becoming a Chartist through his "overpowering thought": "rich and poor; why are they so separate, so distinct, when God has made them all? It is not His will, that their interests are so far apart. Whose doing is it?" (219). Reason, however, fails Barton's uneducated mind. He must resort to feeling, and the only emotion "that remained clear and undisturbed in the tumult of his heart, was hatred to the one class and keen sympathy with the other" (219).

Emotion without wisdom, however, "with all its effects, too often works but harm" (219). Gaskell's Unitarianism is most apparent in this statement, which stops short of a complete rethinking of the failure of religion for Barton. Unitarianism, as the title of Dennis Wigmore-Beddoes' book asserts, is a "religion that thinks" (*A Religion that Thinks: A Psychological Study*). Reason, as well as spirit and sentiment, is the responsibility of the individual who seeks to live a Christian life, and indeed underlies the very basis of Christian society. Within Unitarianism one is as likely—perhaps more likely given the Unitarian denial of the essential depravity of human nature—to be wrong-headed as wrong-hearted.[9] This is Barton's flaw, for he does not have the capacity to act out of wisdom (which Gaskell attributes to education); rather he acts "to the best of his judgement, but it was a widely erring judgement" (219).

Thus if we return to the passage in which Barton "became a Chartist, a Communist," we see that despite the religious troping and the sympathetic tone of the comparison of Chartists to visionaries and men of souls, also at work is the condemnation of such activity—a condemnation the passage itself attempts to soften by expounding on the positive rather than the pejorative effects of being "wild and visionary." Nevertheless, the passage comes at the end of an extended comparison between the working classes—whom Gaskell calls "the uneducated"—and Frankenstein's monster, who despite "many human qualities" was "ungifted with a soul, a knowledge of the difference of good and evil." Rising up to life, writes Gaskell, the people "gaze on us [the middle classes] with mute reproach: Why have we made them what they are: a powerful monster, yet without the inner means for peace and happiness?" (219–20). Though Chartist activity may indicate that the working classes, despite their "creation" by the middle classes, are not without souls (the soul being for Gaskell the seat both of sympathy and of the knowledge of good and evil), they are still "creatures," and attempting a political rather than a religious solution. Whatever the intent of the Chartists, because their activities are politically and not religiously informed they are effectively without reason, or at least without right reason, and thus their efforts must inevitably lead to confrontation rather than communication.

One immediately sees both the disturbing and reassuring effects such a representation must have had on the manufacturing classes in 1848. On the one hand is the justification of a class structure which places some above others; for whatever reason, be it innate ability, or industriousness, or the intercession of Providence, good things can happen to members of the working classes. Mr. Carson, formerly a factory operative, becomes one of the most successful mill owners in Manchester, and Jem Wilson looks bound to recreate the narrative of Carson's success in the "uncompromised New World" (Williams, *Culture and Society* 91). This creates a flexibility within the class structure, and further justifies the positions in society of those who have risen. They are there, the argument goes, because they are more able, because they are *meant* to be in positions of authority.

On the other hand is *Mary Barton*'s questioning of the factory system as it is run by those who have risen to authority. In many ways this is much more disquieting to middle-class sensibilities than an outright attack on the system such as one reads in a work like *Helen Fleetwood* or *Michael Armstrong*. Gaskell's narrator, though critical of the abuses of the system, is after all mediating her observations from a middle-class perspective. She speaks of the manufacturing classes of Manchester as "us." The working classes "gaze on us," she writes; they "ask us" why everyone does not suffer during hard times. She knows that this is an uninformed perspective from which the working classes judge their employers. She knows the "truth in such matters." But knowing the truth does not mitigate the conditions of the poor, nor does it correct their perceptions of the middle classes. Rather, it makes the factory system seem all the more constraining to both manufacturer and operative, and it makes the threat of violence all the more imminent.

Gaskell's solutions to the problems she raises in *Mary Barton* have often been criticized, and it has become a commonplace to speak of the "failure of Gaskell's art."[10] Certainly it is difficult to ignore the contrivance of the narrative resolution: Barton dies, guilty but redeemed. Carson, through his suffering and from talking with Job Legh and Jem Wilson after Barton's confession, becomes a manufacturer who works toward the fulfillment of what has come to be his greatest wish: "that a perfect understanding and complete confidence and love, might exist between masters and men" (460). Jem Wilson and Mary move to Toronto to begin a new life together in a clean, spacious world where the past has no force. Even Jem's attempts to protect Mary from his mother's irritability and possibly misspoken word by not telling the old woman of John Barton's part in Harry Carson's murder is an unnecessary precaution. Years later, after a chance reference to the event, Jem questions his mother and finds she has known of the details of the crimes for years and has never once used it against Mary. This example of the lack of the past's influence on the Wilsons' present circumstances, together with the removal of the Wilsons to Toronto, completes a theme of nostalgia that runs throughout the novel, from the scene in Green Heys Fields, to old Alice's reminiscences and delirium, to a final pastoral ideal that can also accommodate industrialization.

Despite what might be considered literary sleight of hand at its close, *Mary Barton* contributes to the entire discussion of the problems raised by industrialism in a way that most novels dismiss. This novel represents industrialization as a fact of life that cannot, in itself, be significantly changed. It shapes the lives of workers and manufacturers, and it can be interpreted and understood only in its effects on those lives. Thus, for the workers the factory system is both livelihood and enslavement; for the manufacturers it is the source of their wealth but also the breeder of a force that could destroy the status, privilege, and power that wealth has purchased. For both classes, industrialization is neither completely benevolent nor malevolent; it contains its own negative.

In confronting the negative, in seeing what good can come from it, *Mary Barton* offers the possibility of communication, community, and solution to the difficulties each class faces. Like most middle-class observers of the problems of the Victorian poor, Gaskell relies heavily on the belief that what is in the best interest of the middle classes is in the best interest of society as a whole. But unlike *Alton Locke*, which seeks to raise the working classes to the spiritual and intellectual level of their employers, or *Michael Armstrong*, which represents the manufacturing classes as deserving of retribution, *Mary Barton* reforms representations of industrialization by presenting the factory system as problematic for all classes, and by demonstrating that one class is as committed to its interpretation of the successes and deficiencies of the system as the other. At the end of the novel, when Jem, Job, and Mr. Carson meet to go over the facts of the murder and fall into a conversation as to the cause of Barton's actions, Carson is depicted as a reasonable, just man, who, like most men, has his own best interests at heart. Yet he is not a Bounderby any more than Barton was ever an Owenite. This novel is not concerned with presenting what would have been considered the extremists in each class, but those who are well informed of their personal and their class's interests and who are themselves typical members of their class. It is among these people that dialogue must take place, so that if the "system" of industrialization cannot change, then as Job Legh says, at least there will be "the inclination to try and help the evils which come like blights at times over the manufacturing places" (458).

When Gaskell writes that the duties "connected to the manufacturing system" are not yet completely understood, and that she is unable to perceive how the "evils" associated with it might be remedied, though "there is no harm in directing the attention to the existence of such evils," she highlights *Mary Barton*'s interpretive enterprise, which is to bring to a common understanding the attitudes of worker and mill owner toward the *necessity* of industrialization. And while she is continually concerned to mediate between the interpretations of the two classes, and thus accommodates her narrative to that mediation, the fact remains that in attempting such a negotiation, she calls the very project of the social-problem novel to account. Yet despite the criticism of some, such as Coral Lansbury, who has argued that the weakly resolved plot lines of *Mary Barton* demonstrate the failure of Gaskell's inquiry into the factory system to provide the answers for improving the conditions of the poor (22), such failures do little to dampen the spirit of inquiry that such a novel fosters. After *Mary Barton* there are no easy solutions; there is no reverting to an idyllic past. For many the past becomes instead the standard against which to measure the present, as Gaskell indicates in *North and South* when she writes of manufacturers who "defy the old limits of possibility, in a kind of fine intoxication, caused by recollections of what had been achieved and what yet should be" (45). It is as though there is no longer any way to think about the world— past, present, or future—without considering the effects of the industrial system.

It is in novels such as *Mary Barton* and *Alton Locke* that we get ways of reading those effects that provide new ways of organizing and interrogating the world of Victorian England. In each of these novels, the discourse of industrialization does not *replace* other important discourses, but rather becomes the object of interpretation and inquiry by them. Thus, while we may speak of industrialization shaping the everyday lives of the people of Victorian Great Britain, we must also remember that industrialization—at least as some sort of monolithic public discourse—is evaluated, rethought, and at some level even accepted in these social-problem novels of the second quarter of the nineteenth century. The other interpretive enterprises it mingles with certainly are shaped by it; the paradoxical yet undeniable connections between Chartism and religion are a perfect example; but as we see in *Alton Locke* and *Mary Barton*, there is no such thing as the "discourse of industrialism" per se. Rather, through the efforts of these two works we see there are many variants, ways of understanding the concept of industrialism that reformulate it along the paradigmatic lines of a number of discourses. It is in this way that we can speak of the "novelistic reformation of British industrialism," for in becoming part of the discourse of the novel in nineteenth-century England, industrialism in some ways becomes more accessible, more understandable, even if the material effects it generates cannot be solved in the pages of a novel. And it is in this combination of discursive possibilities that Victorian culture and society is generated as much as it is "reflected."

Epilogue

In the epigraph to the first chapter of *Daniel Deronda*, George Eliot writes that we "can do nothing without the make believe of a beginning. Even Science, the strict measurer, is obliged to start with a make believe unit. . . . No retrospect will take us to the true beginning." Her story sets out, she says, with "but a fraction of that all presupposing fact" (35). So it is too with endings. Even when something is at an end, in many ways its conclusion is only illusory, a convenient place to stop but by no means a finale. Rather, endings serve as peaks of observation, places to pause, to examine what has come before, and—perhaps—to serve as make-believe places for yet other beginnings.

Because this study has concerned itself with a particular moment in cultural history and is not a study of the development of the novel per se, I want to forego what might seem the obligatory closing: suggestions about how novels published after 1850 were engaged in interpretive competition with other discourses. Instead I want to return to some of the theoretical and textual implications that *Novel Possibilities* has raised. The issues that have surfaced in the preceding pages, concerns with class, morality, and the formation of both subjectivity and agency, are directly linked to my conviction that novels in the nineteenth century, especially in those years between the first Reform Bill and the demise of Chartism, function constitutively; in effect they function as discourse. Institutionalized, however loosely, they do cultural work that is more than epiphenomenal, and more than "merely" interpretive. And while they may indeed help to resolve temporarily some ideological contradictions within the cultural matrix, they also are instrumental in the formation of that matrix. Their interpretive achievements create possibilities for action, both resistive and consensual, as well as offer paradigms of understanding and being. Thus novels, and in this study specifically social-problem novels, go one better than Raymond Williams's claim that they make sense of a changing world; they help to make the very world they presume to interpret. By providing representational strategies to other, competing interpretive enterprises, from parliamentary politics to religion, novels serve ontological as well as epistemological functions.

One of the most important of these functions is the formation of identity that runs like a leitmotif throughout this work. Implicit in each of the separate parts of *Novel Possibilities* is the issue of the construction of individual subjectivities upon models that strive to reach across class boundaries even as they are continually inscribing them. In "Trading Places" political agency shifts from empowerment by the aristocracy and the voices of Peel, Macaulay, and Disraeli via Harry Coningsby, to empowerment by the emerging middle classes. Class identity for the political subject remains aristocratic, but agency resides in the class below. "Observation, Representation, and the *Report on the Sanitary Condition*" figures both political agency and subjectivity as clearly aligned with a middle-class identity, but the *object* (and, as Judith Butler might argue, the abject) of politics is the working poor. Written as moral and cultural failures when they do not affiliate themselves with middle-class assumptions, these people are nevertheless also always written *as* working class, even when their subjectivities are thoroughly constructed according to middle-class ideologies. Part III, "Washed in the Blood of the Lamb," implies that the move from Chadwick's *Report* to *Alton Locke*'s "respectable" Chartists to Gaskell's idealized national community that subsumes the two nations and is based upon mutual suffering is tantamount to making the working class, rather than the middle class, the model of national community.

The slippage of class identity that occurs in these works is always articulated from a middle-class perspective. Even when the poor "speak" in Chadwick's text, their voices are heard through a class-biased filter. In all these texts some sort of containment is continually at work, restraining how far it is possible to rethink class as a category of identification. Yet there is also always the impetus to attempt that rethinking. The movement between these two impulses is itself a problematizing of class that both allowed for change and kept new ways of thinking about who one was from entirely upsetting the order of things. *Mary Barton* is a perfect illustration of the tension between maintaining the status quo and realizing that things must change. By making the working classes more potentially dangerous—Chartism, political murders—and yet also more selflessly philanthropic, Gaskell writes working-class identity as a subject position that is both socially disruptive and ameliorative. The working classes have farther to go toward "civilization" than the middle classes, but also are apparently able to assimilate middle- class communal ideals more readily and successfully than the middle classes themselves.

The perceived gap between the "two nations" that infuses all these works, from Peel to Gaskell, and their attempts to overcome that schism while maintaining class distinctions, point to the cultural difficulties that attend a bifurcated national identity. This may have seemed an insular problem in the 1840s and perhaps even soluble with appropriate types of reform. Of course as Mary Poovey implies in her work on Chadwick as well as in her important *Uneven Developments*, the emerging discussion of the juridical subjectivity of women complicates the problem of conceiving of any type of national identity. Further, as I have argued in my own analysis of Chadwick and gender, even after the "age of equipoise," class considerations, though perhaps more subtle, still exerted substantial pressure on subject formation. Just as important are the ways in which race enters into the mix after the middle of the century. With the extension of the Empire both economically and politically, issues of "Englishness" (as well as "Britishness") move beyond national boundaries and take on global significance.

I would avoid claiming that there is some sort of development, in the evolutionary sense, from the identity issues forged in the texts taken up in these pages to the more complex discourses over identity that emerge in the later part of the century. Nevertheless, I do maintain that the form of many of the concerns and claims of those later discourses are rehearsed in the texts of the 1840s and discussions of class. The novel, while providing a site of containment for these potentially volatile discourses and their ideological assumptions, is also the place where many of these assumptions are challenged, where the fundamental shape of discourse changes, and how a new and different statement enters into and contributes to new ways of thinking and knowing. Novels become alternative ways of forming culture as well as alternative ways of knowing and even being in culture.

Reading and evaluating those alternatives through texts that may seem all too culturally mainstream, if not necessarily canonical, require one to remember that however useful certain heuristic generalities like "discourse" or "class" are for discussion, all texts in some way challenge whatever general tendencies we may wish to impute to them. Just as no texts are produced outside society, neither does any "dominant" discourse completely subsume a text. Practicing criticism in this way necessarily means increasing one's familiarity with historical particularities; it means realizing that what may be considered the most minor statement has constitutive force; it means recognizing that the documents one chooses to investigate as texts, in my case works like *The Report on the Sanitary Condition*, *Coningsby*, or *Mary Barton*, not only partake of practices such as politics, religion, and industrialization, they also contribute to the way politics, religion, and industrialization may be imagined, thus experienced and lived. It means attempting to come to terms not only with the objects of literary study as agents of change but with our own critical practices as, in their best moments, challenges to epistemological and ontological boundaries. It reminds us of our own cultural work and the novel possibilities that work presents.

Notes

Introduction

1. Compare William James's description of pragmatic method, which must not be content to rest on closure, or what he called a "solving name" such as "God," "Reason," or the "Absolute." Instead pragmatism must "bring out of each word its practical cash-value, set it at work within the stream of [one's] experience. [The pragmatic method] appears less as a solution, then, than as a program for more work, and more particularly as an indication of the ways in which existing realities may be *changed*" (31–32). James implies that the world we make with our ways of seeing is only one of any number of possible realities; yet it is, once made, a reality that may be felt, experienced, described, and changed.

2. See also Judith Newton, "History as Usual? Feminism and the 'New Historicism,'" and Ellen Pollak, "Feminism and the New Historicism: A Tale of Difference or the Same Old Story?"

3. Admittedly, Gaskell's novels have been steadily recuperated since Winifred Gérin's *Life* and Coral Lansbury's *Elizabeth Gaskell* appeared in the mid 1970s and the cultural and literary history done in books like Hilary Schor's excellent *Scheherezade in the Marketplace* (1992) has helped to renew interest in *Mary Barton*. *Coningsby* has not fared so well, however; discussions of that first installment of the Young England trilogy have been the domain primarily of political historians and Disraeli biographers. Similarly, critiques of *Alton Locke*, at least until quite recently, have been relegated mostly to encyclopedic histories of the novel. There are, of course, some very notable exceptions such as Catherine Gallagher's *The Industrial Reformation of English Fiction*, Louis Cazamian's *The Social Novel in England, 1830–1850*, and Raymond Williams's *Culture and Society*.

4. See Catherine Gallagher, *The Industrial Reformation of English Fiction 1832–1867* (1985); Daniel Cottom, *Social Figures: George Eliot, Social History, and Literary Representation* (1987); D. A. Miller, *The Novel and the Police* (1987); Nancy Armstrong, *Desire and Domestic Fiction: A Political History of the Novel* (1987); Rosemarie Bodenheimer, *The Politics of Story in Victorian Social Fiction* (1988); and Mary Poovey, *Uneven Developments: The Ideological Work of Gender in Mid-Victorian England* (1989).

5. According to this reasoning the very term "Victorian" should be abandoned, for it insinuates far more than the temporal boundaries of a period of study; it suggests an undifferentiated set of social, political, and economic practices and standards that misrepresents the variety, competition, and turmoil of public and private languages that were nineteenth-century England. No doubt it is the un-

problematized use of the term by a large number of literary critics that made the title, not to mention the subject matter, of Steven Marcus's book *The Other Victorians* so effective. On the other hand, of course, for a great many literary critics and historians the term "Victorian" does not and never has suggested a homogeneous world-view but rather underscores the diversity of the period. Walter Houghton's *The Victorian Frame of Mind*, however unfortunate contemporary critics may believe its title to be, exemplifies this second usage of "Victorian."

6. In this sense I share the intentions, if not the results, of some of the "new historicists." Certainly I agree with Louis Montrose when he writes that the new historicism is new "in its refusal of unproblematized distinctions between 'literature' and 'history', between 'text' and 'context'; new in resisting a prevalent tendency to posit and privilege a unified and autonomous individual—whether an Author or Work—to be set against a social or literary background" (6).

7. The issue of totality in Marxist theory is far more complex than I present it here. Jameson's statement about dynamic totalities is explicitly traceable at least as far back as to Georg Lukács, who in 1948 writes, "The materialist-dialectical conception of totality means first of all the concrete unity of interacting contradictions . . . ; secondly, the systematic relativity of all totality both upwards and downwards (which means that all totality is made of totalities subordinated to it, and also that the totality in question is, at the same time, overdetermined by totalities of a higher complexity . . .) and thirdly, the historical relativity of all totality, namely that the totality-character of all totality is changing, disintegrating, confined to a determinate, concrete historical period" (*The Tasks of Marxist Philosophy in the New Democracy* 12; qtd. in Bottomore et al. 479). Of course not all Marxist critics agree. For example, Ernesto Laclau and Chantal Mouffe in their book, *Hegemony and Social Strategy: Towards a Radical Democratic Politics*, argue that "the incomplete character of every totality necessarily leads us to abandon, as a terrain of analysis, the premise of '*society*' as a sutured and self-defined totality. 'Society' is not a valid object of discourse. There is no single underlying principle fixing—and hence constituting—the whole field of differences" (111). For them the order of society is only "the unstable order of a system of differences that is always threatened from the outside." While this partly rebuts the Lukács-Jameson position, it raises certain questions as to whether any "system"—even a system of differences—is not itself a totality. For more on this issue see Martin Jay, *Marxism and Totality: The Adventures of a Concept from Lukács to Habermas.*

8. Some case can be made for Bulwer's *Paul Clifford* as an early political novel, although its political theme is really more an allegory than a direct dealing with politics as a *topic* of the novel. *Coningsby* is, to my knowledge, the first major work of fiction in which politics is not only a topic but the focus of the novel.

9. Friedrich Engels's *The Condition of the Working Class in England, 1844* demonstrates that in places like Manchester, however, the middle and upper orders did their best to avoid the lower classes.

Chapter 1

1. This is especially true in light of the July Revolution in France. See Elie Halévy's first chapter in *The Triumph of Reform*.

2. Contexts are not constituted only linguistically, though they are mediated linguistically to those outside them (i.e., historians or literary critics). See Fredric Jameson 82. See also Pocock 13.

3. For a discussion of calling one's own paradigm into account see Kuhn, *The Structure of Scientific Revolutions*; on antagonism creating meaning possibilities see Pêcheux, *Language, Semantics, and Ideology: Stating the Obvious*.

4. In a speech of July 5, 1831, Macaulay discusses his notion of "true statesmanship, which at once animating and gently curbing the honest enthusiasm of millions guides it safely and steadily to a happy goal" (*Speeches* 28–29). In this speech Macaulay is comparing "true statesmanship" to any type of political extremism. When in the speech of March 19, 1832 he accuses the Tories of placing general doctrines before practical considerations, he is including them in his definition of extremism, making them—in Macaulay's view—no better statesmen than the most ardent radicals (see *Hansard* 11:457).

5. After the repeal of the Corn Laws, Macaulay relented in his severe criticism of Peel, hailing him as a great commercial reformer. Nonetheless, Macaulay never "forgot or forgave the way Peel had dealt with the Catholic question. It was this that made the Tories for him a party that would conduct 'a pertinacious, vehement, provoking opposition to safe and reasonable change, and that [would] then, in some moment of fear or caprice. . .bring in, and fling on the table in a fit of desperation or levity, some plan which will loosen the very foundations of society'" (Hamburger 40).

6. By no means do I intend to suggest that other groups using other idioms of political language did not exist in Parliament during this period. The Philosophic Radicals, O'Connell's infamous tail, and the ultra-Tories all exerted considerable influence within the legislature; but within the scheme I have set out these groups can best be understood as employing idioms either more or less historically oriented, or more or less willing to instigate change than those in the political middle.

7. "In the practice of politics . . . there are certain truly incorporated modes of what are nevertheless, within those terms, real oppositions, that are felt and fought out. Their existence within the incorporation is recognizable by the fact that, whatever the degree of internal conflict or internal variation, they do not in practice go beyond the limits of the central effective and dominant definitions. This is true, for example, of the practice of Parliamentary politics, though its internal oppositions are real" (Williams, *Problems* 40).

8. See Kuhn, *The Structure of Scientific Revolutions*; Richard Rorty, *Consequences of Pragmatism*; Stanley Fish, *Is There a Text in This Class?* and Nelson Goodman, *Ways of Worldmaking*.

Chapter 2

1. Before the opening of the 1844 Parliament, Peel snubbed Disraeli by not sending him the customary circular summons to attend the meeting of Parliament. Disraeli was much affected and remonstrated with Peel. Peel replied that Disraeli's past opposition had led him to believe he was justified in not sending him the party summons, adding however that it gave him great satisfaction "to infer from your letter—as I trust I am justified in inferring—that my impressions were mistaken and my scruples unnecessary" (quoted in Monypenny and Buckle 2:187).

2. Although Wellington, Lyndhurst, Peel, and other prominent political figures are important to Disraeli's discussion of contemporary politics, they never really appear as characters in the novel.

3. Disraeli is particularly heavy handed in this. In chapter 2 of Book IV, Coningsby, while visiting Manchester, meets a Mr. G. O. A. Head who speaks of time in the new language of the railroads, "Well, there's a late train . . . 3.15; you will be there by 4.30"; and who insists that while Manchester is a "booked place" and looked upon "as a sort of mother, and all that sort of thing," the town "is behind the times . . . and won't do in this age. The long and short of it is, Manchester is gone by" (181–83). This trip and his side trip to Millbank are directly juxtaposed in Book IV to his first visit to the ancestral seat that bears his name, Coningsby Castle, where the marquess has established a household reminiscent of times gone by. The old noble receives Coningsby "with a dignity of affection that would have become Louis XIV, and then, in the high manner of the old court, kissed him on each cheek" (208).

4. That Sidonia is using the accepted Utilitarian interpretation of "democracy" and not (at that time) Mill's is evident from the context of Mill's own work on the subject up to the composition of *Coningsby*. By the publication of "The Spirit of the Age" in 1831, Mill had already begun to doubt certain aspects of democratic representation, and nowhere in "Civilisation" does he mention representative government. In 1829 his faith in his father's "conception of philosophical Method" had been shaken by Macaulay's review of the "Essay on Government," and the younger Mill had begun to rethink his own approach to politics, concluding that "politics must be a deductive science" and distancing himself from the principles shared by most radicals (see *Autobiography* 96).

For Mill, the institution of representative government does not necessarily mean democracy. In fact, as he says he learned from de Tocqueville, one of the dangers of representative democracy is the possibility of its "degeneration into the only despotism of which in the modern world there is a real danger—the absolute rule of the head of the executive over a congregation of isolated individuals, all equals but all slaves" (116). The impetus for democracy, then, "the government of public opinion," is "the spirit of the age"; and the possibility for preserving the validity of public opinion depends on the efficacy of culture and the "march of the mind." Yet Mill makes the limits he would impose on the franchise quite clear in his writings from the period, including the 1839 "Reorganization of the Reform Party," in which he upbraids fellow radicals for committing themselves to universal suffrage when it is neither necessary nor desirable to give the working classes political power in their present state of culture. See also his "Thoughts on Parliamentary Reform," published as a pamphlet in 1859, but composed in part on the occasion of the first Reform Bill. In it he offers his scheme of plural voting and proportional representation, which even further alienated him from the radicals.

Chapter 3

1. There is no substantive evidence that Disraeli ever read Carlyle. According to Blake, Disraeli "did not read much contemporary literature apart from works of friends like Bulwer—and very few of his friends belonged to literary circles, which he tended to despise" (191). Regardless, there is little way someone as attuned to public attitudes as Disraeli could have escaped at least a cursory knowledge of Carlyle's thought and his more notable phrasings.

2. At one point in *Coningsby*, Everingham takes a glass of Seltzer, thus emphasizing his clear-headed, cold-blooded, and rather abstemious character.

3. Disraeli's comments are perceptive and similar criticisms have been the focus of much discussion of Bentham's ideas. At one point Bentham himself sharply criticized Locke for reducing ethics to a question of definition (see James Steintrager, *Bentham*). As for the notion of competition among interests, many have argued that Bentham believed in a natural convergence of separate interests, that the greatest happiness of the greatest number automatically results. This is Elie Halévy's view when he writes, "Since it is recognized that the predominating motives in human nature are egoistic, and further that the human species lives and survives, it must be admitted that the various egoisms harmonize of their own accord and automatically bring about the good of the species" (*The Growth of Philosophical Radicalism* 15). This interpretation, however, fails to explain the main objective of Bentham's life work: to teach the legislator that "the proper and only useful business of Morality & Legislation is to establish and illustrate this connection between private and public interest" (University College Bentham Manuscripts, box 71; quoted in Steintrager 21). See also Mary Mack, *Jeremy Bentham: An Odyssey of Ideas 1748–1792* and David Lyons, *In the Interest of the Governed*.

4. Of course, Henry Sidney's argument is every bit as guilty of begging the question as Everingham's. It is not at all clear that an English peasantry *ever* existed in the ways that Sidney (and Disraeli, of course) assert. And while *Coningsby* works at making its fictive representations seem more veracious than the "real" representations of parliamentary party politics, it depends on a "history" of England that is every bit as fictitious and tendentious as the novel itself.

5. Disraeli goes to great lengths to establish the original mechanisms of existing political institutions. For example, in chapter 3, Book I, he offers his explanation for the principle of representation, basing it on his notions of the "true estates of the realm." See also *Vindication* 68–85.

6. The character Sidonia, apparently a composite of Baron de Rothschild and Disraeli himself, says to Harry in the portion I have deleted from the quota-

tion: "It was not Reason that besieged Troy; it was not Reason that sent forth the Saracen from the Desert to conquer the world; that inspired the Crusades; that instituted the Monastic orders; it was not Reason that produced the Jesuits; above all, it was not Reason that created the French Revolution." If, as, the novel tells us, Sidonia had "seen and read everything," he must have had a penchant for Carlyle and a particular dislike of Hegel.

7. The term "press" is problematic. In one sense, it no doubt means simply "news media." However, given the increase in the reading public and the increase in publishing that I have already documented as well as the goals described in Disraeli's 1849 preface to *Coningsby*, it seems more appropriate to understand the term to mean all publicly available printed matter, whether newspaper, novel, poem, or pamphlet. As for the efficient and fair representation of public opinion expressed in the press, one should remember that although literacy was on the rise in England and Scotland, the periodical press especially was owned and controlled by the middle classes. Quarterlies such as the *Edinburgh*, *Westminster*, and *Quarterly Reviews* were closely allied to parties or factions. And while daily newspapers were extremely popular, taxation made them prohibitively expensive for the working classes. Unstamped papers, such as Henry Hetherington's *Poor Man's Guardian*, often successfully filled the need for newspapers which represented working-class interests. In 1836, however, the Whigs reduced the newspaper stamp to a penny, and the price of London dailies fell to fivepence. Now in direct competition with affordable "legitimate" newspapers, the unstamped press was deprived of the margin that had made it profitable to risk prosecution. As a result, almost all untaxed papers went out of business, depriving the most impoverished readers of their newspapers and their voice in the periodical press. See Patricia Hollis, *The Pauper Press: A Study in Working-Class Radicalism of the 1830s*, Joel H. Weiner, *The War of the Unstamped: The Movement to Repeal the British Newspaper Tax, 1830–1836*; Stephen Koss, *The Rise and Fall of the Political Press in Britain: The Nineteenth Century*; and Robert K. Webb, "The Victorian Reading Public," in *The New Pelican Guide to English Literature: From Dickens to Hardy*.

8. Fish has considerably modified the position he took when this paper was first delivered as a lecture at Columbia University in 1984. There he offered a general theory of change:

> Change of one kind occurs when already-in-place principles of relevance and noticeability cause an interpretive attention to be paid to something new, which is not really new at all since it is immediately seen as an instance or modification of a relationship internal to the community. And (2) change of another, and in some sense deeper, kind occurs when the principles of relevance and noticeability are themselves altered by confronting those who hold them with principles of a greater generality and arguing that a commitment to those principles requires that more be taken into account than had hitherto been assumed. ("Change" 13)

My thanks to Professor Fish for allowing me to quote from the unpublished version of his paper.

9. This is not the only similarity between Fish and Disraeli; both argue that theory follows from particular situations rather than vice versa; compare "What I want to say is that theories, rather than governing practices, are always the consequences of practices already in place and really are interim reports that codify recognized practices; otherwise, the theory couldn't even be read or understood" ("Theory and Consequences: An Interview with Stanley Fish" *Critical Texts*, 2,1 [1984]: 5) and "It would appear that this scheme [of forming political institutions on abstract principles of theoretic science] originated in the fallacy of supposing that theories produce circumstances, whereas the very converse of the proposition is correct, and circumstances indeed produce theories" (*Vindication* 15).

Chapter 4

1. There seems little doubt, however, that Dickens made a good deal more use of the *Report* when he wrote *Our Mutual Friend* some twenty-two years later. Consider the following descriptions from the *Report*:

> In one part of the street there is a dunghill—yet it is too large to be called a dunghill. I do not misstate its size when I say it contains a hundred cubic yards of impure filth, collected from all parts of town. It is never removed; it is the stock-in-trade of a person who deals in dung; he retails it by the cartful. (119)

And:

> The dungheaps received all filth which the swarm of wretched inhabitants could give; and we learned that a considerable part of the rent of the houses was paid by the produce of the dungheaps. . . .The dwellers in these courts had converted their shame into a kind of money by which their lodging was paid. (98)

In *Our Mutual Friend* these dunghills are transformed into Boffin's Mounds; far from being farmyard-like dunghills, for Boffin these heterogeneous heaps of refuse are a source not only of money but also of a certain beauty and a continuity of life:

> Ay, ay, that's another thing. I may sell *them*, though I should be sorry to see the neighbourhood deprived of 'em too. It'll look but a poor dead flat without the Mounds. Still, I don't say that I'm going to keep 'em always there for the sake of the beauty of the landscape. . . . I ain't a scholar in much, Rokesmith, but I'm a pretty fair scholar in dust. I can price the Mounds to a fraction, and I know how they can be best disposed of, and likewise that they take no harm by standing where they do. (185)

2. See Gertrude Himmelfarb, *Idea of Poverty* 155–76; and Finer, 73–89. For a discussion of the Malthusian world of *Oliver Twist* see Marcus, *Pickwick to Dombey* 64–67.

3. The success (or at least the availability) of the *Sanitary Condition Report* was even greater than that of the Poor Law *Report*. One tradition has it that Chadwick ordered 100,000 copies of an edition he had printed in quarto size. Other, more reliable sources indicate that 10,000 copies were sold or given away. Chadwick told Brougham in July 1842 that "upwards of 20,000 copies of the Report have been sold." This number does not include the more than 3,000 copies that were distributed free by the Commission in the first two months. Certainly Chadwick was determined to see that the *Report* was distributed. Having published the *Report* in July 1842, in September Chadwick made inquiries as to advertising it in the *Times* and the *Morning Chronicle* (Finer 55).

4. Patrick Brantlinger, "Bluebooks, the Social Organism, and the Victorian Novel"; also his *The Spirit of Reform: British Literature and Politics, 1832–1867*, which discusses the relation between novels and bluebooks in terms of the political consequences of each. See also Sheila Smith, "Blue Books and Victorian Novels" and her book-length work *The Other Nation: The Poor in English Novels of the 1840s and 1850s*.

5. See also H. S. Nelson, "*Our Mutual Friend* and Mayhew's *London Labour and the London Poor*"; Himmelfarb, "The Culture of Poverty" in *Idea of Poverty*, 307–70, and Christopher Herbert, "Rat Worship and Taboo in Mayhew's London."

6. Despite the rather small amount of critical commentary on *Sketches by Boz*, more of the same can be adduced for both contemporaneous and more recent criticism. For example, John Forster in his *Life* writes of the *Sketches*: "Things are painted literally as they are. . . . It is a book . . . containing unusually truthful observation of a sort of life between the middle class and the low. . . . It was a picture of every-day London at its best and worst, in its humours and enjoyments as well as its suffering and sins, pervaded everywhere. . . with the absolute reality of the things depicted" (1:93). "As an example of what is now called 'documentary,' " writes Thea Holme in her introduction to the Oxford Illustrated Edition, "the *Sketches* deserve a unique place in literature. . . . More than half this volume's contents are facts: facts observed with an astonishing precision and wealth of detail" (viii).

Chapter 5

1. See Ruth Richardson, *Death, Dissection, and the Destitute* for more on the connections between the poor and the dissecting table.

2. The link to panopticism is historical as well as Foucauldian and theoretical. Chadwick was particularly enamored of the concept of the panopticon and based his recommendations for the organization of Poor Law unions and workhouses upon its principles—recommendations that were only slightly modified in their acceptance. When Chadwick began to collect the data for the *Report on the Sanitary Condition*, he utilized the Poor Law bureaucracy and his position as secretary of the Poor Law Commission to amass vast amounts of information about the poor in England, Wales, and Scotland.

3. For more on the advent of an inspectorate see David Roberts, *Victorian Origins of the British Welfare State*.

4. See Herbert, "Rat Worship and Taboo in Mayhew's London"; Stallybrass and White, "The City: The Sewer, the Gaze, and the Contaminating Touch" in *The Politics and Poetics of Transgression*; H.J. Dyos and D. A. Reeder, "Slums and Suburbs" in *The Victorian City*; Gareth Stedman Jones, *Outcast London*; and A. S. Wohl, "Unfit for Human Habitation," in *The Victorian City*.

5. For discussions of the use of metonymy in realism see Arac, *Commissioned Spirits*, especially "Metaphor and Metonymy in Little Dorrit," 34–47; J. Hillis Miller, "The Fiction of Realism: *Sketches by Boz, Oliver Twist*, and Cruikshank's Illustrations"; and two seminal works by Roman Jakobson, "Two Aspects of Language and Two Types of Aphasic Disturbances" and "Closing Statement: Linguistics and Poetics."

6. Recourse to drink was one of the most disabling and widespread habits of the lower classes. Kay's statistics on Manchester inns and licensed gin shops find that more than two thirds of these establishments were located in six of the town's fourteen districts. Four of these districts, writes Kay, "may be conceived to represent most correctly the exclusively labouring population;" the two others, though not so heavily populated by the lower classes, were immediately adjacent to at least one of these four (58). Nor did these lack for business. One of Kay's informants observed "the number of persons entering a gin shop during eight successive Saturday nights, and at various periods from seven o'clock until ten," on average, was 412 per hour (58).

Kay's findings hardly allow for extrapolation, but at that rate, the 674 liquor- or beer-serving establishments in the six districts Kay names could serve over 833,000 people in three hours on any given Saturday evening. The population of the township of Manchester in 1831 was estimated at 142,000.

7. In a section of the *Report* entitled "Contrast in the Economy of Families" Chadwick provides 10 comparative instances of the ways in which one family, though earning less than its counterpart, manages to live "decently." The following is typical of the comparisons and is Chadwick's third example:

> John Salt of Carr Bank (labourer), wages 12s. per week; a wife, and one child aged 15: he is a drunken, disorderly fellow, and very much in debt. George Hall, of Carr Bank (labourer), wages 10s. per week; has reared ten children; he is in comfortable circumstances.

8. It is not clear from Chadwick's evidence whether the numbers he cites are from London or Westminster or both. Nor is it clear when he cites the instance of the Bollington baths, in which "25 to 70 or 80" baths are taken weekly, how significant a portion of the entire working population of Bollington these numbers are. See p. 317 of the *Report*.

9. Hans-Georg Gadamer in *Truth and Method* comments upon what he identifies as the dialogue between interpreter and text, arguing that as meanings emerge from the encounter between interpreter and text, the interpreter must continually change his or her expectations to adapt to these emergent meanings and the ever-revealed newness of the text. Such changes in expectations are necessary if the

interpreter is to avoid "recitation," or addressing to the text questions to which she or he already knows the answers. Gadamer compares this to an instructor examining a student. There is no authentic inquiry; the "conversation" is teleological and determined (497). If one can describe the reports of the investigators whom Chadwick questions as texts (once removed from observation, of course), then we see that Gadamer's description of inauthentic dialogue fits such instances quite well. Even better examples are those in which Chadwick himself questions members of the working class and gets answers that corroborate his assumptions.

Chapter 6

1. See Dorothy Thompson, "Women and Nineteenth-Century Radical Politics: A Lost Dimension" in *The Rights and Wrongs of Women*.

Chapter 7

1. It was not for lack of trying that pews went empty, as Dickens's description of sabbatarian London in *Little Dorrit* demonstrates. Dickens writes that on Sundays "everything was bolted and barred that could possibly furnish relief to an overworked people" (28). As the hour of worship approached, the merciless church bells changed their cadences from the "deadly-lively" importuning "Come to church, Come to church, Come to church," to the low-spirited, slowly hammered out "They *won't* come, they *won't* come, they *won't* come," to the hopeless "groan of despair," which "shook every house in the neighbourhood for three hundred seconds, with one dismal swing per second," until it ceased with the striking of the hour, causing listeners to "Thank heaven" for the silence (29).

2. Catholicism, of course, was also important to Christian worship in the early years of Victorian England, although the church itself was in somewhat dire straits. Politically recuperated by the 1829 Emancipation Act, the Catholic Church in England found itself ill prepared for the unforseen opportunities and unexpected converts with which it was confronted. A particular problem was how to minister to the poor Irish, who made up the majority of Catholic worshippers. Of the 679,000 Roman Catholics living in England in 1851, 390,000 had been born in Ireland; considering the addition of second-generation Irish, it is reasonable to conclude that nearly two thirds of the Catholic population was of Irish descent, most of them members of the working class. Although the Oxford Movement and the conversions that followed from it did much to redeem the respectability of Catholicism, in the 1830s and '40s it was still very much a working-class—and an Irish—religion. Further evidence of the state of Catholic affairs in England in the second quarter of the nineteenth century is given in the 1851 religious census. While only 253,000 of the nearly 680,000 Catholics attended mass on census Sunday, this number far exceeds the number of seatings available (186,111). Edward Pusey and some of his followers were in favor of spending tremendous amounts of money on a

few, large, highly ornate churches, by which even the poor—according to Pusey—would benefit. On the other hand, a large number within the church believed that what was needed were churches, cheap and plentiful, in order to reach the nearly half-million Irish who were not coming to church, in many cases because they had no church to attend. In either case, there was very little money for either group of projects, and bankruptcy was not only a constant threat, it sometimes was an actuality. See Kitson Clark, *Making* 165–66 and O. Chadwick 1:270 passim.

3. By no means did all Anglican clergy prosper financially. According to Harrison the average annual stipend of a curate (in 1840 there were over 5,000) was only £81. Certainly few of the clergy were as well off as the infamous Earl of Guildford, whose name provides a source of great punning in Trollope's *The Warden* and who held simultaneous livings at St. Mary's, Southampton, and Alresford and was master of St. Cross hospital. His duties at St. Cross required him only to sign leases, yet his stipend was £1,500 per annum. In 1850 due to a series of chancery suits he was compelled to resign two of his livings.

4. According to the findings of the 1851 religious census, of all the church and chapel seatings in England and Wales, 5,317,915 were Church of England, and all other denominations together equaled 4,894,648 (see *Census of Great Britain* cxl). In Lancashire, Derbyshire, Cheshire, and Nottinghamshire, seatings in dissenting places of worship far outstripped those in the established church. The actual numbers for Manchester bear this out; of more than 84,500 seatings, only 33,401 were provided by the Anglican churches while dissenting chapels provided 51,117 (Baines 37).

5. The issue of realism was a considerably vexed one for Gaskell. See Hilary Schor's *Scheherezade in the Marketplace*, especially her chapter on *Mary Barton*, for an important discussion of this topic. Also, in all fairness to Kingsley, I should mention that he was never tempted by "realism." In an 1857 letter to his publisher, Alexander Macmillan, he pleads to be allowed to continue, "as I have always done, from *Yeast* and *Alton Locke* till now; show how much of the heroical and tragical element, supposed to be dead, buried and white-washed over, survives in modern society, ready to reassert itself for evil and for good the moment a great cause or a great sorrow appears" (*The Life and Letters of Alexander Macmillan*, quoted in Cripps xv).

Chapter 8

1. It is, however, typical of the social problem novels, at least as Arnold Kettle describes them: "Apart from Elizabeth Gaskell, the [social-problem] novelists did not write about factory workers, though particular scenes in the factories and mills do of course occur. More often, they wrote about the poor of rural areas or of London, where the social situation, though certainly not less intense or explosive, was somewhat different from that of the towns thrown up around heavy industry" (166).

This is indeed the case with writers such as Disraeli, Kingsley, and Bulwer, whom

Kettle is primarily discussing. Kettle's observation, however, while ignoring an entire collection of novels by authors like Mrs. Trollope or Charlotte Elizabeth Tonna that not only were *specifically* about factory life but also were extremely popular and influential in their time, also raises a problem of genre or subgenre. After about 1840 nearly every important or popular novel in some way dealt with what Kettle defines as "social problems." What then, one might ask, are the limits of the social-problem novel during this period?

2. In the chapter "The Tailor Unraveled" in *The Industrial Reformation of English Fiction*, Catherine Gallagher is especially perceptive on Alton's inability to explain himself and the failure of the novel to define either character or narrator (96). Gallagher is particularly concerned to examine Kingsley's rethinking of certain Romantic (especially Carlylean) notions of the self, making them more applicable to the circumstances of the urban working classes who have been deprived of the beauty of nature. This is an excellent starting point for many discussions of *Alton Locke*, but I am less concerned with the development of Alton as character or narrator than with the implications for social, political, or religious reform that may be traced to Alton's attempts to define himself using the discourses available to Kingsley (or Alton).

3. See Thomas Laqueur, *Religion and Respectability: Sunday Schools and Working-Class Culture, 1780–1850.*

4. On the night of April 10, 1848, after Feargus O'Connor had disbanded the huge Chartist demonstration planned for that day and had delivered the petition for the Charter to the House of Commons, Kingsley, John Ludlow, and F. D. Maurice met in London and began to make plans for the publication of their pamphlet, *Politics for the People.* Working through the night, Kingsley drafted a political poster that made an especially crucial point for the Christian Socialists:

> But will the Charter make you free? Will it free you from slavery to ten pound bribes? Slavery to beer and gin? Slavery to every spouter who flatters your self conceit, and stirs up bitterness and headlong rage in you? That, I guess, is real slavery: to be a slave to one's own stomach, one's own pocket, one's own temper. Will the Charter cure *that*? (see Colloms 93–94; Kingsley, *Letters and Memories* 1:156–57)

In his open letters to the English working men published in *Politics for the People*, Kingsley, under the pseudonym Parson Lot, continually returned to the theme: "Be fit to be free, and God will make you free" (Colloms 95).

5. Hilary Schor makes a related argument about *Mary Barton*'s connections between the "detective, the prostitute, and the novelist, the 'romancer' always on the 'qui-vive,' 'collecting and collating evidence'" (31). Like Schor, I too would resist the "fierce discipline" that Miller insists upon for Victorian novels (see Schor 214, n.45).

6. Less sanguine about the efficacy of moral training in the face of destitution was Mrs. Tonna, who in *Helen Fleetwood* describes the gradual "demoralization" of a devout family as their means of subsistence grow increasingly meager. Only the

saintly Helen remains untainted; however, she dies a victim of the factory system and the persecution of others who resent her "methody."

7. This observation has become a commonplace of the criticism of *Alton Locke* and is most often associated with commentary on Alton's and Kingsley's dilemma as to how Alton, as a working-class man of letters, should use his "genius" (see Bodenheimer, *Politics* 139).

8. Much of Kingsley's information about the life of the poor in London is gleaned from Mayhew's articles, beginning with his exposé of the Jacob's Island slum, which appeared in the *Morning Chronicle* on September 24, 1849.

9. Not all the working class engaged in the anti-clerical language of the Chartists. The Irish, although their religious education and needs were inadequately met by a poor and understaffed Catholic Church in England, retained a good deal of their religious traditions. Also, beginning in the late 1830s and early '40s depressed urban areas became the focus of missionary work by Church of England and dissenting evangelicals alike. The establishment of churches in areas such as Bethnal Green, Benwick Street, and Whitechapel corresponds with a decreasing rate of drunkenness and increase in education among the lower classes (see *Means of Divine Worship in Populous Districts*, Parliamentary Papers, 1857–58, vol. 9, no. 5:42–47; 132). Although many of these churches were poorly attended, Owen Chadwick estimates that about one in ten in the great slum parishes of London and the northern industrial cities attended a church or chapel (1:332).

10. The existence of such churches by no means suggests that all within any given congregation were certain as to either the doctrinal or social intentions of their particular church. "Some never knew whether they were attacking Christianity or defending Christianity by attacking the churches which betrayed Christianity. Most of them thought the second" (O. Chadwick 1:334–35).

11. By 1836 the issue of political involvement by Methodist preachers had become an important topic at the Conference, with most members strenuously denouncing *any* political activism, whether conservative, radical, or moderate: "It is no business of ours as 'men of God' who have dedicated ourselves to a kingdom which 'is not of this world' to be very eager or prominent in drawing out these great principles to what we deem right political conclusions (*Minutes of the Wesleyan Methodist Conference*, 1836, 8:105). The Conference concluded that a Methodist minister who engaged in political controversy was "acting contrary to his peculiar calling and solemn engagements" (2:185). Compare the similar attitude adopted by the Congregationalists at a meeting of their union in 1841: "'Christian ministers have no especial concern, and Christian churches and congregations, as such, no proper concern at all' in the redress of civil grievances" (quoted. in Waddington, 553).

12. Despite the association of the Primitive Methodists with Chartism that scholars such as E. J. Hobsbawm have posited, the links between the Primitives and the Chartists are not simple and direct. Like the Wesleyans, officially the Primitive Connexion disapproved of radical activity. At the Primitive Conference of 1821 Hugh Bourne interrupted a speaker, calling him "a speeching Radical, a man who is employed in speaking against the Government, and he must not sit in this place" (quoted. in Wearmouth 212).

13. R. K. Webb has argued most persuasively that to speak of the "Chartist movement" imposes a unity of goals and presuppositions, however complicated, that misrepresents the heterogeneity and diffusiveness that was Chartism. Webb writes that "Chartism was a name applied to many widely differing protests, to competing impulses towards a hundred hazy visions of a better world" (*Modern England* 250). He goes on to describe the Chartism of the '40s as a collection of "competing, hostile, and pathetic protests . . . [that] gave urgency to the social problem, but without even the semblance of unity, they no longer offered the alternative men thought they saw in Chartism of the late thirties" (250).

14. This is not to say that many have not tried. E. J. Hobsbawm, E. P. Thompson, Bernard Semmel, and Gertrude Himmelfarb are only a few of the more noteworthy commentators on the connections between Methodism and the revolutionary impulse in England.

15. His letters to his wife before their marriage indicate that Kingsley was in many ways enamored of the more cathartic aspects of Catholicism, such as self-flagellation. His illustrations (both published and unpublished) for his early play *The Saint's Tragedy* demonstrates the eroticism that such practices evoked for Kingsley.

16. Interestingly, Friedrich Engels writes in the prefatory pages to his work *Socialism, Utopian and Scientific* that "what struck every cultivated foreigner who set up his residence in England was what he was bound to consider the religious bigotry and stupidity of the English respectable middle class." He goes on to say: "In order to find people who dared to use their own intellectual faculties with regard to religious matters, you had to go amongst the uneducated, 'the great unwashed,' as they were called, the working people, especially the Owenite socialists" (xiv).

17. Notably, women are excluded from this attempt. And although Kingsley's "appreciation" of women is well documented, one cannot help but wonder what form such appreciation took in light of remarks such as, "It is strange how little real intellect, in women especially, is required for an exquisite appreciation of the beauties of music—perhaps, because it appeals to the heart and not the head" (*Alton Locke* 238).

18. Such a description is necessary, for at the end of the novel Alton is a "classless" or unattached intellectual. He directs his concerns beyond any particular group to the generally oppressed. As his benefactress Eleanor says, "Freedom, Equality and brotherhood are here" (386). And when she enjoins Alton to "publish, in good time, an honest history of your life; extenuating nothing, exaggerating nothing, ashamed to confess or to proclaim nothing" so that it may "awaken some rich man to look down and take pity on the brains and hearts more noble than his own," Alton is at first tempted to fall at her feet, but "the thought of that common sacrament" that forged a bond between them, "knit not by man, but God, and the peace of God, which passes understanding" (387, 386) keeps him from prostrating himself. He is her equal.

19. The notes to the Oxford edition of *Alton Locke* (1983) give Ecclesiastes 8:11 as the source for the quotation. In the King James version of the Bible—the version Kingsley would have used—Ecclesiastes 8:11 reads: "Because sentence against an evil work is not executed speedily, therefore the heart of the sons of men is fully set

in them to do evil." While this text conveys part of the meaning of the reverend's statement, the words themselves only barely correspond. In Romans 8:6–7, we see a complementary sentiment expressed in words that are more reminiscent of those of the speaker in *Alton Locke*: "For to be carnally minded *is* death; but to be spiritually minded *is* life and peace. Because the carnal mind *is* enmity against God: for it is not subject to the law of God, neither indeed can be." I have been unable to locate the exact quotation, if indeed Mr. Wigginton is quoting. But since *heart* and *mind* are used interchangeably, especially in the Old Testament, it seems to me to be plausible (and particularly fitting) that the minister's admonition of Alton mixes a representation of a distant, adversarial, Old Testament God with an allusion to the evangelicalism of Paul in his Epistle to the Romans. It is even more appropriate that the muddled quotation should come from the lips of Mr. Wigginton, whom Alton's sister eventually marries and who "preached 'higher doctrine,' *i.e.*, more fatalist and antinomian than his gentler colleague—and . . . was much the greater favourite at the chapel." For Alton, Wigginton symbolizes all that is wrong with strict Calvinism. Alton avers, "I hated him—and if any man ever deserved hatred, he did" (15).

20. For an excellent discussion of the efficacy of disseminating the "word of God" see Sue Zemka, "The Holy Books of Empire: Translations of the British and Foreign Bible Society," in *Macropolitics of Nineteenth-Century Literature: Nationalism, Exoticism, Imperialism*.

21. The morals of the unemployed poor were particularly distressing to respectable society. A report incorporated into Joseph Adshead's *Distress in Manchester* (1842) claims: "The moral condition of the unemployed poor is rapidly deteriorating. It is vain, because contrary to all experience, to expect that moral qualities can for any considerable period co-exist with hunger and nakedness" (39). Where the poor do work, such as in the Yorkshire coal mines, the young are woefully ignorant of religion. Eighteen-year-old Ann Eggerly, a hurrier in a colliery, tells one commission: "I have never heard that a good man came into the world who was God's Son to save sinners. I never heard of Christ at all. Nobody has ever told me about him, nor have my father and mother ever taught me to pray. I know no prayer: I never pray. I have been taught nothing about such things." Another girl, Eliza Coats, eleven, says: "I don't know where I shall go if I am a bad girl when I die. I think God made the world, but I don't know where God is. I never heard of Jesus Christ" (First Report of Commissioners. . . Employment and Conditions of Children in Minew and Manufactories, 252–53). Nor were the agricultural poor able to avoid the depravity of their urban cousins. The Reverend. Sidney Godolphin Osborn (Kingsley's brother-in-law) reports in 1843: "As to the moral condition of the wives and children of agricultural laborers, I must at once affirm that it is far below what it ought to be, but it is not worse than, under the circumstances, we have a right to expect" (*The Assistant Poor Law Commissioner's Reports*, 72).

Chapter 9

1. As Engels himself points out in his chapter "The Great Towns," a good deal of his introduction is taken from Peter Gaskell's *The Manufacturing Population of England* (London, 1833). See translator's note 1 in *The Condition of the Working Classes in England*, trans. Henderson and Chaloner, p. 9. See also p. 78 of the same edition.

2. Steven Marcus discusses these opening pages of *The Condition of the Working Class in England* in some detail in *Engels, Manchester, and the Working Class* (133–39). As Marcus points out, Engels's construction of a pre-industrial way of life for the English is a myth and fraught with empirical inaccuracies. Historical precision, however, while always a concern, is not of primary importance here. More significant is Engels's need to present an historical background in order to examine how change takes place. As Marcus writes of the passage in which Engels describes the workers as intellectually and spiritually dead and the Industrial Revolution as the event that compels them to think for themselves, "It may not be excessive to suggest that in this passage, at this moment, a new mode of conceptual reflection and analysis has been turned upon English events and history. . . . For what Engels has done here, in the opening pages of the work, is to bring the Hegelian method of thinking to bear upon this momentous development in English history" (136–37).

3. In her essay "Private Grief and Public Acts in *Mary Barton*," Rosemarie Bodenheimer argues for the primacy of grief and loss as an organizing trope. She writes that "*Mary Barton* is a novel about responding to the grief of loss or disappointment. Its pages are filled with domestic disaster; the sheer accumulation of one misfortune after another is the organizing principle of the first half of the narrative" (195). Bodenheimer's main concern is with the movement of the "split" narrative and the "structures" of conflict that shape it (196). Also, for Bodenheimer, *Mary Barton* starts and ends "always with personal grief," so that "the novel is only secondarily about politics as such" (213). Although there are obvious affinities between Bodenheimer's reading and my own, my concern is not primarily with the domestic spaces and discourses of the novel, but rather with precisely the ways that suffering, as an interpretive discourse, informs the public, political arena that Bodenheimer sees as secondary.

4. Hilary Schor's *Scheherezade in the Marketplace* provides an especially good discussion of the implications of such "truth telling" and its limits in terms of the issues of authorship and authority that Gaskell faced as one "almost frightened at [her] own action of writing [*Mary Barton*]" (see Schor 26–28).

5. Gérin's remark is problematic since as Asa Briggs has demonstrated in *Victorian Cities*, Manchester was the "shock city" of the period—especially the '30s and '40s—and by 1851 the shock had begun to wear off. Perhaps Gérin is referring to first-hand experiential knowledge of Manchester, and if this is her meaning then there is some validity to her statement; certainly there would have been many Londoners (as well as other southern, more provincial readers) who would never have actually traveled to Manchester despite having read a good deal about it.

6. Hilary Schor comments lucidly on how this trope works to bind the

novel's readers to the community of the poor. In *Scheherezade in the Marketplace* she writes that "the speeches the workers deliver make sense to them—and to us—because they mirror the experience we have been witnessing. When starving workers explain their poverty in terms of dying children, readers who have watched children die for two hundred pages will be moved; the empty talk of foreign markets lacks validity for us, as for them" (17).

7. Although Chartist rhetoric is the obvious exception, there was in early Victorian Britain a tradition, or at least it was perceived as a tradition by the wealthier classes, of the poor's suffering in silence. See E. Chadwick, *Sanitary Condition Report*, 92.

8. For a full treatment of Unitarian doctrine see Dennis Wigmore-Beddoes, *Yesterday's Radicals: A Study of the Affinity between Unitarianism and Broad Church Anglicanism in the Nineteenth Century*, 64–69. Compare also Susanna Winkworth's letter to the Rev. J. J. Tayler, dated July 1, 1859:

> As it is I feel myself to some extent in union with all; and especially with the Unitarians, in as much as they, more than most others, seem to me to recognize the true ground of Christian union to be spirit and sentiment, not doctrine, and to uphold the duty as well as right of free search after truth and intellectual veracity. (Margaret J. Shaen, *Memorials of Two Sisters: Susanna and Catherine Winkworth*, 199)

In the third chapter of *The Industrial Reformation of English Fiction*, Catherine Gallagher discusses the problems of free will and necessitarianism in *Mary Barton* in some length. See pp. 64–87.

9. See, for example, P. J. Keating, *The Working Classes in Victorian Fiction*; John Lucas, "Mrs. Gaskell and Brotherhood," in *Tradition and Tolerance in Nineteenth-Century Fiction*; Raymond Williams, *Culture and Society*, and Catherine Gallagher, *The Industrial Reformation of English Fiction*. Although these critics do not all agree as to the extent of Gaskell's failed attempts at representing the working classes, all find the novel to be either formally or ideologically defective. The notable exception to this list is Rosemarie Bodenheimer, who writes, "A merger of the Bartons and the Wilsons, repairing the decimation of the original families is the proper resolution in a novel that locates its virtues so firmly in family solidarity and tradition" ("Private Grief" 213).

Bibliography

Aarsleff, Hans. *From Locke to Saussure: Essays on the Study of Language and Intellectual History*. Minneapolis: University of Minnesota Press, 1982.

Adshead, Joseph. *Distress in Manchester: Evidence (Tabular and Otherwise) of the State of the Labouring Classes in 1840–42*. London: Henry Hooper, 1842.

Althusser, Louis. "Ideology and Ideological State Apparatuses (Notes Toward an Investigation)." In *Lenin and Philosophy and Other Essays*, trans. Ben Brewster, pp. 127–88. New York: Monthly Review Press, 1971.

———. *For Marx*. Trans. Ben Brewster. Paris: François Maspero, 1965. London: New Left Books; Verso, 1982. First published in Britain by Allen Lane, 1969.

Altick, Richard D. *The English Common Reader: A Social History of the Mass Reading Public 1800–1900*. Chicago: University of Chicago Press, 1957.

Anonymous. "Sir Robert Peel's Address to the Electors of the Borough of Tamworth." *Quarterly Review* 53 (April 1835): 261–87.

———. "A Triad of Novels." *Fraser's Magazine* 42 (Nov. 1850): 574–90. (Review of *Alton Locke*.)

Arac, Jonathan. *Commissioned Spirits: The Shaping of Social Motion in Dickens, Carlyle, Melville, and Hawthorne*. New Brunswick, N.J.: Rutgers University Press, 1979.

———. *Critical Genealogies: Historical Situations for Postmodern Literary Studies*. New York: Columbia University Press, 1987.

———, ed. *Postmodernism and Politics*. Minneapolis: University of Minnesota Press, 1986.

Arac, Jonathan and Harriet Ritvo. "Introduction." In *Macropolitics of Nineteenth-Century Literature: Nationalism, Exoticism, Imperialism*, ed. Jonathan Arac and Harriet Ritvo, pp. 1–11. Philadelphia: University of Pennsylvania Press, 1991.

Armstrong, Anthony. *The Church of England, the Methodists, and Society, 1700–1850*. London: University of London Press, 1973.

Armstrong, Nancy. *Desire and Domestic Fiction: A Political History of the Novel*. New York: Oxford University Press, 1987

Aspinall, A. and E. Antony Smith, eds. *English Historical Documents, 1783–1832*, gen. ed. David C. Douglas. 12 vols. to date, 1955–. Vol. 11. London: Eyre and Spottiswood, 1959.

Austin, Henry. "Metropolitan Movements," *Westminster Review* 36 (1841): 404–35.

Aydelotte, William O. "Parties and Issues in Early Victorian England." In *The Victorian Revolution*, ed. Peter Stansky, pp. 93–118. New York: New Viewpoints, 1973.

Baines, Edward. *The Social, Educational and Religious State of the Manufacturing Districts; with Statistical Returns of the Means of Education and Religious Instruc-*

tion in the Manufacturing Districts of Yorkshire, Lancashire, and Cheshire; in Two Letters to the Right Hon. Sir Robt. Peel, Bart. London: T. Ward, 1843.

Bakhtin, M. M. *The Dialogic Imagination: Four Essays*. Trans. Caryl Emerson and Michael Holquist, ed. Michael Holquist. Austin: University of Texas Press, 1981.

——. *Speech Genres and Other Late Essays*. Trans. Vern W. McGee, ed. Caryl Emerson and Michael Holquist. Austin: University of Texas Press, 1986.

Balibar, Etienne. "The Concept of Class Politics in Marx." *Rethinking Marxism* 1.2 (1988): 18–51.

Barker, Francis et al., eds. *1848: The Sociology of Literature*. Proceedings of the Essex Conference on the Sociology of Literature. Essex: University of Essex, 1978.

Baudrillard, Jean. *Simulations*. Trans. Paul Foss, Paul Patton and Philip Beitchman. New York: Semiotext(e), 1983.

Belsey, Catherine. *Critical Practice*. London: Routledge, 1988.

Bennett, Tony. *Formalism and Marxism*. London and New York: Methuen, 1979.

Benton, Ted. *The Rise and Fall of Structural Marxism: Althusser and His Influence*. New York: St. Martin's, 1984.

Bernstein, Carol L. "Nineteenth-Century Urban Sketches: Thresholds of Fiction." *Prose Studies* 3 (1980): 217–40.

Blake, Robert. *Disraeli*. London: Eyre and Spottiswoode, 1966.

Bodenheimer, Rosemarie. *The Politics of Story in Victorian Social Fiction*. Ithaca, NY: Cornell University Press, 1988.

——. "Private Grief and Public Acts in *Mary Barton*." *Dickens Studies Annual* 9 (1981): 195–216.

Booth, Charles, ed. *Life and Labour of the People in London*. 9 vols. London: Macmillan, 1892–97.

Bottomore, Tom, Laurence Harris, V. G. Kiernan, and Ralph Miliband, eds. *A Dictionary of Marxist Thought*. Cambridge, MA: Harvard University Press, 1983.

Bradford, Sarah. *Disraeli*. London: Weidenfeld and Nicolson, 1982.

Brantlinger, Patrick. "Bluebooks, the Social Organism, and the Victorian Novel." *Criticism* 14.4 (1972): 328–44.

——. *The Spirit of Reform: British Literature and Politics, 1832–1867*. Cambridge, MA and London: Harvard University Press, 1977.

Braun, Thom. *Disraeli the Novelist*. London: Allen and Unwin, 1981.

Brent, Richard. *Liberal Anglican Politics: Whiggery, Religion, and Reform, 1830–1841*. Oxford: Clarendon, 1987.

Briggs, Asa. *The Age of Improvement, 1783–1867*. London and New York: Longman, 1959.

——, ed. *Chartist Studies*. London: Macmillan, 1959.

——. *Words, Numbers, Places, People*. Vol. 1 of *The Collected Essays of Asa Briggs*. Urbana and Chicago: University of Illinois Press, 1985.

——. *Images, Problems, Standpoints, Forecasts*. Vol. 2 of *The Collected Essays of Asa Briggs*. Urbana and Chicago: University of Illinois Press, 1985.

Brown, John. *A Memoir of Robert Blincoe*. Manchester: J. Doherty, 1832.

Bulwer Lytton, Edward. *England and the English*. 2 vols. London: Richard Bentley, 1833.

———. *Paul Clifford*. London: H. Colburn and R. Bentley, 1830.

Burke, Edmund. *Reflections on the Revolution in France*. 1793. New York: Penguin, 1965.

Burrow, J. W. *A Liberal Descent: Victorian Historians and the English Past*. Cambridge and London: Cambridge University Press, 1981.

Butt, John and Kathleen Tillotson. *Dickens at Work*. London: Methuen, 1963.

Buzard, James and Joseph Childers. "Theory and Consequences: An Interview with Stanley Fish." *Critical Texts* 2.1 (1984): 1–6.

Carlyle, Thomas. "Characteristics." *Critical and Miscellaneous Essays*. London: Chapman and Hall, 1887. Vol. 16 of *Thomas Carlyle's Works*. Ashburton Edition.

———. "On History." *Critical and Miscellaneous Essays*. London: Chapman and Hall, 1887. Vol. 15 of *Thomas Carlyle's Works*. Ashburton Edition.

———. "On History Again." *Critical and Miscellaneous Essays*. London: Chapman and Hall, 1887. Vol. 16 of *Thomas Carlyle's Works*. Ashburton Edition.

———. *Past and Present*. London: Chapman and hall, 1886. Vol. 2 of *Thomas Carlyle's Works*. Ashburton Edition.

———. *Sartor Resartus*. London: Chapman and Hall, 1887. Vol. 3 of *Thomas Carlyle's Works*. Ashburton Edition.

———. "Signs of the Times." *Critical and Miscellaneous Essays*. London: Chapman and Hall, 1887. Vol 15. of *Thomas Carlyle's Works*. Ashburton Edition.

Cazamian, Louis. *The Social Novel in England, 1830–1850*. 1903. Trans. Martin Fido. London: Routledge and Kegan Paul, 1973.

Chadwick, Edwin. *The First and Second Reports of the Central Board of H.M. Commissioners appointed to collect information as to the Employment of Children in Factories*. Parliamentary Papers, 1833, nos. 450, 519, vols. 20–21.

———. *Report and Appendices of H. M. Commission for Enquiring into the Administration and Practical Operation of the Poor Laws*. Parliamentary Papers, 1834, no. 44, vol. 29.

———. *Report on the Sanitary Condition of the Labouring Population of Great Britain, 1842*. Ed. M. W. Flinn. Facsimile rpt. Edinburgh: Edinburgh University Press, 1965.

Chadwick, Owen. *The Victorian Church*. 2 vols. New York: Oxford University Press, 1966.

Chartist Circular. Glasgow: Sept. 28, 1839-July 9, 1842. Vols.1–146.

Childers, Joseph. "Carlyle's *Past and Present*, History, and a Question of Hermeneutics." *CLIO* 13.3 (1984): 247–258.

———. "Politics as Interpretation: 'Progress,' Language, and Party in Early Victorian England." *CLIO* 17.1 (1987): 65–80.

Chitty, Susan. *The Beast and the Monk: A Life of Charles Kingsley*. New York: Mason-Charter, 1975.

Clive, John. *Macaulay: The Shaping of the Historian*. New York: Knopf, 1973.

Cohen, Sande. *Historical Culture: On the Recoding of an Academic Discipline*. Berkeley: University of California Press, 1986.

Collini, Stefan, Donald Winch, and John Burrow. *That Noble Science of Politics: A Study in Nineteenth-Century Intellectual History*. Cambridge: Cambridge University Press, 1983.

Colloms, Brenda. *Charles Kingsley: The Lion of Eversely*. New York: Barnes and Noble, 1975.

Cottom, Daniel. *Social Figures: George Eliot, Social History, and Literary Representation*. Minneapolis: University of Minnesota Press, 1987.

Cripps, Elizabeth A. "Introduction." In Charles Kingsley, *Alton Locke, Tailor and Poet*, pp. vii–xxi. New York: Oxford University Press, 1983.

Crow, Duncan. *The Victorian Woman*. New York: Stein, 1971

Dale, Peter Allan. *The Victorian Critic and the Idea of History: Carlyle, Arnold, Pater*. Cambridge, MA: Harvard University Press, 1977.

Davidoff, Lenore. *The Best Circles: Women and Society in Victorian England*. Totowa, NJ: Rowman, 1973.

Davidoff, Lenore and Catherine Hall. *Family Fortunes: Men and Women of the English Middle Class, 1780–1850*. London: Hutchinson, 1987.

Dawson, Carl. *Victorian Noon: English Literature in 1850*. Baltimore: Johns Hopkins University Press, 1979.

Demetz, Peter. *Marx, Engels, and the Poets*. Revised ed. Chicago: University of Chicago Press, 1967.

Dickens, Charles. *American Notes*. 1842. Oxford Illustrated Dickens. Oxford: Oxford University Press, 1987.

——— . *Dombey and Son*. 1846–1848. Oxford Illustrated Dickens. Oxford: Oxford University Press, 1987.

——— . *Hard Times*. 1854. Oxford: Oxford University Press, 1987.

——— . *Nicholas Nickelby*. 1838–39. Oxford Illustrated Dickens. Oxford: Oxford University Press, 1987.

——— . *Oliver Twist*. 1837–39. Oxford Illustrated Dickens. Oxford: Oxford University Press, 1987.

——— . *Our Mutual Friend*. 1864–65. Oxford Illustrated Dickens. Oxford: Oxford University Press, 1987.

——— . *The Pickwick Papers*. 1836–37. Oxford Illustrated Dickens. Oxford: Oxford University Press, 1987.

——— . *Sketches by Boz*. 1836–37. Oxford Illustrated Dickens. Oxford: Oxford University Press, 1987.

Disraeli, Benjamin. *Coningsby, Or the New Generation*. 3 vols. London: Colburn, 1844. Fifth edition with a preface by the author, 1849.

——— . *Contarini Fleming: A Psychological Autobiography*. 4 vols. London: Murray, 1832.

——— . *Sybil, or the Two Nations*. 3 vols. London: Colburn, 1845.

——— . *Vindication of the English Constitution in a Letter to a Noble and Learned Lord*. London: Sanders and Otley, 1835. Facsimile rpt. Westmead, Farnborough, Hants., England: Gregg International Publishers Ltd., 1969.

——— . *Vivian Grey*. 2 vols., published anonymously. London: Colburn, 1826. Vols. 3–5, London: Colburn, 1827.

Dodd, William. *The Factory System Illustrated in a Series of Letters to the Right Hon. Lord Ashley*. 1842 Intro. by W. H. Chaloner. Facsimile rpt. London: Frank Cass, 1967.

Donajgrodzki, A. P., ed. *Social Control in Nineteenth Century Britain*. London: Croom and Helm, 1977.

Dreyfus, Hubert L. and Paul Rabinow. *Michel Foucault: Beyond Structuralism and Hermeneutics*. Afterword by and interview with Michel Foucault. 2nd ed. Chicago: University of Chicago Press, 1983.

Dyos, H. J. and D.A. Reeder. "Slums and Suburbs." In *The Victorian City*, ed. H. J. Dyos and M. Wolff, 1:359–86. London: Routledge and Kegan Paul, 1973.

Dyos, H. J. and M. Wolff, eds. *The Victorian City*. London: Routledge and Kegan Paul, 1973. 2 vols.

Eagleton, Terry. *Criticism and Ideology*. London: Verso, 1976.

———. *Literary Theory: An Introduction*. Minneapolis: University of Minnesota Press, 1983.

Engels, Friedrich. *The Condition of the Working Class in England, 1844*. 1845. Trans. W. O. Henderson and W. H. Chaloner. Stanford, CA: Stanford University Press, 1968.

———. *Socialism, Utopian and Scientific*. London: Swan Sonnenschein, 1892.

The English Chartist Circular and Temperance Record for England and Wales. vols. 1–3 (nos. 1–153). New York: A. M. Kelley, 1968.

Ermath, Elizabeth Deeds. *Realism and Consensus in the English Novel*. Princeton, NJ: Princeton University Press, 1983.

Faulkner, Harold Underwood. *Chartism and the Churches: A Study in Democracy*. 1916. New York: AMS, 1968.

Feltes, N. N. "Realism, Consensus and 'Exclusion Itself': Interpellating the Victorian Bourgeoisie." *Textual Practice* 1.3 (1987): 297–308.

Finer, S. E. *The Life and Times of Sir Edwin Chadwick*. New York: Barnes and Noble, 1952.

Fish, Stanley. "Change." Paper presented at the Conference on the Poetics of Ideology, Columbia University. New York, November 1984.

———. "Change." *South Atlantic Quarterly* 86.4 (1987): 423–44.

———. *Is There a Text in This Class?* Cambridge, MA: Harvard University Press, 1980.

Flinn, M. W. "Preface." In Edwin Chadwick, *Report on The Sanitary Condition of the Labouring Population of Great Britain, 1842*, pp. 1–73. Edinburgh: Edinburgh University Press, 1965.

Flint, Kate, ed. *The Victorian Novelist: Social Problems and Social Change*. New York: Croom Helm, 1987.

Fontana, Biancamaria. *Rethinking the Politics of Commercial Society: The Edinburgh Review, 1802–1832*. Cambridge: Cambridge University Press, 1985.

Forster, John. *The Life of Charles Dickens*, London: Chapman and Hall, 1874. 3 vols.

Foucault, Michel. *Discipline and Punish: The Birth of the Prison*. 1975: Gallimard, trans. Alan Sheridan. New York: Vintage, 1979.

———. *Power/Knowledge: Selected Interviews and Other Writings, 1972–1977*. Ed. and trans. Colin Gordon. New York: Pantheon, 1980.

Frost, Thomas. *The Secret*. In *The National Instructor*. London: 1850.

Fryckstedt, Monica Correa. *Elizabeth Gaskell's "Mary Barton" and "Ruth": A Challenge to Christian England*. Uppsala: Almqvist and Wiksell, 1982.

Frye, Northrop. *Anatomy of Criticism*. Princeton, NJ: Princeton University Press, 1957.

Gadamer, Hans-Georg. *Truth and Method*. Trans. G. Burden and J. Cumming. New York: Crossroad, 1982.

Gallagher, Catherine. "The Body Versus the Social Body in the Work of Thomas Malthus and Henry Mayhew." *Representations* 14 (1986): 83–106.

———. *The Industrial Reformation of English Fiction, 1832–1867*. Chicago and London: University of Chicago Press, 1985.

Gash, Norman. *Politics in the Age of Peel*. London: Longman Group., 1953. New York: Norton, 1971.

Gaskell, Elizabeth Cleghorn. *The Letters of Mrs. Gaskell*, ed. J. A. V. Chapple and Arthur Pollard. Cambridge, MA: Harvard University Press, 1967.

———. *Mary Barton*. 1848. Harmondsworth: Penguin, 1970.

———. *North and South*. 1855. Vol. 4 of Works. 8 vols. London: Smith Elder, 1906.

Gaskell, P[eter]. *The Manufacturing Population of England, Its Moral, Social, and Physical Conditions, and the Changes Which have arisen from the Use of Steam Machinery; with an Examination of Infant Labour*. London: Baldwin and Cradock, 1833.

Geertz, Clifford. *The Interpretation of Cultures*. New York: Basic Books, 1973.

Gérin, Winifred. *Elizabeth Gaskell: A Biography*. Oxford: Oxford University Press, 1976.

Goldstrom, J. M., ed. *Urban Conditions, 1839–1848*. Vol. 2 of *The Working Classes in the Victorian Age: Debates on the Issue from 19th-Century Critical Journals*. London: Gregg, 1973.

———, ed. *Urban Conditions, 1848–1868*. Vol. 3 of *The Working Classes in the Victorian Age: Debates on the Issue from 19th-Century Critical Journals*. London: Gregg, 1973.

Goodman, Nelson. *Ways of Worldmaking*. Indianapolis, IN: Hackett, 1978.

Greg, Samuel. *Two Letters to Leonard Horner, Esq., on the Capabilities of the Factory System*. London: Taylor and Walton, 1840.

Greg, W. R. *An Enquiry into the State of the Manufacturing Population and the Causes and Cures of the Evils Therein Existing*. London: J. Ridgeway, 1831.

———. Review of *Mary Barton: A Tale of Manchester Life*. *Edinburgh Review* 89 (1849): 402–35.

Gregory, Benjamin. *Side lights on the conflicts of Methodism during the second quarter of the nineteenth century, 1827–1852: taken chiefly from the notes of the late Rev. Joseph Fowler of the debates in the Wesleyan Conference*. New York: Cassell, 1898.

Greville, Charles. *The Greville Memoirs, 1814–1860*, ed. Lytton Strachey and Roger Fulford. 8 vols. London: Macmillan, 1938.

Halévy, Elie. *The Birth of Methodism in England*. Trans. Bernard Semmel. Chicago: University of Chicago Press, 1971.

———. *The Growth of Philosophical Radicalism*. Trans. Mary Morris. Boston: Beacon, 1955.

———. *History of the English People in the Nineteenth Century*. Trans. E. I. Watkin. 4 vols. New York: Peter Smith, 1923–48.

Halifax Guardian. May 25, 1839.

Hall, Catherine. "The Early Formation of Victorian Domestic Ideology." In *Fit Work for Women*, ed. Sarah Burman, pp. 15–32. New York: St. Martin's, 1979.

──────. *White, Male, and Middle Class: Explorations in Feminism and History*. London: Routledge, 1992.

Hamburger, Joseph. *Macaulay and the Whig Tradition*. Chicago: University of Chicago Press, 1976.

Harrison, J.F.C. *The Early Victorians, 1832–1851*. New York: Praeger, 1971.

Hart, Jennifer. "Religion and Social Control in the Mid-Nineteenth Century." In *Social Control in Nineteenth Century Britain*, ed. A. P. Donajgrodzki, pp. 108–37. London: Croom and Helm, 1977.

Hartley, Allan John. *The Novels of Charles Kingsley: A Christian Social Interpretation*. Folkestone, Eng. Hour-Glass, 1977.

Hegel, G. W. F. *Lectures on the Philosophy of World History*. Trans. H. B. Nisbet, intro. Duncan Forbes. Cambridge: Cambridge University Press, 1975.

──────. *Reason in History: A General Introduction to the Philosophy of History*. 1837. Trans. and intro. Robert S. Hartman. New York: Bobbs-Merrill, 1953.

Herbert, Christopher. "Rat Worship and Taboo in Mayhew's London." *Representations* 23 (1988): 1–24.

Himmelfarb, Gertrude. *The Idea of Poverty: England in the Early Industrial Age*. New York: Random House, 1983.

──────. *Victorian Minds*. New York: Knopf, 1952.

Hirst, Paul Q. "Althusser and the Theory of Ideology." *Economy and Society* 5.4 (1976): 388–412.

Hobsbawm, Eric J. *The Age of Revolution: 1789–1848*. New York: New American Library, 1962.

──────. *Primitive Rebels: Studies in Archaic Forms of Social Movements in the Nineteenth and Twentieth Centuries*. Manchester: Manchester University Press, 1959

Hollingsworth, Keith. *The Newgate Novel: Bulwer, Ainsworth, Dickens, and Thackeray*. Detroit: Wayne State University Press, 1963.

Hollis, Patricia. *The Pauper Press: A Study in Working-Class Radicalism of the 1830s*. London: Oxford University Press, 1970.

Holme, Thea. "Introduction." In *Sketches by Boz*, pp. i–xxii. Oxford: Oxford University Press, 1987. Oxford Illustrated Dickens.

Horwitz, Howard. "'I Can't Remember': Skepticism, Synthetic Histories, Critical Action." *South Atlantic Quarterly* 87.4 (1988): 787–820.

Houghton, Walter E. *The Victorian Frame of Mind 1830–1870*. New Haven, CT: Yale University Press, 1957.

Howard, Jean E. and Marion F. O'Connor. "Introduction." In *Shakespeare Reproduced*, pp. 1–18. New York: Methuen, 1987.

James, William. *Pragmatism*. Fredson Bowers, textual editor, Ignas K. Skrupskelis, associate editor; intro. by H. S. Thayer. Cambridge, MA: Harvard University Press, 1975.

Jameson, Fredric. *The Political Unconscious*. Ithaca, NY: Cornell University Press, 1980.

Jakobson, Roman. "Closing Statement: Linguistics and Poetics." In *Style in Language*, ed. Thomas A. Sebeok, 98–123. Cambridge, MA: MIT Press, 1966.

──────. "Two Aspects of Language and Two Types of Aphasic Disturbances." In

Fundamentals of Language, ed. Roman Jakobson and Morris Halle, pp. 69–96. The Hague: Mouton, 1956.

Jay, Martin. *Marxism and Totality: The Adventures of a Concept: From Lukács to Habermas*. Berkeley: University of California Press, 1984.

Jones, David. *Chartism and the Chartists*. London: Allen Lane, 1975.

Jones, Ernest. *Women's Wrongs: A Series of Tales*. London: 1855.

Kay (-Shuttleworth), James Phillip. *The Moral and Physical Condition of the Working Classes Employed in the Cotton Manufacture in Manchester*. 1832. Preface W. H. Chaloner. Facsimile rpt. London: Cass, 1970.

Keating, P. J. *The Working Classes in Victorian Fiction*. London: Routledge and Kegan Paul, 1971.

Kent, John. *Jabez Bunting, the Last Wesleyan: A Study in the Methodist Ministry After the Death of John Wesley*. London: Epworth, 1955.

Kettle, Arnold. "The Early Victorian Social-Problem Novel." In *From Dickens to Hardy*, ed. Boris Ford. Vol. 6 of *The New Pelican Guide to English Literature*, pp. 164–81. Harmondsworth: Penguin, 1982.

Kingsley, Charles. *Alton Locke, Tailor and Poet: An Autobiography*. 1850. Oxford: Oxford University Press, 1983.

———. "Preface to the Undergraduates of Cambridge." 1862. Reprinted in *Alton Locke: Tailor and Poet*. New York: Dutton, 1970.

———. *Charles Kingsley: His Letter and Memories of His Life*. 2 vols. Ed. Frances Eliza Kingsley. London: Henry S. King, 1877.

———. *Politics for the People*. London: Parker, 1848.

———. *Sanitary and Social Essays*. Vol. 18 of *Works*. London: Macmillan, 1880.

———. *Yeast*. 1848. London: Parker, 1851.

Kitson Clark, George. *Churchmen and the Condition of England, 1832–1885*. London: Methuen, 1973.

———. *An Expanding Society: Britain, 1830–1900*. Melbourne: Melbourne University Press, 1967.

———. *The Making of Victorian England*. Cambridge, MA: Harvard University Press, 1962.

———. *Peel and the Conservative Party: A Study in Politics, 1832–1841*. 2nd ed. London: G. Bell and Sons, Ltd., 1929. London and Liverpool: Frank Cass, 1964.

Koss, Stephen. *The Rise and Fall of the Political Press in Britain: The Nineteenth Century*. London: Hamish Hamilton, 1981.

Kovacevic, Ivanka. *Fact into Fiction: English Literature and the Industrial Scene, 1750–1850*. Chatham: Leicester University Press, 1975.

Kovacevic, Ivanka and S. Barbara Kanner. "Blue Book into Novel: The Forgotten Industrial Fiction of Charlotte Elizabeth Tonna." *Nineteenth-Century Fiction* 25.2 (1970): 152–173.

Kovalev. I. V. *An Anthology of Chartist Literature*. Moscow: Izdvo Literatury na inostrannykh Iazykakh, 1956.

Kuhn, Thomas S. *The Structure of Scientific Revolutions*. Chicago: University of Chicago Press, 1962.

LaCapra, Dominick. *History, Politics, and the Novel*. Ithaca, NY: Cornell University Press, 1987.

Laclau, Ernesto and Chantal Mouffe. *Hegemony and Socialist Strategy: Towards a Radical Democratic Politics*. London: New Left Books, 1985.

Langland, Elizabeth. "Nobody's Angels: Domestic Ideology and Middle-Class Women in the Victorian Novel." *PMLA* (March 1992): 290–304.

Lansbury, Coral. *Elizabeth Gaskell: The Novel of Social Crisis*. New York: Barnes and Noble, 1975.

Laqueur, Thomas. *Religion and Respectability: Sunday Schools and Working-Class Culture, 1780–1850*. New Haven, CT: Yale University Press, 1976.

Levine, George. *The Realistic Imagination: English Fiction from Frankenstein to Lady Chatterley*. Chicago and London: University of Chicago Press, 1981.

Lovett, William. *The Life and Struggles of William Lovett in His Pursuit of Bread, Knowledge, and Freedom*. London: Tarbour, 1876.

Lucas, John. *The Literature of Change: Studies in the Nineteeth-Century Provincial Novel*. 2nd ed. Brighton: Harvester, 1980.

———. "Mrs. Gaskel and Brotherhood." In *Tradition and Tolerance in Nineteenth-Century Fiction*, ed. David Howard, John Lucas, and John Goode, pp. 161–74. New York: Barnes and Noble, 1967.

Lyons, David. *In the Interest of the Governed*. Oxford: Clarendon, 1973.

Macaulay, Thomas Babington. "History." *The Works of Lord Macaulay*. Ed. by his sister Lady Trevelyan. 8 vols. Vol. 5, pp. 122–61. London: Longmans, Green, 1879.

———. "Southey's Colloquies on Society." *The Works of Lord Macaulay*. Ed. by his sister Lady Treveylan. 8 vols. Vol. 5, pp. 330–368. London: Longmans, Green,, 1879.

———. *Speeches*. Ed. by himself. London: Longmans, Brown, Green and Longmans, 1854.

MacDonagh, Oliver. "The Nineteenth-Century Revolution in Government: A Reappraisal." In *The Victorian Revolution*, ed. Peter Stansky, pp. 5–28. New York: New Viewpoints, 1973.

Macdonnel, Diane. *Theories of Discourse: An Introduction*. Oxford: Basil Blackwell, 1986.

McGowan, John P. *Representation and Revelation: Victorian Realism from Carlyle to Yeats*. Columbia: University of Missouri Press, 1986.

Macherey, Pierre. *A Theory of Literary Production*. 1966. London: Routledge and Kegan Paul, 1978.

Mack, Mary. *Jeremy Bentham: An Odyssey of Ideas, 1748–1792*. London: Heinemann, 1962.

Manners, Lord John. *A Plea for National Holy-Days*. London: Painter, 1834.

Marcus, Steven. *Dickens from Pickwick to Dombey*. New York: Basic Books, 1965. New York: Norton, 1985.

———. *Engels, Manchester, and the Working Class*. New York: Random House, 1974.

———. *The Other Victorians: A Study of Sexuality and Pornography in Mid-Nineteenth-Century England*. New York: Basic Books, 1966.

Martineau, Harriet. *Autobiography*. 3 vols. 2nd ed. London: Smith, Elder, 1877.

——. *Harriet Martineau on Women*, ed. Gayle Graham Yates. New Brunswick, NJ: Rutgers University Press, 1985.

——. *Household Education*. London, E. Moxon, 1849.

——. *Illustrations of Political Economy*. 9 vols. London: C. Fox, 1832–34.

——. *Poor Laws and Paupers, Illustrated*. 4 vols. London: C. Fox, 1833–1834.

——. *The Rioters, or A Tale of Bad Times*. London: Wellington, Salop, Houlston, 1827.

Mather, F. C., ed. *Chartism and Society: An Anthology of Documents*. London: Bell and Hyman, 1980.

Mayhew, Henry. *The Forgotten Mayhew: Selections from the Morning Chronicle, 1849– 1850*. Ed. E. P. Thompson and Eileen Yeo. London: Penguin, 1984.

——. *London Labour and the London Poor*. 1861–62. Intro. John D. Rosenberg. 4 vols. New York: Dover, 1968.

Miall, Arthur. *Life of Edward Miall*. London: Macmillan, 1884.

Mill, John Stuart. *Autobiography*. Ed. Jack Stillinger. Boston: Houghton Mifflin, 1969.

——. "Bentham." 1838. In *Mill on Bentham and Coleridge*, pp. 39–98. Cambridge: Cambridge University Press, 1950.

——. "Civilisation." *London and Westminster Review*, April 1836. In *Essays on Politics and Culture*, ed. Gertrude Himmelfarb, pp. 45–66. Gloucester, MA: Peter Smith, 1973.

——. "Coleridge." 1840. In *Mill on Bentham and Coleridge*, pp. 99–168. Cambridge: Cambridge University Press, 1950.

——. "Reorganization of the Reform Party." *London and Westminster Review*, April 1839. In *Essays on Politics and Culture*, ed. Gertrude Himmelfarb, pp. 268–303. Gloucester, MA: Peter Smith, 1973.

——. "The Spirit of the Age." *Examiner*, January 6–May 29, 1831. In *Essays on Politics and Culture*, ed. Gertrude Himmelfarb, pp. 1–44. Gloucester, MA: Peter Smith, 1973.

——. "Thoughts on Parliamentary Reform." Pub. as pamphlet in 1859. In *Essays on Politics and Culture*, ed. Gertrude Himmelfarb, pp. 304–33. Gloucester, MA: Peter Smith, 1973.

Miller, D. A. *Narrative and Its Discontents: Problems of Closure in the Traditional Novel*. Princeton, NJ: Princeton, University Press, 1981.

——. *The Novel and the Police*. Berkeley: University of California Press, 1987.

Miller, J. Hillis. "The Fiction of Realism: *Sketches by Boz*, *Oliver Twist*, and Cruikshank's Illustrations." In *Dickens Centennial Essays*, ed. Ada Nisbet and Blake Nevius, pp. 85–143. Berkeley: University of California Press, 1971.

Minutes of the Wesleyan Methodist Conference 1836. London: 1836.

Mitchell, Austin. *The Whigs in Opposition: 1815–1830*. London: Clarendon, 1967.

Montrose, Louis. "Renaissance Literary Studies and the Subject of History." *English Literary Renaissance* 16 (1986): 9–12.

Monypenny, William Flavelle and George Earle Buckle. *The Life of Benjamin Disraeli, Earl of Beaconsfield*. 6 vols. New York: Macmillan, 1910–20.

Mozley, Tom. "The Religious State of the Manufacturing Poor." *British Critic* 28 (1840): 334–371.

Nelson, H. S. "*Our Mutual Friend* and Mayhew's *London Labour and the London Poor*." *Nineteenth-Century Fiction* 20.3 (1965): 207–22.

Newton, Judith. "History as Usual? Feminism and the 'New Historicism.'" In *The New Historicism*, ed H. Aram Veeser, pp. 152–67. New York: Routledge, 1989.

Norich, Anita. "Benjamin Disraeli's Novels: Personal and Historical Myths." Ph.D. diss., Columbia University, 1979.

Norman, E. R. *Church and Society in England, 1770–1970*. Oxford: Oxford University Press, 1976.

O'Kell, Robert. "Disraeli's *Coningsby*: Political Manifesto or Psychological Romance?" *Victorian Studies* 23.1 (1979): 57–78.

Parliament of the British Empire. *Hansard's Parliamentary Debates*. Third series, vol. 25. July 10, 1834–August 15, 1834. Fifth (And Last) Volume of the Session. London: T.C. Hansard, 1834.

———. *Hansard's Parliamentary Debates*. Third series, volume 36. January 31, 1837–March 6, 1837. First Volume of the Session. London: T. C. Hansard, 1837.

———. *Hansard's Parliamentary Debates*. Third series, volume 47. April 15, 1839–June 5, 1839. Third Volume of the Session. London: T. C. Hansard, 1839.

———. *Census of Great Britain, 1851. Religious Worship in England and Wales*. Parliamentary Papers 1852–53, no. 1690 vol. 89.

———. *Means of Divine Worship in Populous Districts*. Parliamentary Papers, 1857–58, no. 5, vol. 9.

———. *Select Committee Report on Education*. Parliamentary Papers, 1835, no. 465, vol. 7.

———. *First Report of Commissioners for Inquiring into the Employment and Condition of Children in Mines and Manufactories: Appendix to First Report of Commissioners: Mines, Pt. 1*. Parliamentary Papers, 1842, no. 381, vol. 16.

———. *The Assistant Poor Law Commissioner's Reports on the Employment of Women and Children in Agriculture*. Parliamentary Papers, 1843, no. 510, vol. 12.

Pearson, Robert and Geraint Williams. *Political Thought and Public Policy in the Nineteenth Century: An Introduction*. New York: Longman, 1984.

Pêcheux, Michel. *Language, Semantics, and Ideology: Stating the Obvious*. Trans. Harbans Nagpal. London: Macmillan, 1982.

Peel, Sir Robert. *The Memoirs of the Right Honourable Sir Robert Peel*. London: John Murray, 1857. Includes reprint of "Address to the Electors of the Borough of Tamworth."

Pocock, J. G. A. *Virtue, Commerce, and History*. New York: Cambridge University Press, 1985

Pollak, Ellen. "Feminism and the New Historicism: A Tale of Difference or the Same Old Story?" *Eighteenth Century Theory and Interpretation* 29.3 (Fall, 1988): 281–86.

Poovey, Mary. "Domesticity and Class Formation: Chadwick's 1842 *Sanitary Report*." In *Subject to History: Ideology, Class, Gender*, ed. David Simpson, pp. 65–83. Ithaca, NY: Cornell University Press, 1991.

————. *Uneven Developments: The Ideological Work of Gender in Mid-Victorian England*. Chicago: Chicago University Press, 1989.

Report of A Committee of the Manchester Statistical Society, on the Condition of the Working Classes in an Extensive Manufacturing District in 1834, 1835, and 1836: Read at the Statistical Section of the British Association for the Advancement of Science. Liverpool, Sept. 13th 1837. London: James Ridgway and Son, 1838.

Richardson, Ruth. *Death, Dissection, and the Destitute*. London: Routledge and Kegan Paul, 1987.

Ritchie, Robert. *Observations on the Sanitary Arrangements of Factories*. London: John Weale, 1844.

Roach, John. *Social Reform in England, 1780–1880*. London: B.T. Batsford, 1978.

Roberts, David. "Tory Paternalism and Social Reform in Early Victorian England." In *The Victorian Revolution*, ed. Peter Stansky, pp. 147–68. New York: New Viewpoints, 1973.

————. *Victorian Origins of the British Welfare State*. New Haven, CT: Yale University Press, 1960.

Roberts, Elizabeth. *A Woman's Place: An Oral History of Working-Class Women, 1890–1940*. Oxford: Basil Blackwell, 1984.

Robson, Robert, ed. *Ideas and Institutions of Victorian Britain: Essays in Honour of George Kitson Clark*. London: G. Bell and Sons, 1967.

Rorty, Richard. *Consequences of Pragmatism*. Minneapolis: University of Minnesota Press, 1982.

Rothfield, Lawrence. *Vital Signs: Medical Realism in Nineteenth-Century Fiction*. Princeton, NJ: Princeton University Press, 1992.

Said, Edward W. *The World, the Text, and the Critic*. Cambridge, MA: Harvard University Press, 1983

Saville, John. *Ernest Jones: Chartist. Selections from the Writings and Speeches of Ernest Jones*. London: Lawrence and Wishart, 1952.

Schor, Hilary M. *Scheherezade in the Marketplace: Elizabeth Gaskell and the Victorian Novel*. New York: Oxford University Press, 1992.

Schoyen, A. R. *The Chartist Challenge: A Portrait of George Julian Harney*. Toronto: Heinemann, 1958.

Semmel, Bernard. *The Methodist Revolution*. New York: Basic Books, 1973.

Shaen, Margaret. *Memorials of Two Sisters: Susanna and Catherine Winkworth*. London: Longmans and Green, 1908.

Sharps, J. G. *Mrs. Gaskell's Observation and Invention*. Fontwell, England: Linden Press, 1970.

Smith, Sheila. "Blue Books and Victorian Novels." *Review of English Studies* 21.81 (1970): 23–40.

————. *The Other Nation: The Poor in English Novels of the 1840s and 1850s*. London: Clarendon, 1980.

Soloway, R. A. *Prelates and People: Ecclesiastical Social Thought in England, 1783–1852*. London: Routledge and Kegan Paul, 1969.

Stallybrass, Peter and Allon White. *The Politics and Poetics of Transgression*. Ithaca, NY: Cornell University Press, 1986.

Stedman Jones, Gareth. *Languages of Class*. Cambridge: Cambridge University Press, 1983.

———. *Outcast London*. Oxford: Clarendon, 1971.

Steintrager, James. *Bentham*. Ithaca and New York: Cornell University Press, 1977.

Storch, Robert D. "The Plague of the Blue Locusts: Police Reform and Popular Resistance in Northern England, 1840–1857." *International Review of Social History* 20.1 (1975): 61–90.

———. "The Problem of Working-Class Leisure. Some Roots of Middle-Class Reform in the Industrial North: 1825–50." *Social Control in Nineteenth Century Britain*, ed. A. P. Donajgrodzki, pp. 138–62. London: Croom Helm, 1977.

Strachey, Lytton and Roger Fulford, eds. *The Greville Memoirs, 1814–1860*. 8 vols. London: Macmillian, 1939.

Taine, Hippolyte. *Notes on England*. Trans. and intro. Edward Hyams. London: Thames and Hudson, 1957.

Tholfson, Trygve R. *Working Class Radicalism in Mid-Victorian England*. New York: Columbia University Press, 1977.

Thomas, William. *The Philosophic Radicals: Nine Studies in Theory and Practice, 1817–1841*. London: Clarendon, 1979.

Thompson, Dorothy. *The Chartists*. London: Temple Smith, 1984.

———. "Women and Nineteenth-Century Radical Politics: A Lost Dimension." In *The Rights and Wrongs of Women*, ed. Juliet Mitchell and Ann Oakley. Harmondsworth, Penguin, 1976.

Thompson, E. P. *The Making of the English Working Class*. New York: Vintage, 1966.

———. *The Poverty of Theory*. New York: Monthly Review Press, 1978.

Tillotson, Kathleen. *Novels of the Eighteen-Forties*. London: Oxford University Press, 1954. Rpt. Hong Kong: Oxford University Press, 1985.

Tonna, Charlotte Elizabeth. *Helen Fleetwood*. 1839–40. Vol. 1 of *Work*, intro. by Harriet Beecher Stowe. 7th ed. 2 vols. New York: M. W. Dodd, 1849.

Townsend, W. J., H. B. Workman, and George Eayrs. *A New History of Methodism*. London: Hodder and Stoughton, 1909.

Trollope, Frances. *The Life and Adventures of Michael Armstrong, the Factory Boy*. London: Henry Colburn, 1840.

Uffelman, Larry K. *Charles Kingsley*. Boston: Twayne, 1979.

Waddington, John. *Congregational History, 1800–1850*. London: Longmans, 1878.

Wearmouth, Robert F. *Methodism and the Struggle of the Working Class, 1800–1850*. Leicester: E. Backus, 1954.

Webb, Robert K. *Modern England: From the 18th Century to the Present*. 2nd ed. New York: Harper and Row, 1980.

———. "The Victorian Reading Public" In *The New Pelican Guide to English Literature: From Dickens to Hardy*, ed. Boris Ford, pp. 198–219. Harmondsworth, Eng.: Penguin, 1982.

Webb, Sydney and Beatrice Webb. *English Poor Law History*. London: Longmans, Green, 1927–29.

Weiner, Joel H. *The War of the Unstamped: The Movement to Repeal the British Newspaper Tax, 1830–1836*. Ithaca, NY: Cornell University Press, 1969.

Wigmore-Beddoes, Dennis. *A Religion That Thinks: A Psychological Study.* Belfast: Ulster Unitarian Christian Association, 1972.

——. *Yesterday's Radicals: A Study of the Affinity Between Unitarianism and Broad Church Anglicanism in the Nineteenth Century.* Cambridge: James Clarke, 1971.

Williams, Raymond. *Culture and Society, 1780–1950.* 1958. New York: Columbia University Press, 1983.

——. *The English Novel from Dickens to Lawrence.* London: Chatto and Windus, 1970. London: Hogarth, 1984.

——. *Problems in Materialism and Culture.* London: Verso, 1980.

——. *Writing in Society.* London: Verso Press, 1984.

Wohl, A.S. "Unfit for Human Habitation." In *The Victorian City,* ed. H. J. Dyos and M. Wolff, 2:603–24. London: Routledge and Kegan Paul, 1973.

Young, G. M. and W. D. Handcock, eds. *English Historical Documents, 1833–1874.* Gen. ed. David C. Douglas. Vol. 12–1. 12 vols. to date. 1955–. New York: Oxford University Press, 1956.

Zemka, Sue. "The Holy Books of Empire: Translations of the British and Foreign Bible Society." In *Macropolitics of Nineteenth-Century Literature: Nationalism, Exoticism, Imperialism,* ed. Jonathan Arac and Harriet Ritvo, pp. 102–37. Philadelphia, University of Pennsylvania Press, 1991.

Index

University of Pennsylvania Press
NEW CULTURAL STUDIES
Joan DeJean, Carroll Smith-Rosenberg,
and Peter Stallybrass, Editors

This book has been set in Galliard. Galliard was designed for Mergenthaler in 1978 by Matthew Carter. Galliard retains many of the features of a sixteenth-century typeface cut by Robert Granjon but has some modifications that give it a more contemporary look.

Printed on acid-free paper.